December 13 2006

John:
    Happy Birthday!
        Love,
    Mom & Dad

GRUDGES GUTS & GLORY

By Les Krantz

SportingNews
BOOKS

CONTRIBUTING WRITERS
Paul Adomites, David Aretha, Bill Chastain, Tim Knight, Rob Rains

BOOK DESIGN
Peg Esposito

PRINTED IN SINGAPORE

10 9 8 7 6 5 4 3 2 1

To my brother Dick,
who thought up the
name of this thing.

ACKNOWLEDGEMENTS

The author is grateful to the many individuals who helped and inspired including the *Sporting News* folks: Kathy Kinkeade, John Rawlings, Dale Bye, Bob Parajon, Marilyn Kasal, Michael Garavalia, Fred Barnes, and Corrie Anderson. Others include my contributing writers listed on the opposite page, DVD producer Jack Piantino, AP Wideworld agent Marilyn Rader, Collegiate Image Vice President Mark Geddis, USOC representative Tamera Reub, ESPN's Jay Rizick, Fox Movie Tone's Peter Bregman, Major League Baseball's Dan O'Connor, ITN's Sara Bower, TWP representative Martha Oresman, Ellen Labrecque, Lou Boudreau, Jr., Mush Sterneck, and Toby Schuring.

PHOTO CREDITS

All the photographs were provided by AP Wideworld photos, except the following:
From Corbis Images: 36, 47, 108, 131
From Collegiate Images: 124, 133–135
From The Image Works: 20
From Hockey Hall of Fame: 64, 68
From *Sporting News*: 29, 30, 40–42, 112–114, 118, 145–147, 157, 159

CONTENTS

Chapters are ranked according to their places among the greatest all-time grudge matches.

Rank: 1
See page 10

Rank: 15
See page 52

25. DOUBLE-A TRILOGY: Affirmed vs. Alydar, 1978
After beating Alydar in the Kentucky Derby (by a length) and the Preakness (by a neck), Affirmed edges his rival by a head in the Belmont to win the Triple Crown.

26. THE VALENTINE'S DAY MASSACRE: Jake La Motta vs. Sugar Ray Robinson, February 14, 1951 . .85
Robinson pummels La Motta in their sixth matchup, but the conquered hero avoids a knock-down. "You couldn't put me down, Ray," La Motta says.

27. RUNNING FOR GOLD: Sebastian Coe vs. Steve Ovett, 1980 Olympics
In the 1980 Olympics, these record-shattering Brits finally face each other, with Ovett winning gold over his rival in the 800 meters and Coe prevailing in the 1,500.

28. McENROE VS. WIMBLEDON: John McEnroe at Wimbledon, 1981
Tennis bad boy John McEnroe ends Bjorn Borg's five-year championship run, but he infuriates Wimbledon officials in the process.

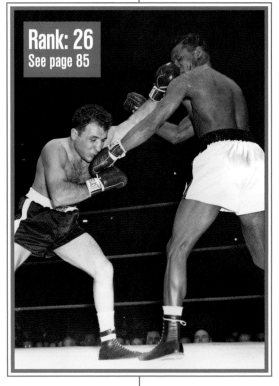

Rank: 26
See page 85

29. A FIGHT TO THE DEATH: Emile Griffith vs. Benny Paret, March 24, 1962
Paret's intimately personal verbal attacks infuriate Griffith, who takes out his anger in the ring during their third matchup. Paret dies from the blows.

30. MILITARY MIGHT: Army vs. Navy, December 2, 1950
In perhaps the most memorable battle between these storied rivals, Navy pulls off a shocking 14-2 upset. Thousands of fans storm the field in triumph.

31. JUST CRAZY!: North Carolina vs. Duke, February 2, 1995

College basketball's greatest rivalry peaks as the Cameron Crazies cheer the Blue Devils to a 102-100 double overtime win over North Carolina.

32. BASKETBRAWL: New York Knicks vs. Miami Heat, 1997-2000 NBA playoffs
Miami comes back to win the fight-filled 1997 Eastern Conference finals, the first of four straight bitterly contested playoff series between these two teams.

33. A WIN FOR THE GIPPER: Notre Dame vs. Army, November 10, 1928
The Irish don't seem to stand a chance against rival Army until coach Knute Rockne's "Win one for the Gipper" halftime speech inspires them to a come-back victory.

34. A THREAT TO THE DYNASTY: Boston vs. Los Angeles, 1969 NBA Finals . . .109
The Lakers enter the 1969 NBA Finals having lost five out of five championship series to the Celtics since 1959. Boston wins this one, too—in seven games.

35. 'DEM BUMS' GET IT DONE: Brooklyn Dodgers vs. New York Yankees, 1955 World Series
After losing four World Series to their crosstown nemeses, the rival Brooklyn Dodgers finally win their first fall classic, shutting out the Yankees in Game 7.

36. RECKLESS DRIVING: Alain Prost vs. Ayrton Senna, 1988-1994
The legendary rivalry between these two Formula One racers comes to a head at Suzuka in 1989, as they force each other off the track in their quest for the championship.

37. NAMATH AGAINST THE WORLD: New York vs. Baltimore, Super Bowl III, January 12, 1969
In this rivalry of the AFL vs. the NFL, upstarts vs. the establishment, Namath guarantees victory—and prevails.

Rank: 40
See page 127

INTRODUCTION

Will Rogers used to say, "I never met a man I didn't like," and that gave away a number of things about him. For one, that he wasn't a professional athlete; second, that he never met Howard Cosell. It was Cosell, the legendary sportscaster, who helped make Muhammad Ali such an interesting character—not that Ali himself didn't have a lot to do with it, too.

It was Cosell who opened up my eyes about a few things. One of them was that you can respect someone for being good at what he does and hate him at the same time. And you can even enjoy watching him, loathing almost every word that spews from his mouth as he insults his way through America's sports arenas.

Though I never met Cosell, I felt I had a special connection to him. During his heyday as a sportscaster, he was frequently interviewed at the magazine at which I was working in the early 1970s, *Esquire*. His battle cry at that time was for reinstatement of Ali's boxing license and title after they were stripped from him in 1967 because he had refused to answer an Army draft call. Cosell lead a veritable campaign for Ali until the deposed champion got another shot at the title in the legendary and No. l-rated grudge match in this book, "The Fight of the Century," in which he fought with another undefeated champion, Joe Frazier. *Esquire* also championed Ali's cause. Like Cosell, the editors of the magazine posited argument after argument about why he deserved to fight again.

Well, Ali got his chance, and it happened to come when I was working at *Esquire*, on March 8, 1971. The fight was an event around my office. Everyone there went to see the closed-circuit telecast, gladly paying the outrageous sum of $20.00, which in 1971 was a lot of money—*a lot*!

I remember so vividly when one of the secretaries walked by a group of us guys as we were congregating to leave for the fight after closing time. She shouted at us, shaking her head in disapproval as she said it, "I can't understand how anyone would pay *20 bucks* to watch a couple of gorillas beat the #@%* out of each other."

I've often reflected on that comment—it was classic! Barbara, the secretary who made the statement, was expressing the ultimate "nonappreciation" of sports. Anyone reading this book obviously would have felt differently about getting the opportunity to see such a history-making event. It had all the elements: two undefeated champions, big talk, a world watching, a world title at stake, political overtones, social relevance, and, above all, media hype.

The prefight antics saturated the media; even old grandmas and women who worked in flower shops knew about it. What's relevant about their historic match-up is how the feelings of resentment between them contributed to the excitement of the event. Add to that the countless newspaper and magazine articles that went with it, and the countless hours of radio and television time that were devoted to reporting their feelings for each other, and you had an irresistible sporting event, the ultimate grudge match.

What's remarkable about this first Ali-Frazier fight is that it took place long before the introduction of the new electronic sports media, namely network cable, sports radio, and the Internet, which spread the venom that begrudged competitors use to build the box office draw. Cosell, who was never exactly considered Mr. Nice Guy—yet was one of the top sportscasters in his day—added even more to the equation. He was a constant reminder that respect is due, even when love and admiration are not, which is how Ali and Frazier felt about each other.

Add up all the above—Cosell, Ali, and Frazier, and later a new expanded universe of media perfect for venting anger and hyping an event—and the face of athletic competition changed drastically. Sports began to provide thrills with the absence of good manners and friendly competitors. For better or worse, the definition of "sportsmanlike conduct" was changed, maybe forever. Competitors were no longer prized for being gentlemen. *Braggadocio* became the watchword. Ferociousness became a substitute for self-confidence, not just in the boxing ring, but on ice rinks, basketball courts, ballfields and almost everywhere serious athletic competition was being played and watched. The fans loved to watch a gut-wrenching grudge play itself out, and the competitors knew it and catered to it. And the media hyped it!

This book, *Grudges, Guts, and Glory*, documents what's at the heart of this phenomenon, starting with some of the earliest examples of the most bitter of competitions that also helped set the stage for what today is considered the ultimate sports event—a "grudge match."

My contributing writers and I, with help from John Rawlings, *Sporting News* Senior VP/Editorial Director, ranked the matches from 1-50. Even the last-place grudge match, "Beanball Memories" (the 2000 World Series), is an example of how angry competitors with a score to settle can ignite the fans. Hopefully—and by design—you too will be set afire as you read about them and view the DVD, which has many examples of the world's greatest, most ballyhooed spectator events—sports' all-time greatest grudge matches.

Les Krantz

SPORTS' 50 ALL-TIME GREATEST GRUDGE MATCHES

THE FIGHT OF THE CENTURY
Muhammad Ali vs. Joe Frazier, March 8, 1971

For the first time in history, two undefeated boxers were battling for the heavyweight title, and the action was ferocious. "This is the most torrid heavyweight championship of all time," announced TV analyst Don Dunphy during the middle of the fight.

Round after round, Muhammad Ali—the bombastic, "draft dodging" Black Muslim—rifled one two jabs at Joe Frazier's head. Smokin' Joe responded with crushing hooks to the head and body. "Don't you know I'm god?" pronounced Ali during the heat of the battle. "God, you're in the wrong place tonight," Frazier shot back.

Not since Joe Louis kayoed Nazi poster boy Max Schmeling in 1938 had the world anticipated a heavyweight bout this much. Ali-Frazier at New York's Madison Square Garden, on March 8, 1971, was dubbed the "Fight of the Century," and no one disputed it. Ali, the former world champion, entered the match at 31-0 with 25 knockouts. Frazier, the reigning champ, boasted a record of 26-0 with 23 kayos. Yet their perfect records were only one aspect of the full story.

Ali, 29, had captivated fans since 1964, when, still known as Cassius Clay, he "shocked the world" with a TKO victory over seemingly indestructible champion Sonny Liston. "I float like a butterfly and sting like a bee," boasted Ali, who could get away with his vanity because of his talent and charm. What many couldn't stomach, however, was his disdain for the American government. Citing his religious beliefs, Ali refused to be inducted in the Army and fight in the Vietnam War. "I ain't got no quarrel with them Viet Cong," he said. His indignant stance earned him a ban from boxing from 1967 to 1970, during which he became a hero to black militants and to young Americans who opposed the war.

Though an Olympic gold medalist like Ali, the 27-year-old Frazier was the antithesis of his rival. While Muhammad relied on speed and panache, Joe pounded foes into submission. (As a teenager, he had used sides of beef as "punching bags" while working in a slaughterhouse.) Moreover, Frazier was quiet and low-key, preferring to read the Bible rather than spout poetry about himself like his opponent did.

Though Ali-Frazier already was a match made in heaven, Muhammad hyped it even further with his outrageous insults. "Joe Frazier is too ugly to be champ," Ali spewed. "Joe Frazier is too dumb to be champ. The heavyweight champion should be smart and pretty like me." The trash talk didn't end there. Ali unfairly called Frazier the "establishment's champion" and even an "Uncle Tom." "Any black person who is for Joe Frazier is a traitor," he said.

Ali's vicious remarks enraged his foe. "A white lawyer kept him out of jail [for draft dodging]," Frazier wrote in his autobiography. "And *he's* going to Uncle Tom me. THEE Greatest, he called himself. Well, he wasn't The Greatest, and he certainly wasn't THEE Greatest. ... It became my mission to show him the error of his foolish pride. Beat it into him."

In the early weeks of 1971, Ali-Frazier captivated fans across the globe. The Garden, which seated more than 20,000 for boxing, sold out weeks before the fight. Ringside tickets fetched $150, with scalpers demanding as much as $700. More than 300 million people worldwide would watch the event on closed-circuit television. On fight night, celebrities strolled in as if it were the Academy Awards. Bill Cosby, Barbra Streisand, and Sammy Davis Jr. took their seats, as did Hugh Hefner and a Playboy Bunny. Even "Ol' Blue Eyes," Frank Sinatra, was in the house.

As the early rounds unfolded, Ali and Frazier revealed their strategies. To conserve energy, Muhammad refrained from his customary "dancing." Instead, he peppered Joe's face with one-two combinations. Frazier fought from a crouch, countering Ali's jabs with heavy hooks. Throughout, Ali jabbed

Already ahead in points, Joe Frazier sealed his victory with a booming left hook in Round 15, which sent Muhammad Ali to the canvas.

Joe Frazier lands a left to the jaw of Muhammad Ali. Durng a prefight rant, Ali had raised Frazier's ire by calling him an "Uncle Tom."

and mocked his opponent. When Smokin' Joe would land a hard punch, Muhammad would look at the crowd and shake his head, as if saying "That was nothin.'"

The fighters maintained a furious pace through the first 10 rounds, with each doling out and absorbing tremendous punishment. Frazier was the most aggressive, especially in the sixth round when he pounded Ali repeatedly while he sagged against the ropes. In the 11th, Frazier hammered the former champ with a pair of hooks in the final minute. Ali collapsed into the ropes and, a little later, stumbled backward. The bell may have prevented a knockout. "I was thinking it was a miracle he survived that round," said his fight doctor, Ferdie Pacheco. "No one had ever hurt Muhammad before."

Exhausted and battered, their faces both swollen, Ali and Frazier battled in agony through the 12th, 13th, and 14th rounds. Sensing he needed a knockout to win, Muhammad went after Smokin' Joe in the 15th and final round. But in his haste, Ali left his face unguarded, and at 2:34 Frazier cashed in with a roaring left hook. Muhammad fell backward, crashing loudly on the canvas.

Ali pounced back up, but by that time the fight

Joe Frazier hugs his manager, Yancey Durham, after the decision is announced. It would be Joe Frazier's only triumph over Muhammad Ali in three tries.

was lost. Referee Arthur Mercante scored the bout eight rounds for Frazier, six for Ali, and one even. The two judges gave the fight to Frazier, 11-4 and 9-6. By unanimous decision, Smokin' Joe Frazier remained the heavyweight champion of the world.

Ali was unavailable for comment after the fight, as he was transported to the hospital for X-rays of his jaw. Reporters, though, had plenty to write about, many claiming that this was one "Fight of the Century" that truly—literally—lived up to its billing.

Three years after the epic bout, Ali avenged the loss with a close unanimous-decision victory over Frazier. Then in 1975, he outlasted Frazier in the heat of the Philippines, winning the "Thrilla in Manila." Ali described his last win of the trilogy as the closest thing to dying he had ever experienced.

Although Ali often taunted and insulted Frazier, even calling him a gorilla, he held the highest respect for him. In a rare moment of humility, he revealed in a BBC interview: "I always bring out the best in the men I face, but Joe Frazier, I'll tell the world, brings out the best in me. That's one hell of a man."

The Thrilla in Manila

Although many historians rate the first Muhammad Ali–Joe Frazier fight as the greatest heavyweight bout in history, the "Thrilla in Manila"—their third and final battle—also ranks as an all-time classic.

Hosted by Philippines President Ferdinand Marcos, the 15-round fight was set for October 1, 1975. This would be the decisive battle of the trilogy, as Frazier had won the first fight and Ali the second. Ali's prefight hijinks reached a new low when he repeatedly waved a rubber gorilla while referring to Frazier. "It's gonna be a thrilla and a chilla

and a killa when I get the gorilla in Manila," he said.

The bout took place in a virtual sauna, as the indoor temperature reached an estimated 95 to 110 degrees. Heat, humidity, and age (both Ali and Frazier were in their 30s) sapped the combatants of energy, so the fight turned into a flat-footed slugfest. Ali opened aggressively but began to tire around the fifth round. The middle rounds belonged to Frazier, who beat Ali mercilessly in the 11th.

Despite the oppressive conditions, Ali

found a second wind. From the 12th through the 14th, he butchered Smokin' Joe. Blood flowed from Frazier's mouth, and his eyes were nearly swollen shut. Ali sent Frazier's mouthpiece flying in the 13th, and he punched until he was spent through the 14th. Somehow, Frazier remained standing.

Before the 15th and final round, Ali told his trainer, Angelo Dundee, that he was through. Dundee ignored him. In the other corner, Frazier's trainer, Eddie Futch, ended the fight by conceding defeat. "But I want him, boss," Frazier protested. "Sit down, son," Futch replied. "It's all over. No one will ever forget what you did here today."

FIGHTING THE NAZI POWER

Joe Louis vs. Max Schmeling, June 22, 1938

Late in the afternoon of June 22, 1938, hours before he was set for his rematch against German Max Schmeling at Yankee Stadium, Joe Louis and two friends went for a walk along the Harlem River.

"How do you feel, Joe?" Louis was asked by his friend Freddie Wilson.

"I'm scared," Louis said.

"Scared?" Wilson questioned.

"Yeah, I'm scared I might kill Schmeling tonight," Louis answered.

For two years and three days, Louis had been tormented by the only loss of his professional boxing career. Schmeling had knocked him out in the 12th round of their previous bout, capitalizing on a flaw in Louis' boxing style; Schmeling had observed from films that Louis often kept his left hand too low.

Louis also had been victimized by his own haphazard training, and by overestimating himself and underestimating his opponent, mistakes he vowed not to make as he prepared for the rematch.

Before the fight, Louis was quoted by Murray Lewin of the *New York Daily Mirror* as saying, "I am out for revenge. All I ask of Schmeling is that he stand up and fight without quitting. I'll give him enough to remember me for life and make him hang up his gloves for all time. I've waited for two years for this chance and now my time has come."

When Louis and Schmeling had stepped into the ring for the first time on June 19, 1936, the stakes were much lower. That fight had been viewed by almost all observers only as a bout between a black man and a white man. The fact Schmeling was from Germany and Louis was the son of Alabama sharecroppers who had moved to Detroit when he was 12 years old had mattered little.

Racial inequities in the United States had prompted some white Americans and some of the white press to root for Schmeling. When Schmeling won, he received hundreds of telegrams of congratulations from Americans. He also received congratulations from Adolf Hitler, back home in Germany.

The German government had taken little interest in the fight beforehand, no doubt fearing that a loss by Schmeling would reflect badly on their regime. When he won, however, Hitler and his aides were quick to rally behind Schmeling and parade him before the public as the embodiment of Aryan superiority and claim his victory as a triumph for their country.

When the victorious Schmeling returned to Germany, Hitler invited him, his wife, and mother to lunch. An autographed portrait of Hitler was placed in a spot of honor in Schmeling's home. As the political turmoil in Germany became more intense, the rest of the world began to take notice. Especially in America, the attitude of the press and public—a portion of which had been behind Schmeling—began to erode.

Joe Louis hovers over his prey after his first of three knockdowns of the "Aryan Superman" in Round 1. The Brown Bomber won by TKO just 124 seconds into the fight.

As the two boxers prepared for the rematch, the stakes this time were raised. It was no longer simply a prizefight between a black man and a white man. This was now the first battle between America and Germany. It was freedom against fascism. The fact that Louis was black was now far less important than the fact that he was an American and willing to step up and take on Hitler and Germany.

Louis had rebounded from his loss to Schmeling to win the heavyweight title of the world with an eighth-round knockout of Jim Braddock in 1937. Louis was defending that title and trying to prevent Schmeling from becoming the first fighter in history to regain the title after he had lost it. Schmeling had won the crown in 1930, but lost it to Jack Sharkey two years later.

As the fight neared, President Franklin Roosevelt invited Louis to the White House. FDR reportedly gave the prizefighter's biceps a sqeeze and said, "We need muscles like yours to beat Germany."

Schmeling noticed the change in the attitude of the American people as soon as he arrived in New York to begin training for the rematch. His arrival drew picketers, and reporters peppered him with questions about Hitler and the political situation in Germany, not just about how he planned to attack Louis.

Louis had spent his time preparing for the fight by studying films of the first bout and learning how he had left himself open to Schmeling's attack. He also determined that he was going to attack from the opening bell, believing that if he came out aggressively and immediately put Schmeling on the defensive, it would give his opponent no time to retaliate.

Louis wanted to score a decisive victory to erase the negative feeling that he still harbored from the first fight. He had developed a personal grudge against Schmeling, and he did not hide his anger at the German from reporters.

Several days before the fight, the U.S. government indicted 18 American citizens, Germans and German-Americans all, accusing them of acting as spies for the Nazis, thus adding an even greater diplomatic backdrop to the fight.

This tension between the two fighters, and now between their two countries, made the rematch one of the most anticipated sporting events of its time. Scalpers were asking $100 for $30 ringside seats, and a crowd of more than 70,000 filled Yankee Stadium for the Wednesday night bout.

Clem McCarthy broadcast the fight live over the NBC Radio network throughout the United States, and the fight was also heard around the world in German, Spanish, French, and Portuguese.

As he had promised, Louis was the aggressor in the fight, pounding Schmeling from the opening bell. *The New York Times* described what happened:

"Like flashes from the blue, the Bomber's sharp, powerful left started suddenly pumping into Schmeling's face. The blows tilted Max's head back, made his eyes blink, unquestionably stung him. The German's head was going backward as if on hinges."

Three times Louis knocked Schmeling to the canvas. Twice, Schmeling managed to make it to his feet before the referee's count reached 10.

"But Schmeling was helpless," *The Times* reported. "He staggered drunkenly for a few backward steps, the crowd in an uproar as Louis stealthily followed and measured his man. Max was an open target. His jaw was unprotected and inviting. His mid-section was a mark for punches. The kill was within Louis' grasp. He lost no time in ceremony."

In just two minutes and four seconds, the fight was over, at the time the second-shortest heavyweight title fight in history. (In 1908, Tommy Burns kayoed Jem Roche in just 1:28.) The 24-year-old Louis had not only defeated his own personal demons; he had defended his title and scored the first knockout of the Second World War.

According to *The Fight of the Century*, Louis said in his dressing room, post-fight,"Now I feel like the champion, I've been waiting a long time for this night. I sure do feel pretty glad about everything."

Exploding the Nordic myth

The reaction to Joe Louis' victory over Max Schmeling was predictable. In Germany, the nation was stunned. Residents had stayed awake until after the 3 a.m. curfew to hear the bout, and could not believe what had happened. The German media and citizens immediately began making excuses for the defeat.

Where the media had been quick to claim Schmeling as a national hero after his 1936 victory, one German newspaper now said "the defeat of a boxer does not mean any loss of national prestige."

In the United States, there was jubilation.

At his post-fight news conference, Louis said, "It wasn't just Joe Louis defending the championship against Max Schmeling. It was international, like the Olympic Games. I just couldn't let that crown get out of this country and I aim to keep it here for many years."

In the *New York World-Telegram*, the famed writer Heywood Broun tried to take a historical approach to the fight results.

"One hundred years from now some historian may theorize, in a footnote at least, that the decline of Nazi prestige began with a left hook delivered by a former unskilled

automotive worker who had never studied the policies of Neville Chamberlain and had no opinion whatever in regard to the situation in Czechoslovakia," Broun wrote.

"And possibly there could be a further footnote. It was known that Schmeling regarded himself as a Nazi symbol. It is not known whether Joe Louis consciously regards himself as a representative of his race and as one under dedication to advance its prestige. I can't remember that he has ever said anything about it. But that may have been in his heart when he exploded the Nordic myth with a boxing glove."

Just seconds into their legendary fight on June 22, 1938, Joe Louis lands a right to the body as Max Schmeling cowers toward the corner.

A LOW BLOW
Tonya Harding vs. Nancy Kerrigan, 1994

It was January 6, 1994. Nancy Kerrigan, the cool, aloof, dedicated 24-year-old figure skater and bronze medal winner at the 1992 Olympic Games, had just completed her practice in Detroit's Cobo Arena for the next night's United States Championships when she was attacked by a burly man dressed in a black cap, black coat, and tan trousers. The man ran at her, swung some sort of stick, striking her right knee, then continued running. The blow knocked her over.

Kerrigan, who was favored to win the U.S. competition and among the favorites at next month's Olympics, could say only one word over and over again: "Why? Why? Why?"

Kerrigan couldn't skate in the U.S. championships. The winner in her stead was Tonya Harding, who had finished fourth in the '92 Games. Harding was a feisty, truck-driving woman as different from Kerrigan's prim persona as anyone could be. Within a week four men had been charged with involvement in the assault. One was Harding's "bodyguard." Another was her ex-husband.

The country was stunned. The graceful, balletic world of figure skating seemed as far from directed brutality as ice hockey is from lacy underwear. But the reality is that figure skating has an ugly side. In fact, it can be a cutthroat business. Olympic gold for figure skaters, particularly female skaters, means huge money. According to Kerrigan's agent, she could reap as much as $10 million for an Olympic victory. The reason: We love our lady figure skaters. They become cultural icons of beauty and grace. The first was Norwegian Sonja Henie, who turned three consecutive Olympic gold medals in the '20s and '30s into a career as a Hollywood movie star. Peggy Fleming, Dorothy Hamill (who seemed to change the way every girl under 15 wore her hair), and Kristi Yamaguchi were later incarnations.

There is a lot at stake on the ice at the Olympics. And now the attack on Kerrigan made it clear how far some people were willing to go to push the odds in their favor. When the ever-direct Harding returned home to Portland, Oregon, after the U.S. championships, she was asked for her thoughts on the Olympic Games. According to *The New York Times*, Harding replied, "To be perfectly honest, what I'm really thinking about are dollar signs."

The Nancy–Tonya event played out en route to the Olympics in several ways. One was the support of Kerrigan by her potential teammates, who reportedly asked that she be able to join the skating team even though she hadn't formally qualified. Another was in the upper echelons of amateur sport. The FBI grilled Harding for more than 10 hours, but she maintained she did not find out about her "friends'" actions until afterward. The U.S. Olympic Committee finally agreed to let her participate if she would drop a $25 million lawsuit she had filed against them when they tried to prevent her from skating in the Olympics. The USOC made the announcement, permitting Harding to skate, on the day of the opening ceremonies.

But perhaps the most interesting was the response of the American people. They divided themselves rather quickly into Tonya or Nancy fans. One writer called the skate-off "a Rorschach of how America sees itself." The article was titled "The Ice Queen vs. The Darling of Dysfunction."

Kerrigan was the polite victim who fought back to go for the glory, the graceful and elegant Massachusetts girl. *The New York Times* described her Olympic short program outfit as "cocktail-dress-like." Some people loved that. Others found her too perfect, too distant. One man said, "I think Kerrigan's too wholesome. She's like Barney."

Left: Harding's bodyguard, Shawn Eckhardt (*pictured*), admitted taking part in the assault on Kerrigan. *Right:* Kerrigan makes her first public statement about the incident.

Tonya Harding (*left*) and Nancy Kerrigan pass each other during practice in Hamar, Norway, on February 17, 1994—just six weeks after the attack on Kerrigan.

Harding was an asthmatic who smoked cigarettes, played pool, and shot her first deer when she was 14. To some she was a scrapper who never had it easy and had to keep fighting against all odds. Her mother had married six times. Harding pushed potatoes at Spud City to pay for rink practice time. To Kerrigan fans she was merely a bad girl with criminal tendencies. *The Times* on Harding's attire? "Over-rouged and dressed in beads and feathers like a Las Vegas showgirl."

Olympic rules state that teammates must share practice space, so Kerrigan and Harding skated on the same rink, politely, during the leadup to the competition. After the first night, a *New York Times* reporter commented: "Nancy Kerrigan skated the best short program of her life. Tonya Harding skated one of the worst of hers." Kerrigan was first, Harding 10th.

In the long program, Harding created even more drama. She was six seconds away from being disqualified when she finally showed up and began to skate. She began her first leap, but didn't complete it. She skated over to the judges, threw her right leg on the railing in front of their seats and pointed to her skate. She had broken a lace during practice and couldn't find a replacement. She tried a shorter one but realized it wouldn't work,

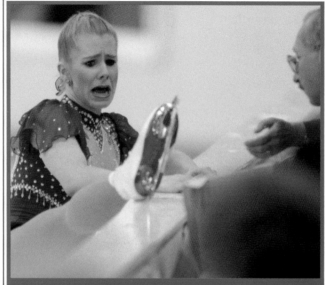

Few mustered any sympathy for Tonya Harding when she complained of a broken shoelace just before her long-program performance at the 1994 Olympic Games.

and she feared injury. She begged the judges for time to find a suitable lace. They granted it, moving her back on the slate of skaters. She skated decently, and was in second place when she left the ice. But the big stars hadn't yet skated. Harding would finish eighth overall. Kerrigan finished second by a pug nose to the effervescent Ukrainian Oksana Baiul.

A week later Harding was assaulted near a friend's apartment in Oregon. Two days later after the assault Kerrigan was given a parade in her hometown. Two weeks after that, Harding pleaded guilty to one count of conspiring to hinder a prosecution. She was given three years of probation, fined $100,000, plus court costs, legal fees, and a $50,000 donation to the Special Olympics, and was told to perform 500 hours of community service. She was also banned for life from the U.S. Figure Skating Association. With no trial, and no further investigation, it is impossible to know how much she was involved in the Kerrigan attack. In 1999 she finished second in a (nonsanctioned) ESPN professional skating championship. Four years later she was back in the news trying to make it as a pro boxer. Latest reports indicate that Kerrigan is a happy mom of two.

Attacks on female athletes

The Nancy Kerrigan incident was hardly the first time a female athlete had to deal with dangerous threats or actual assaults. The public nature of the lives these women must live can often attract individuals with twisted psyches, whether they're seeking to cause bodily harm or express "deep feelings."

Before the attack on Nancy Kerrigan, Tonya Harding herself felt she needed a bodyguard after she received a death threat

in her home town of Portland in November 1993. The incident upset her so much she withdrew from the northwest regional skating competition.

Monica Seles, tennis star, was stabbed as she waited for a changeover during a match in April of that same year. The attacker said he wanted to keep Monica from playing so that his "idol," Steffi Graf, would hold the No. 1 spot in the world. The assault kept Seles from competition for

more than two years. When she returned, she was never able to reach the heights of excellence she had attained before.

Another ice skating legend, Katarina Witt, was harassed by an over-the-edge "fan." He stalked her and sent her obscene mail. When he was captured, he was sentenced to more than three years in a mental hospital. Witt also had to forego the common practice of accepting flowers from fans after performances when one such character offered a bouquet, then grabbed her arm to try and pull her into the stands with him.

BLOODBATH
Hungary vs. the Soviet Union, December 6, 1956

In the fall of 1956, members of the Hungarian water polo team sequestered themselves from the real world. Nestled at a mountain retreat in their homeland, the athletes focused on the task at hand: preparing for the Summer Olympic Games, to be held in November/December in Melbourne, Australia. Led by 21-year-old sensation Ervin Zador, the team seemed poised to repeat as the Olympic gold medalists.

Yet between training sessions, the players noticed disturbing sights and sounds in the distance. In the capital city of Budapest, gunfire erupted for days while an excessive amount of smoke rose to the sky. What was happening? The players didn't know for sure, but they sensed something was terribly wrong.

Keeping the athletes in the dark, communist Hungarian officials whisked the team out of the country, first to Czechoslovakia and eventually to Australia. In Melbourne, the Olympians heard and read the details of the tragedy that had played out in their beloved country.

Hungary, an Eastern Bloc satellite of the Soviet Union, had been clamoring for independence since the summer. On October 23, thousands of Hungarians tore down a statue of Joseph Stalin, the deceased ruler of the USSR who had raised an "Iron Curtain" over Eastern Europe in the aftermath of World War II. The protesters melted the statue with blowtorches while chanting, "Russians go home! Russians go home!"

Later, demonstrators recited the national poem:
> Stand up, Hungarians, your country calls.
> The time for now or never falls.
> Are we to live as slaves or free?
> Choose one. This is our destiny!

For five days after the demonstration, Hungarian

On October 23, 1956, enraged Hungarians used blowtorches to topple a statue of former USSR dictator Joseph Stalin, a symbol of oppression in the Soviet satellite state.

"freedom fighters" battled the Soviet Red Army in the streets of Budapest. Reformer Imre Nagy took over as Hungary's leader, ousting the Soviet-aligned Erno Gero. On October 31, the Soviets withdrew troops and Nagy announced the triumph of the revolution.

Tragically, the USSR was not retreating but merely regrouping. In early November, 200,000 Soviet troops and 4,000 tanks rolled into Hungary to crush the resistance. Overall, an estimated 25,000 to 50,000 Hungarians and 7,000 Soviet troops were killed in the crackdown. Hungarians lost not just their lives and their loved ones, but any hope of personal freedom.

Peter Fryer, author of *Hungarian Tragedy*, explained what Hungarians had to look forward to: "Hungary was Stalinism incarnate. Here in one small, tormented country was the picture, complete in every detail: the abandonment of humanism, the attachment of primary importance not to living, breathing, suffering, hoping human beings but to machines, targets, statistics, tractors, steel mills, plan fulfillment figures ... and, of course, tanks."

In Melbourne, Hungary's Olympians burned with emotion. They worried about their loved ones back home, and they seethed with anger at their Soviet oppressors. In the Olympic Village, officials flew the communist Hungarian flag—which infuriated Hungarians. One night, vandals took down the flag and removed the red star of communism, reportedly replacing it with the Kossuth Arms, the traditional symbol of Hungary.

Despite (or because of) the turmoil, the water polo team remained focused throughout the tournament, overpowering their first four opponents. As they entered the fifth round, the Hungarians were in first

Officials finally ended the fight-filled match after a punch by USSR's Valentin Prokopov opened a gash above Ervin Zador's eye.

place, one point ahead of Yugoslavia and two ahead of the USSR. Fatefully, Hungary drew the Soviets.

Water polo is a high-energy, often violent sport, but on December 6, 1956, the Hungarian team entered the pool ready for war. As Zador later explained to *Sports Illustrated,* "We felt we were playing not just for ourselves but for every Hungarian. This game was the only way we could fight back."

Among the packed crowd of 5,500 at the natatorium were hundreds of Hungarian expatriates. They waved flags, taunted the Soviets, and chanted, "Go Hungarians!" From the opening whistle, the teams battled ferociously. Hungary's Dezsö Gyarmati scored the first goal, and in the process nearly knocked out a Soviet defender. Soon afterward, a referee penalized the Soviets' Vyacheslav Kurennoi for slugging.

More fisticuffs followed, including a second-half bout between Hungary's Antal Bolvari and the USSR's Boris Markarov. By that time, fights had begun to break out all over the pool. Soviet troops may have stormed the streets of Budapest, but this Hungarian team refused to allow a Soviet goal. Late in the game, Hungary led 4–0. Then, after play was stopped by a referee's whistle, the USSR's Valentin Prokopov blind-sided Zador with a brutal punch above his right eye.

The water turned red as Zador's blood poured into the pool. Suddenly, all hell broke loose. Hungarians in the stands charged toward the pool ready to retaliate. Police ran in to contain the crowd, while officials called off the match. As the Soviet players, under police escort, headed for safety in the locker room, hostile fans cursed them along the way. Miklós Martin, a member of Hungary's 1952 Olympics water polo team, said about the Soviets, "They play their sports just as they conduct their lives—with brutality and disregard for fair play."

Declared the victors of their literal bloodbath against the Soviets, the Hungarians advanced to the final, where they defeated Yugoslavia 2–1 for the gold medal. As the team ascended the victory stand during the medal ceremony, Zador began to sob. "I was crying for Hungary," he said, "because I knew I wouldn't be returning home."

Zador was one of dozens of Hungarian Olympians who defected after the Games. Some stayed in Australia, while others sought refuge in other countries. Nearly all had wished to go home, but home wasn't what it used to be. The Soviet Red Army made sure of that.

Warm hearts in a Cold War

As the Summer Olympics commenced in fall 1956, the Cold War continued to rage between the world's two superpowers, the Soviet Union and the United States. On May 1, U.S. Secretary of Defense Charles Wilson asserted that the Soviets were ahead of the United States in the production of long-range bombers capable of delivering hydrogen bombs. And on November 18, at a diplomatic reception in the Kremlin, Soviet leader Nikita Khrushchev frightened Americans when he proclaimed, "Whether you like it our not, history is on our side. We will bury you."

As in 1952, the '56 Summer Olympics were a political grudge match. The Soviet Union proved itself superior with 98 medals (37 gold) compared to 74 medals (32 gold) for the U.S. Yet amid the Cold War tensions, a remarkable love story developed in the Olympic Village. Harold Connolly, an American hammer thrower, became smitten with Olga Fikotová, a discus thrower from Czechoslovakia, a Soviet satellite state.

To Connolly, Olga was the prettiest discus launcher he had ever seen—with a smile that could warm the chilliest of Cold War hearts. Connolly escorted Fikotová (who happened to win the gold medal in '56) around the Village, and after the Games the two lovebirds kept in touch with letters. Eventually, Connolly went to Prague to ask permission of the Czech president to marry Olga and bring her to the U.S.

After some delay, and help from the U.S. State Department, the Czech government consented to the marriage. Harold and Olga married in 1957, had four children, and competed in the Olympics together through 1968—each time as American teammates.

HUMILIATING HITLER
Jesse Owens vs. Hitler, 1936 Berlin Olympics

The grudge match between Jesse Owens and Adolf Hitler was more like a silent feud, an African/Aryan Cold War. At the 1936 Olympic Games, the two adversaries exchanged only a wave. They never talked to each other and apparently rarely talked about each other. Yet Owens' four victories in August 1936 at the Berlin Games were a screwdriver to the belly of Hitler's ideology: that nonwhites—specifically those of African and Jewish descent—were subhuman.

The son of an Alabama sharecropper, Owens never dreamed he'd become an immortal hero, especially because he had endured several bouts of pneumonia as a child. After the Owens family moved to Cleveland, the track coach at Cleveland East Tech High School noticed Jesse's extraordinary running and leaping skills. As a senior, Owens actually tied the world record in the 100-yard dash (9.4 seconds).

As a nonscholarship athlete at Ohio State, Owens competed in 42 events and won them all. At the 1935 Big Ten Championships in Ann Arbor, Michigan, the "Buckeye Bullet" stunned the nation. While nursing a tailbone injury, he tied his world record in the 100-yard dash and broke world records in the 220–yard dash, the 220 low hurdles, and the long jump. Yet on road trips in segregated Middle America, Owens had to sleep and eat in "blacks-only" hotels and restaurants. If nothing else, America's racism hardened him for his chilling experience in Nazi Germany.

In 1936, Hitler was busy building his war machine and plotting ways to dominate Europe and eradicate as many Jews as possible. The Olympics, which had been promised to Berlin before Hitler became chancellor in 1933, would be a great PR opportunity for the fiendish *Führer*. By playing the part of benevolent host, he could give the illusion that his Nazi Party was not as villainous as portrayed abroad. He could lull the world into complacency.

Before the Summer Games, Hitler ordered the removal of vicious anti-Jewish signs throughout Berlin, such as "Jews are not wanted in this place." He even allowed one German Jew (a blonde half-Jew named Helene Mayer) to participate in the Olympics. It was a token gesture, because all other German Jews were banned from the Games. Hitler's Opening Ceremonies were the grandest ever held, climaxed by the release of 20,000 birds that soared to the sky wearing colored ribbons.

Owens quickly sensed the ugliness of Nazi racism. One German official groused that the Americans were letting "nonhumans, like Owens and other Negro athletes," compete. On the first day of the Games, Hitler congratulated gold medalists but left the stadium before African-American Cornelius Johnson received his first-place medal in the high jump. Olympic officials informed Hitler that for the rest of the Games, he must greet all the winners or none at all. He chose the latter option.

Adolf Hitler hands his autograph to a happy spectator. The Nazi leader, who considered blacks subhuman, was on hand when Jesse Owens won his first gold.

On August 3, Owens won his first gold medal, prevailing in the 100 meters, while Hitler stewed in his box. The next day, officials seemingly tried to sabotage Owens in the long jump, ruling that his warm-up run was a foul (three fouls meant disqualification). Blond German long jumper Luz "Lutz" Long then advised Jesse to leap several inches before the takeoff board on his final jump so that officials couldn't disqualify him for "touching" that line.

Owens took Long's words to heart, and he went on to win the gold with a world-record leap of 26′ 5½″. As

Jesse Owens salutes after winning the gold medal in the long jump—one of his four during the Games. Silver medalist Luz "Lutz" Long (*right*), a German, gives the Nazi salute.

he recalled in *Jesse Owens, Champion Athlete*: "I decided I wasn't going to come down. I was going to fly. I was going to stay up in the air forever." In broad daylight, Owens displayed his gratitude for Long. "Hitler must have gone crazy watching us embrace," Owens said, according to ESPN.

After Owens won his third gold medal, in the 200-meter dash, on August 5, he and Ralph Metcalfe replaced Marty Glickman and Sam Stoller (both Jews) on the 4 X 100-meter relay team. Reportedly, Nazi heavies had asked U.S. officials to make the switch, for they didn't wanted to be humiliated by America's blacks *and* its Jews. So Owens ran, and he captured his fourth gold medal.

In his autobiography, Owens recounted his only exchange with Hitler during the Games: "When I passed the Chancellor he arose, waved his hand at me, and I waved back at him." After their encounter, both men headed down seemingly unfathomable personal paths.

Hitler went on to incite World War II, which resulted in the deaths of 62 million people, including six million Jews exterminated by Hitler's Nazis and their collaborators. With his defeat imminent, Hitler committed

Jesse Owens blasts off in a 200-meter heat during the Berlin Games. Owens copped gold in the 100 meters, 200 meters, long jump, and 400-meter relay.

suicide on April 30, 1945.

After his victories, Owens was hounded for autographs on the streets of Berlin and was honored in New York with a ticker-tape parade. Yet for his post-parade reception at the Waldorf-Astoria, Owens was forced to ride the freight elevator because he was black. President Franklin Roosevelt did not acknowledge Owens' feats, and his skin color prevented him from landing any endorsement deals. To support his family, Owens stooped to participating in novelty exhibitions, such as running against racehorses and motorcycles. Eventually, he made a successful living as a public speaker, then started his own public relations company.

Late in life, and after his death in 1980, Owens finally received his due. President Gerald Ford awarded Owens the Presidential Medal of Freedom in 1976, and the city of Berlin named a street and a school after him. In 1990 President George H.W. Bush honored Owens posthumously with a Congressional Gold Medal. Bush called his victories under the hateful eyes of Hitler "an unrivaled athletic triumph, but more than that, a triumph for all humanity."

Bursts of greatness

In the liberal community of Ann Arbor, Michigan, and in the heart of Nazi Germany, Jesse Owens proved himself as the greatest track star the world had ever seen. A look at his accomplishments:

Big Ten Championships, May 25, 1935
- Runs the 100-yard dash in 9.4 seconds, tying his own world record.
- Soars 26′ 8½″ in the long jump, establishing a world record that lasts for 25 years.
- Breaks the record in the 220-yard dash with a sprint of 20.3 seconds.
- Becomes the first person ever to break the 23-second barrier in the 220-yard low hurdles, clocking in at 22.6.

Summer Olympics, August 3–9, 1936
- Wins a gold medal in the 100-meter dash with a time of 10.3 seconds.
- Cops gold in the long jump with a leap of 26′ 5½″, breaking the Olympic record.
- Earns a gold medal in the 200-meter dash with an Olympic-record time of 20.7 seconds. Mack Robinson, the older brother of baseball legend Jackie Robinson, wins the silver.
- Runs leadoff on the 4 X 100-meter relay team, sparking the quartet to a gold medal. Their world-record time of 39.8 seconds lasts for 20 years.

THE GOAL OF THE CENTURY

England vs. Argentina, 1986 World Cup

Twenty years before the 1986 World Cup, England, on its own soil, had defeated Argentina in a heated match en route to winning the 1966 tournament. It was the first such championship for the British, and a terrific example of the cross-continental rivalry that has long existed between England and Argentina. Every match between the two soccer-rich countries seems to bring a new level of intrigue, an enticing contrast in styles, and some of the most passionate fans on the globe. It was a military showdown, however, not an athletic one, that elevated the England–Argentina football grudge to a fever pitch entering their quarterfinal date in the 1986 World Cup.

Four years earlier, the nations had waged war over the Falkland Islands, a series of two main isles and several smaller ones in the South Atlantic, 300 miles off Argentina's coast. Ownership of these islands had long been contested between the governments of Great Britain and Argentina, but the dictatorship of Argentine General Leopoldo Galtieri had decided to settle matters in 1982. There had been growing civil unrest in Argentina, and with it a fear that, without an external enemy, the people might turn on their own leaders. So Galtieri, largely in a quest for his own political survival, sent thousands of troops to invade and secure the islands Argentina claimed were its own. Despite being outnumbered, the British prevailed in less than 11 weeks, suffering about 250 casualties while capturing 11,000 Argentine prisoners. About 650 Argentine soldiers were killed by the time their side surrendered in June 1982.

Against this backdrop, the proud national football clubs of England and Argentina advanced to face each other in the quarterfinal round of the 1986 World Cup in Mexico City. The teams and their fans had opposed each other since a 1950s match at Wembley Stadium in London, England, developing a tension unusual for countries so far apart geographically. Never had that tension been so tangible as it was in the oppressive heat of Estadio Azteca Stadium on June 22, 1986.

Diego Maradona rises above England's Peter Shilton to score his "Hand of God" goal.

Argentina, which had hosted and hoisted the 1978 World Cup, fielded a talented team powered by Diego Maradona, who at 25 years old had already established himself as perhaps the greatest player in the world. His wizardry with the ball and ability to put it in the net from angles other players would not even consider gave his country a unique dimension. England had routed Paraguay in the round of 16, its second 3–0 decision of the tournament, with Gary Lineker scoring five goals in four games. The British entered the quarterfinal feeling their disciplined style and rigid defense gave them a legitimate chance not only to defeat Argentina, but to contend for the Cup.

The heat did not deter 114,580 fans from setting a frenzied tone, and the decibel level went up when each team had a glorious scoring chance in the opening 12 minutes. Maradona was brought down 30 yards from the English goal on an early burst, and keeper Peter Shilton steered a deflected free kick outside the post. An early rush for England gave Peter Beardsley a shot even closer to the goal, but it missed the mark and settled into the side of the net.

Argentina gained control of the tempo after that early chance for the British. Maradona's footwork gave him a series of free kicks from just outside the box, and one of them grazed the goalpost from 25 yards away. Using flawless technique, quick passes and its usual dash of creativity, Argentina felt it was only a matter of time before it gained the upper hand on the scoreboard. It happened in the second half, in a four-minute span that remains unparalleled in World Cup history.

Argentina collected a 1–0 lead five minutes into the second half on what became known as the "Hand of God" goal. In reality, it was the hand of Maradona that knocked the ball across the line, but the officials did not see the illegal touch. The Argentine star had tried to play the ball into the penalty area, but midfielder Steve Hodge beat him to it and lofted the ball

After losing the war in the Falkland Islands to England, Argentines looked to their soccer team to restore their country's honor.

back to keeper Shilton. Maradona refused to give up on the play, jumped toward the ball and knocked it into the net with the back of his left hand. The English fans howled and whistled in protest, but to no avail. It was ruled a goal. "The hand of God" knocked it in, Maradona would say.

Just four minutes after fans had watched one of the most controversial goals in World Cup history, they witnessed what most consider to be the greatest one. Dancing between opponents on his own side of the midfield stripe to begin the memorable play, Maradona freed himself to dribble along the right sideline, leaving British pursuers in his wake. Cutting inside one defender and outside a final one, he was in front of the keeper with a snap decision to make. In a similar situation against England six years earlier at Wembley, Maradona had shot wide instead of trying to go around the English keeper. This time, he faked a shot, rounded Shilton as the keeper came out to make a play, avoided a tackle from behind and kicked a low 10-yarder into the vacated goal, setting off a wild celebration among Argentina's players and fans. "The goal of the century," it remains called today.

"That first goal was dubious," British coach Bobby Robson told the Associated Press. "The second one was a miracle, a fantastic goal. It's marvelous [for soccer] that every now and then the world produces a player like Maradona. I didn't like his second goal, but I admire it."

England would not go down without a fight. Lineker scored his sixth goal of the tournament at the 78-minute mark to make it 2–1, but an equalizer was not to be. Argentina went on to defeat Belgium and West Germany to claim the World Cup, but it was the match with England that would forever be remembered by these rival nations. "That was a final for us," Maradona noted on FIFA's Official World Cup website. "It was about knocking out the English."

The World Cup

A visionary named Jules Rimet and a group of French football administrators came up with a novel idea in the 1920s to hold a tournament among the world's strongest soccer countries. Rimet's name appeared on the original World Cup trophy, which was awarded three times in the 1930s before World War II halted the tournament for a 12-year stretch. Since then, it has grown in both popularity and prestige, capturing the world's sporting attention every four years. Following is a chronology of FIFA World Cup competition, with year, host country and final score.

1930 Uruguay: Uruguay 4, Argentina 2
Note: United States finished third, its best-ever showing.

1934 Italy: Italy 2, Czechoslovakia 1

1938 France: Italy 4, Hungary 2

1950 Brazil: Uruguay 2, Brazil 1
Note: Tournament resumed after 12-year hiatus during World War II.

1954 Switzerland: West Germany 3, Hungary 2

1958 Sweden: Brazil 5, Sweden 2
Note: Brazil's Pele debuted at age 17 and scored six goals in four matches.

1962 Chile: Brazil 3, Czechoslovakia 1

1966 England: England 4, West Germany 2

1970 Mexico: Brazil 4, Italy 1
Note: By rule, Brazil's third title allowed it to keep the Rimet Cup. The FIFA World Cup Trophy would be introduced in '74.

1974 West Germany: West Germany 2, Holland 1

1978 Argentina: Argentina 3, Holland 1

1982 Spain: Italy 3, West Germany 1

1986 Mexico: Argentina 3, West Germany 2

1990 Italy: West Germany 1, Argentina 0

1994 United States: Brazil 0, Italy 0 (3-2 on penalty kicks)
Note: First American-hosted Cup is the first decided on penalty kicks.

1998 France: France 3, Brazil 0

2002 Korea/Japan: Brazil 2, Germany 0

Argentina's Diego Maradona celebrates with the cup after defeating West Germany 3–2 in the final game of the 1986 World Cup.

New York's Aaron Boone completes his home run trot in the 11th inning of Game 7 of the ALCS. Yankees pitcher Mariano Rivera celebrates at the mound.

CURSED

Boston Red Sox vs. New York Yankees, October 2003

A portly 72-year-old man was grabbed by the head and flung to the ground during a bench-clearing shoving match. A grounds crew member in the visiting team's bullpen was beaten up by two players because he was cheering on his team. And, by the way, an edgy, bruising ballgame was being played.

The Yankees and Red Sox have more than a rivalry; they have a war. And it has lasted a long time. Sure, it hasn't always been obvious; there were many years when it was merely smoldering and sputtering, in fits and starts. Sometimes it's just quaint and curious, more like a cartoon than a full-blown disaster. But when it explodes, it explodes white-hot.

The Yankees didn't come into existence until 1903, when the American League Baltimore franchise shut down. The Sox already had two pennants before the Yanks were three seasons old. In 1914 the Boston team purchased a young lefty from the minors, a kid named Babe Ruth, and won three pennants in four years. But Boston owner Harry Frazee was stretched tight with regard to cash, often investing in Broadway shows. He needed dough to stay afloat, and before long began selling off his players to the wealthier Yankee organization.

Ruth was one of them, and the others weren't too shabby: Carl Mays (he of the Ray Chapman beanball incident in 1920), Red Ruffing, Dutch Leonard, Ernie Shore, Duffy Lewis, "Jumpin'" Joe Dugan, Herb Pennock, and Waite Hoyt. With many of their best players sold off, the Sox only once finished above last from 1924 through 1930. New York won three pennants and two World Series titles during that time.

Do you wonder why Boston hates New York?

What's worse is that the Yankees stayed great and the Sox lumbered. Only twice did they both field good teams at the same time: in the late '40s and the late '70s. Then, starting in 1998, the rivalry came to a full boil. The Yanks and Sox finished 1–2 six years in a row

In Game 3 of the 2003 ALCS, Boston starting pitcher Pedro Martinez (*right*) and New York hurler Roger Clemens (*left*) were at the center of a bench-clearing brawl.

through 2003. The Sox lost to the Yankees in the 1999 LCS, and to Cleveland in the '98 Divisional Series.

In other words, by the time the 2003 ALCS began on October 8, these teams were not news to each other. Both were playing at a high level and had been for years. In today's baseball world it's harder to reach the World Series, so comparing these two teams to the all-time greats is a tough dog to scratch. Each team had at least two legitimate Hall of Fame candidates (Boston's Pedro Martinez and Manny Ramirez, and New York's Roger Clemens and Derek Jeter), with a fistful of All-Stars alongside them. Both Martinez and Clemens were intense competitors (probably two of the more intense players ever) and not afraid to pitch inside.

Boston took the first contest behind the baffling knuckleball of Tim Wakefield. Yankees quoted after the game either snarled or simpered at their inability to deal with the floater. The Yanks handed the ball to iceman Andy Pettitte for Game 2; he had to button up and squeeze his way out of some jams, but that was his style. The Yanks tied the Series with a 6–2 win.

The third game, matching Pedro and Clemens, was raucous. Ramirez, the mercurial Sox slugger, rapped home two first-inning runs with a single. The Yankees had taken the lead with single runs in the second, third, and fourth when a fourth-inning Martinez pitch plunked Karim Garcia in the upper back, near the head. Garcia said he was certain Pedro was throwing at his head. Garcia took his base, then when the Sox turned a subsequent double play (which scored another run), slid especially hard into Todd Walker. Words were exchanged and the benches cleared.

In the bottom of the inning, Ramirez overreacted to a high Clemens fastball and tried to charge the mound. "Big Papi" David Ortiz held him back, but the benches cleared. That's when the portly, aged Don Zimmer went charging at Pedro Martinez. Zimmer tried to wind up to throw a big left hook when Pedro grabbed the coach by the head and tossed him to the ground. His nose bloodied, the dazed Zimmer sat on the ground for a few moments. It was an awful, embarrassing sight, but in truth Pedro settled the issue with a minimum of fuss. It could have been worse. After things calmed down, both pitchers pitched well, but the Yankees took the game 4–3.

Game 4 replayed Game 1. The Knuckle Kid, Wakefield, baffled the Bronxmen again. The Sox hit two solo homers and won 3–2. Game 5 was dominated by plump pitcher David "Boomer" Wells, who shut down the Sox 4–2. The boys from Boston responded the next game with a thundering 9–6 victory, as Nomar Garciaparra had four hits.

Game 7 was supposed to be another fierce Clemens/Pedro match-up, but this time neither pitcher was at his best. Clemens didn't get an out in the fourth inning, putting his team in a 4–0 hole. But though two solo home runs by previously slumping Jason Giambi got them closer, things were looking dim for manager Joe Torre's men as they headed into the bottom of the

The Red Sox hadn't won a World Series since selling Babe Ruth to the Yankees. New Yorkers loved to rub "The Curse" into Red Sox fans' faces.

eighth down 5–2. But in a flash, Pedro self-destructed, allowing three doubles and a single with one out before being lifted (which ultimately cost Sox manager Grady Little his job and started a discussion about managerial strategy that continues in Boston to this day). The Yankees got three home to tie the game at 5.

Neither manager was holding anything back. Mike Mussina, who had already started twice in the series, replaced Clemens for New York, and later on, the other starter, Wells, replaced Mussina. The new pitcher facing the Yankees in the 10th was their two-time nemesis, Tim Wakefield. He set them down in order. The Sox didn't mount a threat in their ups.

Leading off for New York in the bottom of the 11th was Aaron Boone, who had some power but better bloodlines, being the brother of Bret, son of Bob and grandson of Ray—big leaguers all. He decided not to wait and jumped on the first Wakefield pitch he saw. The line drive cleared the left field fence in a hurry, and the Yankees were going to the World Series for the 39th time.

The "Idiots" unravel "The Curse"

The Yankees-Red Sox feud continued with a vengeance in 2004. After Boston lost a bidding war with New York for superstar free agent Alex Rodriguez, A-Rod mixed it up with Sox catcher Jason Varitek during a bench-clearing brawl on July 24. A contentious regular season led up to a classic Boston-New York post-season confrontation.

After sweeping the Angels in the LDS, the Red Sox came up against their long-time nemeses, the Yankees, in the ALCS New York promptly belted Boston in three straight games to start the Series. But the "grinders" delivered improbable comebacks and last-inning heroics to win in Games 4 and 5.

In Game 6, Red Sox starter Curt Schilling provided the world with one of game's most indelible images ever: blood on his sock. His ankle had a dislocated tendon, and surgeons had to stitch the skin around it back together enough for him to pitch; the blood was clearly visible. But Schilling threw seven tough innings and the Sox won 4–2. The Red Sox had accomplished the heretofore impossible. Twenty-five times before a team had been down three games to none in the postseason. Not one had ever made it to Game 7.

But Schilling's blood was emblematic of his team's unwillingness to quit. They called themselves "grinders," "idiots" filled with a goofy confidence born of sheer energy and orneriness. And in Game 7, the Sox rolled to a surprisingly easy 10–3 win that made them A.L. champs for the first time in 18 years.

Next step: St. Louis and the World Series. The Cardinals had won 105 games in the regular season and featured a future Hall of Fame manager in Tony La Russa and a murderous lineup. What they didn't have was the Red Sox' spirit. The Sox slammed the door on La Russa's minions, winning four straight games. They had upended the "curse" forever. After 86 years, the Red Sox were World Champions again.

ANTI-AMERICAN
Pittsburgh Steelers vs. Dallas Cowboys, Super Bowl XIII, January 21, 1979

Butch Johnson had just hauled in a four-yard touchdown pass with 22 seconds on the clock to pull the Dallas Cowboys within four points of the Pittsburgh Steelers, making the score 35–31 in Super Bowl XIII.

An onside kick sat on the horizon and Rocky Bleier knew it.

"I was right in the front [of the Steelers "hands team" front line]," said Bleier in *Steel Dynasty: The Team that Changed the NFL.* "I'm thinking, are they going to drill this kick toward me? They'll probably sort of bounce it. And if that's the case, then I'm going to let it go through and have our backup guys pick it up and I'll just throw a block."

Bleier understood the significance of the contest. This game went deeper than any Super Bowl—it was all about bragging rights for the decade. The Steelers and Cowboys were the best in the NFL and they had been for the duration of the 1970s. The Cowboys were the defending champions after beating Denver in the previous year's Super Bowl, giving them two titles for the decade; the Steelers also had two Super Bowl wins in the decade—including a memorable victory over the Cowboys. Whichever team claimed this game would likely hold the distinction of the "team of the '70s."

Not only did this game pit teams of contrasting styles, it also pitted contrasting cultures of their fans. The large Dallas crowd was perceived as glitzy. Meanwhile, Pittsburgh was blue-collar, shot-and-a-beer, work-at-the-mill folks.

Meanwhile, in the Cowboys' locker room, linebacker Thomas "Hollywood" Henderson questioned the intelligence of Steelers quarterback Terry Bradshaw, among other slights of Steelers players. Henderson's mouth flapped continuously during the 14 days before the big game that would be played at

Miami's Orange Bowl. Steelers linebacker Jack Lambert looked like "a toothless chimpanzee" and "Dracula" to Henderson. To Hollywood's way of thinking, tight end Randy Grossman "only plays when someone dies or breaks a leg" and Bradshaw "couldn't spell 'cat' if you spotted him the 'c' and the 'a.'"

Trash-talking aside, each roster swelled with talent and stability.

Running back Tony Dorsett had joined the Cowboys since the last time they met the Steelers in Super Bowl X and added another facet to their offense, rushing for 1,007 yards during his rookie season in 1977 and 1,325 yards in 1978.

Bradshaw led a Steelers offense that had evolved into a different team. Defense had carried the Steelers to their first two Super Bowl victories. This Steelers team had more balance, because the offense could run the football or strike quickly, thanks to Bradshaw's strong arm.

The Steelers scored their first touchdown in the first quarter on a Terry Bradshaw toss to reliable wideout John Stallworth.

Defensively, the statistics told the story. The Cowboys had allowed an NFC-low 107.6 rushing yards per game; Pittsburgh's defense had allowed an AFC-low 110.9 rushing yards per game. Each team had signed most of the players on their roster out of college.

The Steelers got on the scoreboard first when Bradshaw capped a seven-play, 53-yard drive with a touchdown pass to John Stallworth for a 7–0 lead. A Bradshaw fumble with a minute left in the first quarter led to a Staubach-to-Tony Hill touchdown pass that tied the game at 7. The Steelers quarterback fumbled again early in the second quarter and Mike Hegman carried the football 37 yards for a touchdown and a 14–7 Cowboys lead.

But the Cowboys couldn't stop Bradshaw, who found Stallworth at the Steelers' 35 for what should have been a short gainer. Instead, Stallworth got loose from cornerback Aaron Kyle and sprinted to the end-

The acrobatic Lynn Swann skies for a touchdown reception in the fourth quarter of Super Bowl XIII.

zone for a 75-yard touchdown.

An interception by Steelers cornerback Mel Blount gave Bradshaw the ball back late in the second quarter, and he tossed a seven-yard touchdown pass to a leaping Bleier to put the Steelers up 21–14 at the intermission.

The track meet disguised as a Super Bowl slowed down in the third quarter, which remained scoreless before finding the Cowboys at the Steelers 10 facing a third-and-3. Cowboys coach Tom Landry called for a set using an extra tight end, which gave the impression the Cowboys planned to run. Another confusing slant followed as Dorsett went into motion to give the idea he might become a target in the flat. Surprising the Steelers' defense, Staubach dropped back to pass and spotted tight end Jackie Smith open in the middle of the endzone. He threw him the ball for what appeared to be a gift game-tying touchdown. Inexplicably, Smith dropped the football and the Cowboys had to settle for a field goal. Despite cutting the Steelers' lead to 21–17 with the only score of the third quarter, a momentum shift could be felt.

After a controversial pass interference call on Cowboys cornerback Benny Barnes, the Steelers called Franco Harris' number at the Cowboys 22. The Steelers running back burst off tackle and went untouched for the score that capped an eight-play, 84-yard drive that put the Steelers up 28–17.

On the ensuing kickoff, Steelers kicker Roy Gerela slipped, which caused him to squib the kick. Dallas' All-Pro defensive tackle Randy White picked up the ball, then fumbled, giving the Steelers the football at the

Steve Furness puts the heat on Cowboys quarterback Roger Staubach, who managed three touchdown passes against the "Steel Curtain" defense.

Cowboys' 18. Bradshaw cashed in on the next play when he found Lynn Swann in the endzone for a 35–17 lead.

The game appeared to be over even after Staubach threw a seven-yard touchdown pass to Billy Joe DuPree with just over two minutes on the clock. But the Cowboys onside kick on the kickoff was bobbled by Tony Dungy and the Cowboys recovered at their own 48. The recovery led to Staubach's scoring pass to Johnson that made the score 35–31 and put Bleier and the rest of the Steelers on pins and needles as the Cowboys lined up for another onside kick with time running out.

The kick went directly to Bleier, who overcame his pre-kick anxiety and cradled the football to put the game away for the Steelers.

Time expired and the Steelers had become the first NFL team to win three Super Bowls.

Mr. Smith goes to the Super Bowl

Jackie Smith helped change the perception of tight ends. Before his playing days, tight ends were considered blockers and not a threat to catch passes, particularly deep ones. Unfortunately for Smith, his lasting legacy is more about the pass he dropped in Super Bowl XIII than for the body of his work, compiled primarily as a tight end for the St. Louis Cardinals.

Smith played college football at Northwestern Louisiana State College (now Northwestern State University) before start-ing an NFL career that spanned 210 games. He played for the Cardinals from 1963 to 1977 before moving to Cowboys in 1978. With the Cowboys Smith did not catch a pass during the season and was used only as a blocking tight end.

While with the Cardinals, he caught 480 passes for 7,918 yards and 40 touchdowns. In short, he was considered the standard at tight end. He had great size and he could run well, block, and catch.

The legacy he established before his drop eventually got Smith elected to the Pro Football Hall of Fame in Canton, Ohio, in 1994. Many feel that he should have gone in the first year he became eligible, but the memory of Super Bowl XIII poisoned the vote.

"In my opinion," said former Cowboys teammate Charlie Waters in a *St. Louis Post-Dispatch* article, "[Smith is] the sole reason we made it to the Super Bowl that year. His attitude and his leadership, these are the reasons the Cowboys went to the Super Bowl."

Franco Harris races toward the endzone after making his "Immaculate Reception." Jimmy Ware gets two hands on the powerful halfback but cannot pull him down.

THE IMMACULATE RECEPTION

Raiders vs. Steelers, December 23, 1972

The conclusion to a magical season for the Pittsburgh Steelers appeared near when quarterback Terry Bradshaw got forced out of the pocket by the Oakland Raiders on fourth down with time running out. When the play had begun, at the Steelers' 40-yard line, 22 seconds remained on the clock. Anxious Steelers fans prayed for a miracle, as the Raiders held a 7-6 lead in this 1972 AFC playoff semifinal.

All of Bradshaw's options appeared closed while he scrambled right. Suddenly, he spotted running back John "Frenchy" Fuqua near the Raiders' 35. If he could somehow complete the pass, the Steelers would be in field goal range for Roy Gerela to attempt the game-winner. Bradshaw threw the football and fell to the ground ...

If ever a stadium could will a team to win, Three Rivers Stadium, packed with 50,350 raucous fans, felt like a place that could turn the trick. The shot-and-a-beer, blue-collar crowd possessed an unparalleled exuberance for their team—coming up with playful factions such as "Franco's Italian Army,"

Steelers quarterbacks Terry Bradshaw (*left*) and Terry Hanratty celebrate after the game. Bradshaw's last pass was intended for John Fuqua, but it ricocheted and fell into Franco's hands.

"Gerela's Gorillas," and "Fuqua's Foreign Legion." But a victory looked like a long shot even though their season had been of storybook proportions.

The Steelers caught fire in 1972 thanks largely to running back Franco Harris. The rookie from Penn State rushed for 1,055 yards and scored 11 touchdowns en route to AFC Rookie of the Year honors. The boost to the running game and Bradshaw's continued seasoning led the Steelers' offense to a team-record 343 points. Meanwhile, the defense allowed just 175 points, second only to the unbeaten Miami Dolphins.

After posting an 11-3 record in 1972, the Steelers claimed their first-ever division title in the 40-year history of the franchise, which earned the team its first playoff appearance since 1947. Most of the club's success stemmed from a dominant defense. Opponents scored just one touchdown against the Steelers in the final four games of the season.

Meanwhile, the Raiders had a nasty attitude, an accomplished defense, and a balanced offense paced by seven Pro Bowl nominees. The Raiders and Steelers had played just two times since the NFL and the AFL merged in 1970, so they had not yet truly developed the genuine hatred associated with bitter rivals. But this game would change all that.

After three quarters, the Steelers held a 3-0 lead, which they extended to 6-0 with just over a minute to play. The Raiders' offense lost a fumble and suffered two intercepted passes, which prompted them to make a quarterback change at the start of the fourth quarter.

Crafty Ken Stabler entered the game as the Raiders' quarterback and brought with him the hope that he might be able to generate some offense. Unlike Raiders starting quarterback Daryle Lamonica, Stabler could run the football. He also had a good football mind, and he knew how to exploit a situation—which he did in the final quarter.

"We had played the Raiders a real tough game," said Dwight White in a 2004 interview. "The Raiders were down on our 30-yard-line when I got injured and came out of the game. Stabler was a lefthanded quarterback. [Art] Shell and [Gene] Upshaw were on the left side [of the offensive line]—that was their strong side, which is usually the opposite on a football team. Most quarterbacks are righthanded; the strong side of the line is on the right side with the tight end."

White explained that containment was the No. 1 priority of a defensive end, which had a lot to do with the angle taken when rushing the quarterback.

"I come out for one play, it is fourth down for the Raiders—this is it for them. I come out of the game, they go back to pass, and guess what? My backup, Craig Hanneman, doesn't contain. Stabler pulls the ball down and runs the damn thing in for the touchdown. Can't believe it. We can't believe it." Stabler's touchdown gave the Raiders a 7-6 lead with a 1:13 remaining.

Steelers fans mob Franco Harris after his immortal touchdown. This was Pittsburgh's first playoff game in 25 years, and its first postseason victory ever.

With 22 seconds to go, the game seemed like it was over. It was fourth down, and the Steelers were 60 yards away from the goal line. That's when Bradshaw made his heave of desperation.

Harris recognized that the play was breaking down, so he abandoned his blocking assignment and ran up the field to become another target for Bradshaw. The Steelers quarterback never looked Harris' way, opting instead to throw to Fuqua at the Raiders' 35. Bradshaw's throw and Raiders safety Jack Tatum arrived at the same time, creating a collision while sending the ball ricocheting back 20 yards in the direction of the line of scrimmage.

Harris, who would later say that he had learned at Penn State to always go to the ball, alertly watched the pigskin pop into the air and sprinted toward it in a race with gravity. Harris grabbed the ball in full stride just before it hit the ground at the Raiders' 42. He then sprint-ed all the way to the endzone to put the Steelers up 13–7.

"There was so much pandemonium," White said. "I saw the ball when it was deflected. I didn't really see Franco catch it. But I knew what had happened from the way the crowd was jumping up and down screaming."

Steelers fans and players celebrated while the Raiders vehemently protested.

According to NFL rules at the time, Harris' catch would have been nullified if the officials had judged that the ball had hit Fuqua instead of Tatum—because two offensive receivers were not allowed to touch the ball consecutively. Officials ruled the ball did not get deflected from Fuqua to Harris, which meant the touchdown stood. Pittsburgh would lose the following week to Miami, but Steelers fans would forever cherish Harris' catch—immersed in legend as the "Immaculate Reception."

Pigskin Physics 101

After the "Immaculate Reception" took place, pandemonium broke loose at Pittsburgh's Three Rivers Stadium.

"People were all over the place," said Steelers coach Chuck Noll during a 2005 interview. "We had people on the sidelines who had come down earlier because they thought it was over. Then this happened. [Steelers owner] Art Rooney usually didn't come down, but he was down there, too."

Though the play was controversial and

discussion among the officials followed, Noll said he never got concerned that the call would be reversed because logic told him the right decision had been made.

The play "was a double deflection kind of thing and it was a question of it bounced off one of our players and went back to one of theirs, which would have made it an illegal catch," Noll said. "But as it turned out, and rightfully so, they made the right call. Because if you look at the physics of it ... "

Noll began waving his hands like a traffic cop to illustrate the play.

"Ball coming here and you have [John Fuqua] coming here, both forces are coming this way, then you introduce another force coming this way, which was [Oakland safety Jack] Tatum, now the ball goes back," Noll said. "There's no question in my mind who hit the ball, that's just Physics 101. If the ball had continued this way, I would have thought otherwise. But this one came back from [Tatum's angle] with a great force."

POLITICAL CHESS GAME
Bobby Fischer vs. Boris Spassky, 1972

Brute strength and athleticism defined the typical sporting endeavor between the Soviet Union and the United States during the heyday of the Cold War. Intelligence wasn't a part of this particular sporting battlefield—that is, until the 1972 World Chess Championship.

A great lack of awareness about the sport of chess existed in the United States, where few citizens even knew such a championship existed until the "Match of the Century" was scheduled. Meanwhile, the Soviet Union took great pride in the fact it had ruled the chess world since the storied day in 1948 when Mikhail Botvinnik won the world championship. Brains, not brawn, had led to USSR dominance, which the Soviets believed proved that their country had greater intelligence than any other nation in the world.

The Soviets' Boris Spassky reigned as the world champion in 1972, and the challenger was Bobby Fischer from the United States. The American public viewed Spassky as the enemy—after all, he was a communist. But in reality, he had more endearing qualities to the average American than the challenger. Spassky had the reputation as a well-rounded sort and a friendly man. He enjoyed socializing with friends, and he liked to fish. A chess purist, he embraced the competition with Fischer, referring to the event as a "feast of chess."

Across the table would be the brazen challenger, Fischer, who hailed from Brooklyn. Bobby received his first chessboard at age 6, and he played by himself for a year before joining a local chess club. From there, his progression of learning continued dramatically, until he became the youngest international grandmaster ever at age 15. Fischer dropped out of high school and had few social graces.

In addition to Fischer's hunger to learn the game, he was said to have an insatiable appetite for winning, and chess satisfied that desire. While Fischer had the I.Q. of a genius, his bratty behavior and constant tantrums added a combat mentality to his game. He knew how to play with the heads of his opponents to a point where they were distracted by his antics and could not concentrate on the game in front of them.

Fischer began this mental warfare on the first day of his match with Spassky, on July 11, 1972, in Reykjavik, Iceland. In fact, when Spassky made his opening move, Fischer was not even present. The Russian master sat and waited by himself for seven minutes. Fischer finally arrived, but with an attitude; he was upset about the presence of television cameras. The game lingered until a second day, when Fischer resigned after the 56th move of the match.

Fischer remained adamant that the cameras needed to go, but the sponsorship of the event depended on the money paid for the TV rights. During the second game, played on July 13, the irritable challenger displayed considerable instances of quirky behavior. When the clock started, Fischer was nowhere to be found. Only after arrangements were made to have the cameras removed for the second game did Fischer agree to play. Then the challenger demanded that the clock be reset at zero. When it was not made, the second game was forfeited to the champion.

At this juncture, everybody expected Fischer to quit and return to the United States. He did not. Perhaps his antics were a ruse and he wanted to continue his against-the-grain behavior. In any case, Fischer continued to fool everyone by going against conventional thought. He chose to return for the third game, on July 16, and defeated Spassky for his first win of the match. By the sixth game, Fischer led 3½ games

Bobby Fischer arrived in Iceland to face Boris Spassky on July 4, 1972. The American continuously frustrated officials with his demands for more money and restrictions on TV cameras.

The media portrayed Bobby Fischer as a prima donna and a loner, as well as a chess genius. As a 15-year-old in 1958, he became the youngest-ever international grandmaster.

Boris Spassky and Bobby Fischer play their last game of the match. Despite his constantly disruptive behavior, Fischer won the 21-game match 12½–8½.

to Spassky's 2½ (the fourth game had ended in a draw).

After the seventh game ended in a perpetual check, Fischer won the eighth game, despite the return of the TV cameras. Mentally, the match began to take its toll on Spassky, who had been dealing with Fischer's antics since before the match had even begun. The ninth game began on August 1 and saw Spassky leave the stage after the first couple of moves before the game ended in a draw.

Fischer won the 10th game to take a 6–3 lead, and a draw followed in the 12th game. Fischer won the 13th, and they played to a draw in the 14th. At one point, the Soviets contended that Fischer was somehow benefiting from electronic devices planted inside the building where the match was played, which resulted in the police sweeping the premises to put to rest any such

nonsense. The match came down to the 21st game, which saw Spassky fall badly behind before it was adjourned. In fact, Spassky never returned to finish the game. He instead phoned his concession to Fischer on September 1st. The chess world had a new king.

All told, Fischer won seven of the final 19 games—losing just once during the run—and played to a draw 11 times. His final margin of victory was 12.5 to 8.5.

In the aftermath of his victory, Fischer enjoyed celebrity status in the United States. The sport of chess also benefited from the exposure of the "Match of the Century," and Fischer's name became synonymous for excellence in the "sport of kings."

Fischer never defended his crown. When he did not play Anatoly Karpov in 1975, the International Chess Federation anointed Karpov the champion.

Searching for Bobby Fischer

Bobby Fischer disappeared from public view after defeating Boris Spassky in 1972, which made chess aficionados yearn for a rematch. The pair had become synonymous with chess to a generation.

Finally, two decades after their first match, a rematch was arranged.

Fischer was stripped of the world title in 1975 for refusing to defend it. The eccentric, reclusive champion became a member of an extremist religious sect. Meanwhile, Spassky

continued to compete, but was said to be more interested in playing tennis.

Controversy surrounded the rematch because playing in it defied U.N. sanctions against Yugoslavia. Billed as the "Revenge Match of the 20th Century," the event started in Sveti Stefan but moved, in the middle of the match, to Belgrade. Fischer was 49 and unranked by the FIDE (Federation Internationale des Echecs, a.k.a., the International Chess Federation) and the

55-year-old Spassky ranked below the top 100 when the pair played the highly public rematch for a first prize (based on the first player to win 10 games) of more than $3 million.

The chess played during the second meeting between the two icons was less than inspiring. Fischer won 10–5 with 15 draws, then continued to live as a recluse abroad, while the U.S. government deemed him a fugitive for defying the U.N. sanctions against Yugoslavia.

THE SHOT HEARD 'ROUND THE WORLD
Brooklyn Dodgers vs. New York Giants, October 3, 1951

1951: No pennant race in baseball history has ever been wackier. No ending has ever been more dramatic. And no rivalry in the history of the game has lasted so long, had so much bad blood, and so much intense drama; it actually crossed the continent intact. The Giants and the Dodgers both had amazing battles even when neither of the teams was very good. When they were both of championship caliber, their confrontations were like nothing in the world. In fact, the Brooklyn/New York baseball rivalry predated the Dodgers and Giants by nearly 30 years.

Sal Maglie, a Giants pitcher known for a grim visage and a mean streak to match, said, "I really hated that club. If I could have gotten that feeling [of playing the Dodgers] every time I pitched, I'd have been a lot better pitcher." When Dodger great Jackie Robinson was traded to the Giants, he simply packed his bags and left the game. According to *The Giants and the Dodgers,* Maury Wills said, "Grudges got carried not only from game to game but from year to year." These guys really didn't like each other.

The 1951 season started out as expected. The Dodgers had been the dominant team in the league for several years, winning pennants in 1947 and '49 and missing by the narrowest of margins in '50. The Giants, under the field leadership of former Dodger icon Leo Durocher, had potential; they had finished the previous season just three games behind Brooklyn. But Leo's boys started out poorly. They won two of their first three games, then lost 11 in a row.

They turned that streak around in typical fashion. After trading beanballs with Dodgers pitchers, Maglie low-bridged Jackie Robinson, who bunted down the first base line in the next at-bat and then threw a body block on Maglie. Awakened, the Giants won that game and 14 of their next 21.

Then, a savvy personnel move by Durocher paid off. Superstar-to-be Willie Mays was given the center

Bobby Thomson (*left*) buddies up with Jim Hearn (*center*) and Monte Irvin after clouting the most thrilling home run in baseball history.

field job (he had been batting .477 in Triple A), and Bobby Thomson was moved from center to third. Thomson claimed being at an unfamiliar position (and the hot corner at that) clarified his mind. He had to focus on his defense, so he could relax and let his natural offensive talents take hold. Mays wasn't hitting 50 homers or .350 just yet, but he wasn't far from those numbers.

Yet by August 11, the teams were still 13½ games apart. After sweeping Durocher's boys in an August 8 doubleheader, the Brooklyn men razzed the Giants unmercifully through a wooden door between the Ebbets Field clubhouses. They sang, "Roll out the barrel, the Giants are dead!"

That may have been the final straw; the Giants then really kicked it into gear. After losing on August 11, the Giants won 16 straight games. Durocher claimed he got lucky with some moves; the team picked up on it and began to believe in him. Their confidence translated into exceptional performances, the two fed off each other, and his hunches looked better and better.

Whatever the reason, the Giants were darned near unbeatable. They won 37 of their last 44 regular season games. In fact, the Dodgers wouldn't even have been in the playoffs if Jackie Robinson hadn't put on the hero's hat once again, homering in the 14th inning of the season's final day to force the best-of-three tiebreaker.

You just knew that this wasn't going to be a sleepy best-of-three set. Game 1, on October 1, was the first regular-season baseball game ever televised live across the country. Televisions in more than three million home were tuned to the game.

A two-run homer by Bobby Thomson off Dodger starter Ralph Branca gave the Giants team a 2-1 lead. They held on for a 3-1 victory. Game 2, now in the Polo Grounds, was punctuated by rain showers, but it was the Dodgers who brought the thunder. They slugged four homers and Labine tossed a six-hit shutout. The season

Left fielder Andy Pafko hoped Bobby Thomson's line drive would bang off the wall, but it cleared the barrier by several feet.

315 FT.

that had seen incredible comebacks and last-second heroics was coming down to a final game. The two managers sent out their best starters: Maglie for the Giants, Newcombe for the Dodgers.

A bout of wildness by Maglie led to a first-inning run for Brooklyn. Then "The Barber" settled down, and Newk matched him. A seventh-inning Giant run tied the score. But the Dodgers roared to life against Maglie in the eighth. Four singles wrapped around a wild pitch and an intentional walk (with some sloppy defense by Thomson) gave the Dodgers a huge 4–1 lead. Newcombe had no trouble in the bottom of the eighth, and the Giants came to bat in the bottom of the ninth facing a pitcher who had allowed only four hits through eight innings. Their glorious comeback season looked dismally over.

But Newk stumbled. As one writer said, "After 272 innings of work this season, Newcombe's arm didn't have three more outs in it." Alvin Dark started things by slapping a single to right. Then, in an amazing example of managerial blockheadedness, Dressen had Gil Hodges hold Dark on, even though his run meant

Bobby Thomson is mobbed at home plate following his epic blast. In just six weeks, the Giants overcame a 13½-game deficit to win the pennant.

zilch. Don Mueller, known for his bat control, rapped a single through the place where Hodges should have been. After a pop out, Whitey Lockman doubled to left, driving home Dark. Mueller stopped at third, and in doing so, twisted his ankle and had to be removed from the game.

The two Dodgers warming in the bullpen were Ralph Branca and Carl Erskine. Even though Branca had allowed a homer to Thomson two days before, even though he had pitched eight innings that game, and even though he had warmed up four times earlier in this game, he was Dressen's choice.

Thomson tomahawked Branca's second pitch into the left field seats. Not by much, but it didn't have to be. A Dodger 4–2 lead had been twisted into a 5–4 defeat, a season-ending defeat, on one pitch. The whole city went crazy. Radio announcer Russ Hodges shouted "The Giants win the pennant!" over and over again into his microphone.

But those kinds of things happen when the Dodgers play the Giants.

Were the Giants stealing signs?

Nearly half a century after the Giants' remarkable streak, and Bobby Thomson's miracle, a reporter for *The Wall Street Journal* dug up evidence supporting the contention that the Giants had started stealing opposing catchers' signs from the Polo Grounds centerfield clubhouse on July 20. Everyone involved with the team admitted it was true. Ralph Branca said he knew it was the case, but to blame Thomson's winning homer on cheating would have sounded like whining. Here's how it is said to have worked.

Through a buzzer (one buzz, fastball; two, anything else), the clubhouse spy would signal the bullpen, where a Giants player (usually a catcher) would motion to the batter. Manager Leo Durocher asked each player whether he wanted the signs. About half said yes. Willie Mays and Thomson allegedly said no.

There is no doubt the Giants got hot about this time. But was it because of the sign stealing? The stats show that the Giants put up worse numbers at home that year after the July 20 buzzer installation, not better. Most of the Giants starting line-up had lower averages and production after July 20.

But ... one Giant showed dramatically higher offensive numbers after buzzer day: Bobby Thomson. Even though he disavowed any involvement, Thomson hit 120 points higher, about 90 higher than his lifetime average, during that period.

And did he know what was coming from Branca with two on in the bottom of the ninth? In a TV interview, Branca said he believed so.

But there is another flaw in the sign-stealing story. If the bullpen heard one buzz, they couldn't signal the batter until they were sure there was not a second one. That takes time. By that time the pitch was already being thrown, and the batter had better have his mind on the pitcher, not the bullpen.

RACIAL TENSION
Texas Western vs. Kentucky, March 19, 1966

In another time and place, there would have been no reason for a rivalry between Texas Western and Kentucky, universities worlds apart, in the championship game of the 1966 NCAA basketball tournament. The former, a little-known school in El Paso that had earned a surprising No. 3 ranking despite not beating a top 10 foe, had been to the NCAA Tournament just twice previously, never advancing past regionals. The latter, the top-ranked team in the country, was favored to win its fifth national title under legendary head coach Adolph Rupp. Their March 19, 1966, meeting, however, was no ordinary one. This was a unique setting indeed, painted in black and white.

Rupp was a bearish man and a great coach—perhaps the most respected coach of his era—and fellow white Southerners generally held him in high regard for his stance on black players. Simply put, he wanted nothing to do with them. He had never coached one and never recruited one. If anyone had suggested this was bad policy, Rupp could point to his coaching record as evidence to the contrary. Not that anyone would dare question this stern disciplinarian. The Southeastern Conference remained segregated in 1966. Rupp had even gone so far as to ask newspaper editors to put asterisks next to the names of black high schoolers, so he knew which ones *not* to recruit.

If Rupp had a coaching opposite, it might have been Texas Western's Don Haskins, nearly 30 years his junior. Haskins was not out to break any color barriers by recruiting black players from cities like New York, Houston, or Gary, Indiana. He simply realized there was talent available to help his team. Two years after the Civil Rights Act was passed, blacks still could not play at most Southern schools. They could in El Paso,

Tommy Kron of Kentucky passes over the head of David Lattin to teammate Larry Conley. According to Texas Western's Willie Worsley, the Miners played a more "white" game than the all-white Wildcats.

where Haskins had compiled a 23-1 regular-season record with a club that had seven black players, four whites, and one Latino. Although the prevailing philosophy, even among coaches who *did* allow blacks, was that you needed at least one or two white players on the floor to ensure a "disciplined" approach, Haskins simply started his five best players. That each of those players happened to be black—a first in NCAA Championship history—did not faze the high-strung bench boss, nor did it produce "undisciplined" play, as Kentucky would discover.

Rupp had said before the final that no lineup comprised entirely of black players could beat an all-white team. He felt particularly good about that all-white team being his own. Some called this Kentucky team "Rupp's Runts" because of its lack of size. The Wildcats' top scorers were 6-foot-3 Pat Riley, who went on to become a coaching great himself, and 6-foot Louie Dampier. It was a quick, hot-shooting group that Rupp loved for its teamwork. Many thought the Wildcats' 83-79 victory against second-ranked Duke in a semifinal was the de facto national title game. Beating Texas Western for the championship seemed a foregone conclusion.

Texas Western's players heard about Rupp's comments before the game. They came to downplay the remarks as a motivational factor as time has passed, but there's no question the 1966 title game became something of a grudge match. It was evident from the start, when 240-pound Miners center David Lattin made an early statement with a powerful slam dunk over Riley on his team's second possession. "It was a violent game," Riley recalled to ESPN. "I don't mean there were any fights—but they were desperate and they were committed and they were more motivated than we were."

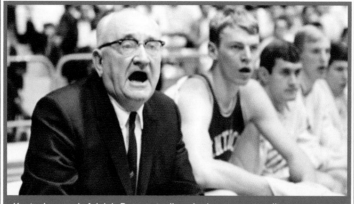
Kentucky coach Adolph Rupp actually asked newspaper editors to put asterisks next to the names of black high school players so he would know whom not to recruit.

If five black players were expected to be undisciplined, no one told the Miners. Their star guard, Bobby Joe Hill, made back-to-back steals midway through the first half, converting both into layups to help Texas Western open a lead. Although nearly three-quarters of the game remained, it was a sequence from which the Wildcats never fully recovered. "Kentucky was a great offensive team," Lattin told writer Marty Strasen. "We were a great defensive team. And if you've been around sports for long enough, you know that a great defense always beats a great offense."

Kentucky's zone defense challenged the Miners to make their outside shots, and the underdogs did just that. The Wildcats trailed by eight in the last few minutes of the first half but cut the deficit to 34–31 by halftime. They clawed to within one point in the second half. Trailing by two during one stretch, they missed three chances to tie the score.

What ultimately sank Kentucky was Texas Western's free-throw shooting. The Miners made 28 of 34 from the stripe, as the "undisciplined" club refused to fold under pressure; it was the ultimate show of discipline. As Willie Worsley says in *And The Walls Came Tumbling Down*, "We were more white-oriented than any of the other teams in the Final Four, We played the most intelligent, the most boring, the most disciplined game of them all."

The final score was 72–65. Texas Western had won the first major American sporting championship ever contested between an all-black lineup and an all-white one. The game was not televised by a major network, and was not seen until the next day in many American cities. Still, its significance was impossible to deny. "If basketball ever took a turn, that was it," Nolan Richardson says in Fitzpatrick's book. Richardson had played for Haskins at Texas Western and followed him into coaching.

Integration became a reality at most schools in the years following the Miners' championship. Rupp had been pressured by Kentucky president John W. Oswald to start recruiting black players. This process had begun in 1964 and '65, although assistants recruited for him. The first blacks Rupp did approach, including home-staters Butch Beard and Wes Unseld, were apparently not interested in playing for a man of his reputation. Finally, in 1970, Rupp dressed Kentucky's first black player, Tom Payne. By the time he coached his last game in '72, Kentucky was all-white again, but times had certainly changed. Joe Gergen quotes Rupp as saying, "Losing to Haskins that year was possibly the biggest disappointment in my life," Rupp once said, "because that was my finest coaching effort."

Milestone miners

The only thing on their minds was winning a basketball game. In doing so against all-white Kentucky in the 1966 NCAA Tournament final, five black starters and their up-and-coming coach not only wrote their names in the history books, they also hastened the pace of integration in college sports.

Coach Don Haskins: Just 36 when his team won its 1966 title, "The Bear" went on to win 719 games at Texas Western, which later became Texas-El Paso. He won seven WAC titles and suffered just five losing seasons in 38 years before retiring in 1999.

Orsten Artis (6-1, G): The third-leading scorer on the '65-66 Miners (12.6 PPG), Artis scored 15 points and grabbed eight rebounds in the final. He later returned to his hometown of Gary, Indiana, and served as a detective for 25 years.

Harry Flournoy (6-5, F): One of the best rebounders in his region during '65-66 (10.7 per game), Flournoy also hailed from Gary, but landed in El Segundo, California, as a sales representative for a baked goods manufacturer and distributor.

Bobby Joe Hill (5-10, G): The Miners' top scorer (15 PPG), defensive ace, and floor general, Hill sparked the title upset with 20 points. His former teammates were stunned and saddened to learn he had died of a heart attack in 2002.

David Lattin (6-7, C): The bruising Lattin was the team's second-leading scorer (14 PPG) and a force in the middle. After college, he returned to his hometown of Houston, where he worked in realty and business and became an avid cyclist.

Willie Worsley (5-6, G): Worsley started over Nevil Shed in the final, as Haskins countered Kentucky's speed with a three-guard lineup. Worsley went on to coach basketball at Spring Valley High School in New York.

Texas Western's David Lattin crawls up the back of Kentucky's Thad Jaracz. The Wildcats struggled all game against Texas Western's tenacious defense.

THE GAME OF THE '70s
Nebraska vs. Oklahoma, November 25, 1971

The game edged toward halftime on Thanksgiving Day of 1971. No. 1 Nebraska held a 14–10 lead and had just kicked off to Oklahoma on the Sooners' home turf, Owen Field in Norman, Oklahoma.

Entering the contest, Oklahoma's potent wishbone attack led college football in rushing, total offense, and scoring. The wishbone was all about running the football, but the pass came to quarterback Jack Mildren's mind after looking up at the pressbox and noticing that assistant coach Barry Switzer—who called the Sooners' offensive plays from the booth—and the other coaches had already made their exit for the locker room at halftime.

Wide receiver Jon Harrison, who had been a high school teammate of Mildren's in Abilene, Texas, approached Mildren after the Sooners got the ball and told him he could beat his man deep. Four plays later Harrison was in the Cornhuskers' endzone after hauling in a 24-yard touchdown pass from Mildren to give the Sooners a 17–14 halftime lead.

For Nebraska it was the first time they had trailed at halftime all year.

Head coach Bob Devaney's Cornhuskers were the defending NCAA champions and had destroyed their first 10 opponents of the 1971 season, scoring 38.9 points a game while averaging 441 yards. Meanwhile, their opponents averaged just 6.4 points against the tough Cornhusker defense.

Nebraska personified balance; they could pass and run while playing stingy defense. Offensively they had halfback/flanker Johnny Rodgers, quarterback Jerry Tagge, and running back Jeff Kinney. Defensively they had middle guard Rich Glover and defensive end Willie Harper.

Meanwhile, Chuck Fairbanks' Sooners had a backfield consisting of Mildren and running backs Joe Wylie, Greg Pruitt, and Leon Crosswhite. Especially

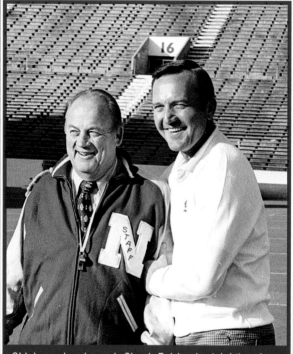

Oklahoma head coach Chuck Fairbanks (*right*) welcomes Nebraska head coach Bob Devaney to Norman. Fifty-five million TV viewers would tune in for the game.

lethal was Pruitt, one of the top breakaway runners in college football. He had a chance to score any time he took the wide pitch from Mildren. Entering the Nebraska game the Sooners were averaging 563 yards and 45 points per game.

Asked to compare the teams, Colorado Associate Athletic Director Fred Casotti was quoted in *Big 8 Football* as saying, "It depends on how you want to die. Oklahoma kills you quick, like a dagger in the heart. Nebraska slowly gives you cancer."

Hype about big games wasn't so much the order of the day in the early 1970s, but this one had been highly anticipated not only by Big Eight aficionados, but also by an entire nation. Paranoid about something going wrong to derail their team, the Cornhuskers not only packed their equipment when they left Lincoln, they also packed their own food for fear of having somebody tamper with the team's.

This game captivated a national television audience from the opening kickoff. The Cornhuskers drew first blood and quieted the Oklahoma band's "Boomer Sooner ... Boomer Sooner" when Rodgers fielded a punt at the Nebraska 28-yard-line and dodged, weaved, dashed, and darted up the field for a touchdown and after the extra point, a 7–0 Nebraska lead. Rodgers returned to the bench to a sea of pats on the back and "attaboys" only to throw up from his exhausting jaunt to the endzone.

Nebraska actually had taken a 14–3 lead in the first half before Mildren led his team to two scores. The cagey quarterback properly read the Cornhuskers' defense that concentrated on taking away the wide pitch to Pruitt and left the Huskers' defense vulnerable to Mildren keepers, Crosswhite dives up the middle, and passes to Harrison. Mildren exploited the weaknesses well and guided the Sooners to the halftime lead.

The Sooners defense gang-tackles Johnny Rodgers. In the end, it would be red-zone runs by Nebraska back Jeff Kinney that would break Oklahoma's back.

An emotional Cornhusker team listened to a Devaney tirade at halftime and responded to the challenge with two touchdowns in the third quarter to take a 28–17 lead. But Mildren answered once again, leading the Sooners to two touchdowns to take a 31–28 lead. By the time the game had ended, the Sooners had chalked up 467 yards of total offense against a defense that had looked impenetrable all season long. Mildren had run for two touchdowns and thrown two.

While all eyes focused on Mildren, Tagge, Rodgers, Pruitt, and company, an epic battle was taking place in the trenches. Glover and All-American Sooner center Tom Braheney went against each other all afternoon and by the end of the game, Glover had completed one of the great big-game performances in college football history by making 22 tackles.

In the midst of the Sooners' comeback, the normally placid Devaney turned to his defense on the sideline and scolded: "Why in the hell don't some of you guys give Glover some help once in a while?"

After the go-ahead touchdown, Nebraska took over at its own 26 with 7:10 to go. The Cornhuskers were a veteran team and did not panic. Knowing they needed a score, they patiently began to move the ball steadily up the field between the tackles with the idea that when they did score, there would be no time left on the clock for the

Nebraska's Johnny "The Jet" Rodgers returned a punt 72 yards for a touchdown in the 1971 Oklahoma game. The following year, he won the Heisman Trophy.

Sooners to answer.

Nebraska faced a critical third-and-8 at Oklahoma's 46 and Tagge coolly found the experienced Rodgers, who had ventured just past the first-down markers.

After the pass, Nebraska went back to their bread-and-butter, Kinney, off-tackle. Two minutes later they found themselves facing a second-and-goal situation at the Sooners' 6. Tagge called time out to organize his thoughts.

Devaney greeted him on the Nebraska sideline and told Tagge there would be no field goals and no ties before asking his quarterback what he thought was the offense's most successful play. The answer was simple: Kinney, off-tackle.

Tagge returned to the huddle and called Kinney's number and he got four yards. Facing third-and-2, Tagge gave the ball to Kinney again and this time he barreled across the goal line for his fourth and most meaningful touchdown of the game. With the extra point, Nebraska had a 35–31 lead.

Oklahoma got the ball back, but could not mount a final charge. Nebraska had taken the "Game of the Century," which had managed to live up to its hype. Afterward there was no trash-talking, just players from both teams shaking hands and offering shows of respect. Both teams left feeling that Oklahoma had not so much lost that day rather Nebraska had found a way to win.

The clip controversy

The 1971 Nebraska-Oklahoma game had so much hype leading up to the contest that living up to the buildup would have been a difficult task for any two teams. However, both squads put together highlight reels during this storied game.

There were many compelling moments, but Johnny Rodgers' electrifying 72-yard punt return for a touchdown—which started

the scoring—is remembered as the best of the best, though some feel the play should have been called back because of a clip.

Even after a great deal of time had passed since the memorable contest, Oklahoma fans still maintained there were one, perhaps even two clips on the play.

One of the alleged clips was a downfield block on the Oklahoma punter, Joe Wylie, by

Nebraska cornerback Joe Blahak. Though it may have looked like a block to the back, Wylie would even say he was diving when the block took place, making the block somewhat irrelevant.

Oklahoma quarterback Jack Mildren saw things differently as he said in a 2001 story in the *Daily Nebraskan*.

"From my vantage point, I saw a clip or two. But as my father the philosopher always said, 'I didn't see a flag. Did you?'"

BATTLE OF THE SEXES
Bobby Riggs vs. Billie Jean King, September 20, 1973

In 1939 Bobby Riggs laid down money with a London bookmaker, claiming he would win that year's singles, doubles, and mixed doubles tennis championships at Wimbledon. Sure enough, he won all three ... and collected $108,000 from the bookie. From that point on, Bobby Riggs reigned as the tennis world's most infamous hustler.

As his skills waned, Riggs' hustles became more outrageous. He bet opponents that he could beat them while carrying a pail of water, while holding a poodle on a leash, and even while tied to his doubles partner. Then in the early 1970s, stated *Time* magazine, this "street-shrewd promoter ... finally found a way to satisfy his gargantuan appetite for both action and attention." In the midst of the feminist era, Riggs would play against a world-famous female opponent. And he'd be a pig about it—a chauvinist pig—creating enough sizzling controversy to attract national interest.

On Mother's Day, 1973, the 55-year-old Riggs played Margaret Court, the No. 1 ranked women's player in the world, on national television. In a sly move, Riggs unnerved Court by handing her a bouquet of roses before the match. His frustrating array of spin shots and lobs kept her off balance, and he won 6–2, 6–1.

For Riggs, the match had been a good gig for a washed-up tennis player. He decided to up the ante. According to the *Washington Post*, Riggs then declared "I want Billie Jean King, " as if he were a boxing contender. "I want the women's lib leader."

King, 29, was a controversial star—a tenacious tennis champion (five Wimbledon singles titles through 1973) and a feminist drum-beater for women's tennis. Ever since 1955, when she was barred from a Los Angeles Tennis Club photograph because she was wearing shorts instead of a skirt, King had tried to improve conditions for female tennis players. At first she didn't want to play Riggs, but the Court match infuriated her. As King told *Time*, "When I finally saw

Bobby Riggs did anything he could to draw attention to himself, including dressing like Little Miss Muffet at a pro-celebrity tennis tournament in New York in August 1973.

the film of the match and watched him present her with those roses and Margaret curtsy, I yelled 'Margaret, you idiot, you played right into his hands!'" she said.

Riggs and King agreed to meet on September 20, 1973, at the Houston Astrodome, with winner-take-all prize money of $100,000. Working with master boxing promoter Jerry Perenchio, Riggs drummed up the event, calling it "the match of the century and the battle of the sexes." He practiced for the match dressed in a "Men's Liberation" T-shirt and spouted deliberately sexist phrases: "Get your biscuit in the oven and your buns in the bed."

Day after day, Riggs hyped the match by talking trash. "I can handle anything she can throw at me," he boasted in *Time*. "I'll psych her out a little bit. I'm psyching her out already. She won't admit it, but I can see her coming apart at the seams."

Riggs' mouth was bigger than Muhammad Ali's. His bravado earned him endorsement deals; he peddled aftershave and Sugar Daddy suckers and he made the cover of *Time*. King mocked him, calling him "Roberta," while her supporters ripped him in the press. In the *Washington Post*, tennis player Rosie Casals called Riggs "an old man who walks like a duck, can't see, can't hear, and besides, he's an idiot."

Riggs indeed was an odd bird. Twice divorced and a father of six, he fancied himself a playboy, despite his John Denver-gone-bad appearance. He boasted of taking 450 pills a day, including 100 soybean-wheat germ pellets and 75 liver-extract pills, as prescribed by his L.A.-based nutritionist.

While Riggs reveled in the spotlight, King felt pressured to beat the chauvinist. "I thought it would set us back 50 years if I didn't win that match," she later told ESPN. "It would ruin the women's tour and affect all women's self-esteem."

King responded with a rigorous training regimen. Upon arriving in Houston, she declined interviews and

Though it appears that Billie Jean King is about to shove her fist down the throat of her male chauvinist opponent, she saved her energy for the main event.

worked on her game in a plastic "Bubble" in the Astrodome parking lot. The Bubble contained the same Sportface floor that would be used in the match. To gear up for night play, King changed her sleeping schedule, waking up late each day.

Match night was an audacious spectacle, attracting 30,472 fans to the Astrodome, a world record for a tennis match. An estimated 50 million viewers, another record for tennis, tuned in on ABC. A brass band trumpeted the combatants' arrival. Four musclemen carried King to the court on a gold litter, as if she were Cleopatra. Six starlets pulled in Riggs on a golden rickshaw.

Billie Jean King rejoices after routing Bobby Riggs 6-4, 6-3, 6-3. King was so dominant that many of her winning shots never touched Riggs' racket.

Exchanging gifts, Riggs gave King a giant Sugar Daddy Sucker, while King bestowed a baby pig on her opponent.

Riggs was a 5-2 favorite to win, indicating that the odds-makers and bettors were predominantly men. Right from the start, King dominated the old man. Understanding that this was a best-of-five-set match, she ran Riggs from baseline to baseline. Her serves, forehands, and backhands were aggressive, hard, and accurate. She waited on Riggs' high lobs and smashed them down his throat. Of King's first 34 winners, 26 didn't even touch his racket. King took the first set 6-4 and got better after that.

"Go, baby, go!" yelled Bill Moffitt (also 55 years old) after every point his daughter won. Both players suffered injuries—King with calf cramps and Riggs hand cramps. A quick massage did the trick for King, while Riggs downed more pills. Nothing could help Riggs, however, who lost the remaining sets 6-3, 6-3. Even Riggs' new pig forsook him, falling asleep on the sidelines. When Riggs hit match point into the net, King tossed her racket in the air. Millions of American women joined her in jubilation, while men stewed silently in their La-Z-Boys.

For Riggs, the hustle and hype were over. He graciously accepted defeat, leaping over the net and embracing King. "You were too good," he told her. For years after, King remained friends with Riggs and grateful for his challenge. Despite his selfish intentions, no other man had done so much to popularize women's tennis.

A league of her own

Bobby Riggs was foolish to think he could psych out Billie Jean King before their "match of the century." In the previous decade, King had made the finals of Grand Slam events 49 times, winning 31 of them. Riggs, meanwhile, hadn't won a Grand Slam title in 32 years. Below is a complete list of their Grand Slam triumphs—39 for King, five for Riggs:

Billie Jean King

U.S. Championship/Open
Singles champion: 1967, 1971, 1972, 1974
Women's doubles champion: 1964, 1967, 1974, 1978, 1980
Mixed doubles champion: 1967, 1971, 1973, 1976

Wimbledon
Singles champion: 1966, 1967, 1968, 1972, 1973, 1975
Women's doubles champion: 1961, 1962, 1965, 1967, 1968, 1970, 1971, 1972, 1973, 1979
Mixed doubles champion: 1967, 1971, 1973, 1974

French Championship/Open
Singles champion: 1972
Women's doubles champion: 1972
Mixed doubles champion: 1967, 1970

Australian Championship/Open
Singles champion: 1968
Mixed doubles champion: 1968

Bobby Riggs

U.S. Championship
Singles champion: 1939, 1941

Wimbledon
Singles champion: 1939
Men's doubles champion: 1939
Mixed doubles champion: 1939

The defensive schemes of Pistons coach Chuck Daly (*left*) and the "whining" of Bill Laimbeer (*right*) frustrated Michael Jordan year after year.

JORDAN RULES
Chicago Bulls vs. Detroit Pistons, 1988-91

The Detroit Pistons–the despised "Bad Boys" of the NBA–had eliminated the Chicago Bulls in the 1988 and 1989 playoffs. Now, in the 1990 Eastern Conference finals, they were crushing the Bulls again. Employing their "Jordan Rules" defense, which suffocated superstar Michael Jordan, and assorted dirty tricks (swinging elbows, shoves, forearm shivers), the Pistons won Game 1 and led by 15 at halftime of Game 2.

Chicago's locker room was dead quiet during intermission, until an unraveling Michael Jordan punctuated the silence. According to Sam Smith's book *The Jordan Rules*, MJ kicked a chair and blurted, "We're playing like a bunch of pussies!" The Bulls still lost Game 2, and Jordan stewed in silence all the way back to Chicago. The Bulls extended the series to seven games, but in the end they fell short, losing the finale 93–74. Chicago forward Scottie Pippen blamed his poor performance in Game 7 on a migraine headache– courtesy, Chicagoans assumed, of those rotten Pistons.

Back on April 3, 1988, the high-flying Jordan had his way with Detroit, pouring in 59 points. Yet, the Pistons had plans to destroy Jordan and the Bulls, both physically and psychologically. Coach Chuck Daly and his assistants devised the "Jordan Rules," more than 10 defensive "sets" intended to squelch the NBA's premier scorer. Basically, defenders swarmed MJ whenever he had the ball.

But that wasn't Detroit's only scheme to derail Jordan. Previously, the Pistons had sent well-edited tapes to the NBA, claiming that Jordan had been drawing too many weak fouls. "Ever since then, the foul calls started decreasing," Jordan complained, "and not only those against Detroit."

All the while, the Pistons were building the toughest

In the 1991 Eastern Conference finals, Piston rebel Dennis Rodman (*right*) shoved Scottie Pippen (*left*), but Chicago prevailed in a four-game sweep.

defense in the history of the NBA. In the backcourt, sweet-talking Isiah Thomas and classy Joe Dumars stuck like glue to their opponents. It was the front line that gave the Pistons their "Bad Boys" reputation. Rick Mahorn, known for his big butt and his mean streak, unloaded forearms like Joe Frazier threw punches. Dennis Rodman, who in later years would become America's most famous rebel, shut down opponents with raw athleticism and occasional cheap shots.

Then there was "the big white guy," Bill Laimbeer. With his flying elbows, incessant whining about fouls, and sarcastic smiles whenever calls went against him, Laimbeer infuriated opposing fans, especially in Chicago. "He didn't even seem human," wrote columnist Jack M. Silverstein. "He was a supervillain, the Devil himself, a life force of pure evil sent to this planet to destroy our heroes, the Chicago Bulls."

And in the 1988 playoffs, Laimbeer and the Pistons did. Jordan may have won the NBA MVP and Defensive Player of the Year awards in 1987–88, but his two most talented teammates, forwards Scottie Pippen and Horace Grant, were both rookies. In the Eastern Conference semifinals, the Pistons blew past Chicago in five games en route to a seven-game loss in the NBA Finals to the Los Angeles Lakers.

After the season, Bulls general manager Jerry Krause made bold moves to improve the team. He replaced head coach Doug Collins with cerebral assistant Phil Jackson. "[Jackson] has extraordinary mental strength," said then-Bulls assistant coach Jim Cleamons, in an nba.com interview. "And, looking back, that's just what the Bulls needed at the time."

Krause also traded for Knicks center Bill Cartwright, who was a tower of strength in the middle both mentally and physically. "His approach rubbed off on the other guys," said former Bulls center Tom Boerwinkle, "and he was more than willing to stand up for himself and his teammates."

In the 1989 playoffs, the Bulls made it all the way to the Eastern Conference finals. But the Pistons, with a franchise-record 63 wins in 1988-89, were tougher than ever. They ousted Chicago in six hard-fought games before sweeping the Lakers for their first NBA championship.

In 1989–90, the Bulls won 55 games, their most in 18 years. Scottie Pippen emerged as a multi-talented superstar, averaging 16.5 points, 6.7 rebounds, and 5.4 assists per game. The Bulls-Pistons match-up in the Conference finals was a brutally physical seven-game war. Pippen's headache and guard John Paxson's ankle sprain meant that all the pressure was on Jordan again. In Game 7, MJ scored or assisted on all of the Bulls' points for the first 22 minutes of the second half. Again, it wasn't enough.

In 1990-91, the Bulls seemingly found their key to success. Assistant coach Tex Winter devised an offensive plan that would prove more famous than the Jordan Rules. It was called the "Triangle Offense," and here's how it worked: When Jordan moved to one spot with the ball, the other four players moved in synch on predetermined angles, creating openings for shots for not only Jordan but for themselves. Beamed Jordan: "It gives us so many options that I'm not sure Tex knows all of them yet."

Suddenly, the Bulls were the NBA's team to beat. Jordan won his fifth straight NBA scoring title (31.5 PPG), while Pippen—now a "point forward"—set personal bests across the board. Grant grabbed 8.4 rebounds per game, Paxson shot 55 percent from the

Joe Dumars (*right*) had contained Michael Jordan in their three previous postseason match-ups, but MJ had a hot hand and great team support in the 1991 conference finals.

floor, and Cartwright ruled the paint defensively. The Bulls won 61 games, including a 108-100 triumph over the Pistons in the regular season finale.

After cruising past New York and Philadelphia in the early rounds, the Bulls faced Detroit in the 1991 playoffs for the *fourth* straight season. But this time, the Bulls were more talented, more sophisticated, more battle-tested, and more determined than ever before. Amid the deafening din of Chicago Stadium, the Bulls stuck it to Detroit in Games 1 (94–83) and 2 (105–97). Even in the Pistons' Palace in Game 3, Chicago prevailed, 113-107. According to Pistons coach Chuck Daily in the *Michael Jordan Scrapbook*, "The whole series is simple to explain. They are just a better team."

In Game 3, it was the Pistons who this time came unglued. Rodman shoved Pippen hard, then threw a basketball into Jordan's stomach. But the Bulls now had the luxury to shrug it off, to sneer like Laimbeer into the Pistons' collective face. Chicago blew out Detroit 115-94.

Watching on TV in Chicago, fans soaked it in when the Pistons acted like babies in the closing moments. With eight seconds to go, Detroit's starters walked off the floor, past the Bulls' bench, refusing to shake hands. The Bad Boys, apparently, were also bad sports. "Outside of Detroit," Jordan is quoted as saying on nba.com, "I think people will be happy they're not champions anymore."

With the Pistons *finally* out of the way, the Bulls rolled over the Lakers in five games in the 1991 NBA Finals. It was their first of three straight NBA titles—and six altogether in the 1990s. The Bulls, and not the Pistons, proved to be the NBA's last dynasty of the 20th century.

MIRACLE ON ICE
United States vs. Soviet Union, February 22, 1980

From their invasion of Afghanistan to their veiled threats of military action against countries outside the communist bloc, the Soviet Union cast a long shadow over the world in 1980. Heading into the 1980 Winter Olympics at Lake Placid, the Soviet national hockey team held a similar aura.

The Soviets had cruised in dominating fashion while taking the 1979 World Championship and they defeated the NHL All Stars in a challenge series, claiming the final game with a 6–0 rout. Dotting the Soviet roster were veterans in their primes such as Vladimir Petrov, Alexander Maltsev, Valery Kharlamov, and Boris Mikhailov, as well as talented youngsters such as Vladimir Krutov and Sergei Makarov. Goalie Vladislav Tretiak was widely acknowledged as the best in the world. They were, in essence, hockey's version of the '27 Yankees.

On the other side of the coin was the U.S. hockey team, the antithesis of the Soviets. Herb Brooks was the man whose task it was to coach the U.S. team. Brooks had been the last play-

Just a week before the 1980 Olympics, the Soviet Union had humiliated the U.S. 10–3. The Americans, many thought, needed a miracle to prevail at Lake Placid.

er cut from the gold medal-winning U.S. team at the 1960 Olympics and later became the head coach of the University of Minnesota, leading the Gophers to three NCAA titles. Finding the players to man the U.S. team that would compete in the 1980 Olympics began with a series of tryout camps and personality evaluations. Eventually Brooks pared the list down to a workable number—which included future NHL players Neal Broten, Mark Johnson, Mike Ramsey, Dave Christian, and Ken Morrow—and then embarked on an ambitious four-month schedule of exhibition games in the United States and abroad.

Brooks stressed the fact that the U.S. team would not stand a chance of competing with any of the world hockey powers if they relied purely on their hockey skills. Brooks' solution came in conditioning. He made the decision his team would be the best-conditioned team in the Games, then pushed them to the limit while positioning himself as the bad guy—thus creating a rallying point for the team to unite against.

The U.S. team seemed to be coming around during the months leading up to the Lake Placid Games until playing a pre-Olympic exhibition against the Soviets. The youngsters on the U.S. team found out what it was like to play the best team in the world and came away 10–3 losers. Any notions Team USA might win a gold medal in Lake Placid were seemingly dispelled. Still, Brooks continued to drive his team relentlessly heading into the Games.

Sweden was Team USA's first opponent at Lake Placid and the Americans managed to forge a 2–2 tie when Bill Baker scored a goal in the final minute of the game. Victories over Czechoslovakia, Norway, Romania, and Germany followed to advance Team USA into the medal round. The Soviet team finished its bracket undefeated after rallying late to win games against Finland and Canada. In the medal round it was scheduled to play the American team first.

Team USA goalie Jim Craig kept his team in the game early when the Soviets peppered him with shots on goal. Despite the fact that the Soviets led just 2–1 in the waning moments of the first period, and the fact that the Americans were playing a far more rugged style than they had in their previous encounter with the Soviets, it appeared to be a foregone conclusion that the Soviets would wear down Craig and turn the game into their typical rout.

But with the clock winding down on the first period, Christian directed a long drive at the great Tretiak, who stopped the shot. Then the puck rebounded away from him and Johnson alertly pounced on it to score

Coach Herb Brooks knew how to push his players' buttons. During an intense practice before the Soviet game, he chided: "You're too young—you can't win this!"

right before the buzzer. The officials debated whether the goal should stand, and the call went the Americans' way, and the score was tied 2-2 after one period.

The Soviets remained on the attack in the second period—but their coach, Viktor Tikhonov, had removed Tretiak from the game. Somehow the red-hot Craig continued to keep the puck out of the net, allowing only Maltsev's breakaway goal that put the Soviets up 3-2 after two periods.

Team USA's young legs took over in the final period. Johnson took possession of a loose puck during an American power play and drove it into the net to tie the score at 3 and the chant began to echo through the arena: "USA! USA! USA!"

Perhaps the most famous moment in America hockey then followed. With approximately 10 minutes remaining in the game, Team USA captain Mike Eruzione found himself alone with the puck in the high slot and let loose with a 25-foot wrist shot that found the net. Plenty of time remained, but the crowd

celebrated Team USA's 4–3 lead.

Meanwhile, Brooks juggled four different lines in staccato shifts that seemed to drive home the fatigue in legs of the veteran Soviet players. For the fans embracing the miracle, the clock couldn't move fast enough. Finally, when the game clock reached five seconds, veteran sportscaster Al Michaels made the now famous call: "Five seconds left in the game! Do you believe in miracles? Yes!"

A celebration erupted on the ice. Craig's teammates mobbed him as the Soviet players watched with stunned expressions on their faces. A sporting miracle of epic proportions had just occurred. Everything had fallen exactly into place and the Americans had come away with the highly improbable win. Among the Americans list of good fortunes was Tikhonov's decision to bench Tretiak, who later wrote the following in his autobiography about the move:

"I don't think I should have been replaced in that game. I had made so many mistakes already, I was confident my play would only improve. [Vladimir Myshkin, his replacement] is an excellent goalie, but he wasn't prepared for the struggle, he wasn't 'tuned in' to the Americans."

Two days after the upset of the Soviets, Team USA defeated Finland to win the gold medal and complete "The Miracle on Ice," which many feel is the single greatest accomplishment in American sports history.

Team USA's captain

Mike Eruzione was the captain of Boston University's hockey team during his senior season and became one of the school's all-time leading scorers with 208 points. Eruzione graduated from BU with a degree in education in 1977 before beginning his career in international hockey.

Eruzione had obvious leadership qualities, which earned him the role of team captain for the USA hockey team during the 1980 Olympics. He scored three goals and recorded five assists during the team's gold medal run—including the game winner against the Soviet Union.

Since the "Miracle on Ice" Eruzione has done a lot of motivational speaking, much of which is based on what Team USA accomplished in the face of great odds. Ironically, Eruzione told Denver's *Rocky Mountain News* he has never watched a replay of the United States' victory over the Soviets.

"It was a great moment in my life, but I know the outcome," Eruzione said. "Plus, if I watch it, I might not have played as well as I thought I played. And if my kids are watching, they'd probably criticize me."

Forward John Harrington watches in delight as Mike Eruzione's 25-foot wrist shot flies past netminder Vladimir Myshkin for the game-winning goal.

SHOCKED AT THE BUZZER

United States vs. Soviet Union, September 9, 1972

In a Lausanne, Switzerland, vault, a group of shiny silver medals waits in storage. The "winners" of those medals have no intention of accepting them, more than three decades after refusing them for the first time. Kenny Davis, the captain of the 1972 United States Olympic basketball team that lost a controversial decision to the Soviet Union in the gold medal game, put a clause in his will stating that even after he dies, his surviving family members cannot receive that silver medal. As Davis told ESPN, "We felt like they just did something to us that was illegal and we didn't know any other way to protest than to say that you're not about to get us to show up to take that silver medal."

The controversy—the biggest in Olympic basketball history— involved the gold medal game's last three seconds. To understand its significance, though, one must look back to the beginning of a run of U.S. dominance. Professionals could not compete in the Games back then. The U.S. sent groups of talented young amateurs to face the best the Soviet Union had to offer. Some called the older Soviets "quasi-professionals." Their training was funded by a government that placed a high priority on developing champions. Their national team of '72 had played hundreds of games together, while the U.S. college stars had been together for just a dozen exhibitions before the Olympic Trials. Still, the U.S. was thought to be invincible in basketball. The Americans had never lost a game in Olympic competition, a run of 63 straight wins that had produced seven gold medals entering the night of September 9, 1972, in Munich.

The rivalry between the U.S. and USSR was far more than an athletic one, of course. The Cold War had seen to that. Politics had come to the forefront at these Games, certainly, when Arab terrorists had massacred 11 members of the Israeli contingent, an attack that had everyone on edge. If the Americans were ever going to lose a game, they sure wouldn't have wanted the Russians to be the team ending the streak.

American star Dwight Jones reaches in vain for the ball against the Soviets. Jones was ejected with 12:18 remaining, costing the Americans their top scorer and rebounder.

Conversely, the Soviet Union wanted to show the world how far it had advanced on the hardwood. It was a talented club that took the floor in Munich. Showing superiority against the Americans would put its Moscow-based sports machine on top of the world. Both teams were 8–0.

That the Americans were more vulnerable than usual became evident early in the game. It was the youngest team the U.S. had ever fielded, and coach Henry Iba had been criticized for not "turning his players loose" early enough to run and press their opponents into submission. Instead, Iba had stressed the tight defensive system that had made him a legend at Oklahoma State University and helped him coach the '64 and '68 teams to Olympic gold medals. The Soviets scored the first seven points. "We played their game, the slow-down game," said American guard Tom Henderson. "We should have ran, and we'd have ran them back to Russia."

The Soviets led 26–21 at halftime. With the margin at 38–34 and 12:18 remaining, Russian reserve Dvorni Edeshko and top U.S. scorer Dwight Jones were ejected from the game after a scuffle. It was a great trade for the Soviets, who extended their lead to 10 points with less than 10 minutes to play. Though not particularly well-versed in playing from behind, the Americans staged a spirited comeback. Guard Kevin Joyce led the charge, and a jumper by Jim Forbes with 40 seconds left sliced the deficit to 49–48. The Soviets ran the clock down to 10 seconds, but Doug Collins intercepted a cross-court pass by Aleksander Belov and was fouled hard as he drove to the hoop for a potential go-ahead bucket. Collins, a 21-year-old, sweet-shooting Illinois State star, was awarded two free throws.

If nothing else, this much is certain about the ending of the game: Collins hit both free throws, the second one despite the sounding of a horn as he released the shot. The U.S. led 50–49. The Soviets quickly inbounded the ball, but Bulgarian referee Artenik

The U.S. celebrates its apparent 50-49 victory over the Soviets. But the referee put three seconds back on the clock, giving the USSR another chance.

Just before the buzzer, Soviet Aleksander Belov caught a long inbound pass and coverted this layup, to shock the Americans, 51–50.

Arabadjan blew his whistle with one second showing on the clock, and an officials conference determined that Soviet coach Vladimir Kondrashkin had called timeout between Collins' foul shots. Three seconds would be put back on the clock. While it was in the process of being reset, though, the Soviets inbounded the ball a second time and a horn sounded. "It's all over!" announcer Keith Jackson told an American radio audience. "Well, what a finish, the United States winning their eighth consecutive gold medal. This place has gone crazy."

While the Americans were celebrating, officials were gathering again. R. William Jones, secretary general of the International Amateur Basketball Federation, ordered that the clock be reset to :03 once again. The Americans were in disbelief. "It was like they were going to let them do it until they got it right," U.S. forward Mike Bantom told ESPN. This time, the long inbound went right to Belov, the man whose pass had been intercepted by Collins. The big Russian caught it near the foul line, sending Americans Forbes and Joyce sprawling. Belov made the winning layup as time expired. The game was over. USSR 51, USA 50.

Days later, a U.S. protest was defeated by a 3–2 vote, but debate would go on far longer. Russians recall the ending as one of their proudest Olympic moments. Americans remember it as "highway robbery." Ivan Edeshko, who threw the final pass to Belov, said he understood the feeling on the U.S. side. "It was the Cold War," he told ESPN. "Americans, out of their own natural pride and love of country, didn't want to lose and admit loss. They didn't want to lose in anything, especially basketball."

Members of the 1972 U.S. team, who voted unanimously not to accept the silver medals, contend they never did lose that game. "If we had gotten beat," Bantom told ESPN, "I would be proud to display my silver medal today. But we didn't get beat. We got cheated."

A history of near perfection

The legacy of the U.S. Men's Basketball team in the Olympic Games.

Berlin 1936
Medal (record): Gold (5–0)
Top scorer: Joe Fortenberry
Note: The final is played outdoors in the rain. U.S. defeats Canada, 19–8.

London 1948
Medal (record): Gold (8–0)
Top scorer: Alex Groza
Note: The U.S. routs France 65–21 for the gold.

Helsinki 1952
Medal (record): Gold (8–0)
Top scorer: Clyde Lovellette
Note: The Soviet Union, in its first Olympics, falls 36–25 in the final.

Melbourne 1956
Medal (record): Gold (8–0)
Top scorer: Bill Russell
Note: The average U.S. victory margin is 53.5 points.

Rome 1960
Medal (record): Gold (8–0)
Top scorers: Oscar Robertson, Jerry Lucas
Note: 10 of 12 U.S. players have NBA careers.

Tokyo 1964
Medal (record): Gold (9–0)
Top scorer: Jerry Shipp
Note: The U.S. defeats a strong Soviet team, 73–59.

Mexico City 1968
Medal (record): Gold (9–0)
Top scorer: Spencer Haywood
Note: Haywood, 19, is the youngest U.S. player ever to make the team.

Munich 1972
Medal (record): *Silver (8–1)
Top scorers: Dwight Jones, Thomas Henderson
Note: The Soviet Union snaps a 63-game U.S. winning streak.

Montreal 1976
Medal (record): Gold (7–0)
Top scorer: Adrian Dantley
Note: The final is U.S. 95, Yugoslavia 74.

Moscow 1980
Note: The U.S. boycotted these Olympics.

Los Angeles 1984
Medal (record): Gold (8–0)
Top scorer: Michael Jordan
Note: Jordan leaps toward stardom.

Seoul 1988
Medal (record): Bronze (7–1)
Top scorer: Dan Majerle
Note: The Soviets dump the U.S. in the semis.

Barcelona 1992
Medal (record): Gold (8–0)
Top scorer: Charles Barkley
Note: The NBA "Dream Team" makes a dominant debut.

Atlanta 1996
Medal (record): Gold (8–0)
Top scorer: David Robinson
Note: A record crowd of 34,600 watches the final.

Sydney 2000
Medal (record): Gold (8–0)
Top scorer: Vince Carter
Note: The U.S. survives some tight games.

Athens 2004
Medal (record): Bronze (5–3)
Top scorer: Allen Iverson
Note: The club's three losses top their previous combined Olympic total.

* Team USA refuses to accept silver medals.

CLASH OF THE TITANS

Wilt Chamberlain vs. Bill Russell, 1959-1969

Wilt Chamberlain joined the NBA in 1959 with the Philadelphia Warriors, bringing a brand of basketball the league had never seen. Chamberlain's impact, although immense, was hardly surprising.

Standing 7-foot-1, with a muscular body and fluid moves to match, Chamberlain attended the University of Kansas. Because of his obvious talents, the NBA felt compelled to decide his future, even though he was just a freshman in 1956; the NBA ruled the Warriors could claim him as a territorial pick because he hailed from Philadelphia—even though his class wouldn't graduate until 1959.

Chamberlain beat the NBA to the draw, electing to leave college early after a storied three-year career at Kansas to play for the Harlem Globetrotters a year before he was eligible to play in the NBA.

Wilt "The Stilt" opened his NBA career against the New York Knicks, and he hardly cut the figure of a timid rookie when he knocked down 43 points and gathered 28 rebounds. By the end of the season, Chamberlain had compiled one of the best seasons in NBA history by averaging 37.6 points and 27 rebounds per game. In recognition of his accomplishments, Chamberlain was voted the NBA's Rookie of the Year and Most Valuable Player. The results foreshadowed a career in which he would win virtually every individual honor possible. Unfortunately for Chamberlain, another result from his rookie season would also serve as a bellwether for his career.

As a rookie, Chamberlain led the Warriors, who without him had finished last during the 1958–59 season, to the Eastern Division finals against the Boston Celtics in 1959–60. Against the Celtics, Chamberlain went toe-to-toe with Bill Russell, perhaps the best defensive player in NBA history, and a man unaccustomed to losing.

While at the University of San Francisco, the 6-foot-9 Russell led the Dons to 55 straight wins and back-to-back national championships. The St. Louis

Against the New York Knicks on March 2, 1962, Wilt Chamberlain scored 100 points—an NBA record that still stands. For the season, he averaged 50.4 points.

Hawks took Russell with the No. 2 pick of the NBA draft, but Red Auerbach of the Celtics was determined that Russell would not play for the Hawks. So Auerbach packaged Cliff Hagan and Ed Macauley in a trade to acquire Russell. In hindsight, St. Louis' trade was probably the worst in NBA history.

Russell believed in team basketball and doing whatever was necessary to ensure victory. He hauled in rebounds, blocked shots, and threw outlet passes that fueled the Celtics' fast-break offense. During his rookie season of 1956–57, Russell grabbed 19.6 rebounds per game on his way to leading the Celtics to their first NBA title. To gauge Russell's value to the Celtics, consider the fact the Celtics lost to the Hawks in the 1958 NBA Finals after he sprained his ankle in the third game of the series.

On November 7, 1959, Russell and Chamberlain met for the first time. The game took place at Boston Garden and served as a microcosm of all their future meetings. Chamberlain scored more points than Russell—30 to 22—while Russell outrebounded Chamberlain 35-28 and the Celtics won the game. During their meeting in the 1960 Eastern Division finals, the trend continued. Chamberlain outscored Russell by 81 points, but the Celtics took the series four games to two en route to claiming the NBA championship.

The Celtics' strategy had been to go for Chamberlain's Achilles' heel—free-throw shooting. "We went for his weakness," former Celtics forward Tom Heinsohn told the *Philadelphia Daily News*, "tried to send him to the foul line, and in doing that he took the most brutal pounding of any player ever. ... I hear people today talk about hard fouls. Half the fouls against him were hard fouls."

That first playoff meeting marked the beginning of what would become one of the most memorable rivalries in sports history. Chamberlain had actually pondered retiring after his rookie season because of the manner in which teams had tried to defend him all season. An intelligent man, Chamberlain was concerned about the toll that would be exacted on his body if he continued to play a game in which he got pounded excessively. And he didn't want to have to fight force with force.

Chamberlain did not retire, instead continuing to compile an unmatched NBA resume in the statistical categories. One of Chamberlain's more eye-popping accomplishments came March 2, 1962, when he set a record against the Knicks that isn't likely to be challenged. He scored 100 points—without benefit of overtime—to lead a 169–147 Warriors win.

Chamberlain's other larger-than-life accomplishments: He averaged 50.4 points during the 1961–62 season, won league scoring titles his first seven seasons, became the only center to ever lead the league in assists, and, astonishingly, never fouled out in 1,045 games. Chamberlain became an American icon and a synonym for *giant*. Yet throughout Chamberlain's career, the public perception of him was as a selfish player who thought more about his own statistics than winning. Much of that perception came because his performance was always compared to Russell's. And Russell and his Celtics teammates were the dominant NBA team of the time. Russell's only

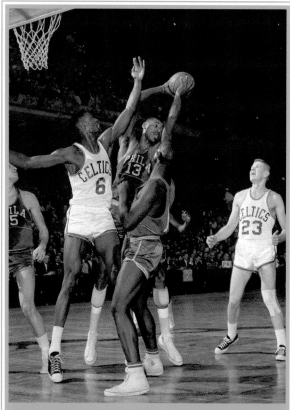

Bill Russell's ferocious defense often neutralized Wilt Chamberlain's scoring. Though blocked shots were not recorded in his day, Russell frequently posted double digits in swats.

label was *winner*.

Before the 1968–69 NBA season, Chamberlain was traded by the Philadelphia 76ers to the Los Angeles Lakers in a deal heralded as the move to end all moves for the Lakers. With Chamberlain in the paint, joining Jerry West and Elgin Baylor, the Lakers were everybody's choice to unseat Russell and the Celtics as the NBA champions.

Russell had a difficult season getting the Celtics to the championship round, while Chamberlain and the Lakers cruised. But once again the Celtics found a way to come away with the NBA title, defeating the Lakers in seven games. Chamberlain spent the last five minutes of Game 7 on the bench, while Russell, the Celtics' player/coach, led the final charge.

Nobody knew it then, but Game 7 of the 1969 NBA Championship would be the final installment of the Russell-Chamberlain rivalry. Russell soon retired.

The final accounting shows that Chamberlain outscored Russell in their meetings by an average of 14 points a game, and outrebounded him by five per game. But Russell's teams held an 86–57 advantage over Chamberlain's teams. And during the period when both played, Russell's teams won nine championships to Chamberlain's one (in 1966-67 over the San Francisco Warriors).

Don't bench Wilt the Stilt

Lakers coach Butch van Breda Kolff found out the hard way that if it came down to a decision between keeping a basketball icon like Wilt Chamberlain and a coach, the icon would win.

Chamberlain joined the Lakers before the 1968-69 season. The coach had no trouble with the team's other "superstars," Jerry West and Elgin Baylor, but Chamberlain made things difficult for van

Breda Kolff. Chamberlain reportedly missed practice on a fairly regular basis; he was also said to have ignored any instructions or advice from the Lakers' coach. Despite the rift between coach and player, the Lakers reached the NBA Finals in 1969. But the problem persisted and came to a head in Game 7.

Chamberlain took himself out of the game after hurting his leg and van Breda

Kolff inserted Mel Counts to take his place. With Chamberlain on the bench, the Lakers got back into the game. In the midst of this run, Chamberlain told van Breda Kolff he was ready to get back into game, to which the coach replied, "Sit down."

Chamberlain never got back into the game, the Lakers lost 108-106, and van Breda Kolff started the next season coaching the Detroit Pistons.

A phenomenal athlete who towered over opponents, Wilt Chamberlain averaged 37.6 points as a rookie in 1959–60. Here he displays his patented finger-roll.

THE ALL-OVERTIME FINALS
Toronto vs. Montreal, 1951 Stanley Cup Finals

Finally, it seemed, emotionally drained hockey fans would catch a breather. Unbelievably, the first four games of the 1951 Stanley Cup Finals, between the Montreal Canadiens and Toronto Maple Leafs, had gone to overtime—with the Leafs winning three of them. But the Canadiens led Game 5 at Maple Leaf Gardens, 2-1, and with less than a minute to go, the series was destined for Game 6 in Montreal. Or so it seemed.

After pulling goalie Al Rollins, the Leafs swarmed the Canadiens' goal. With 32 ticks remaining, Toronto forward Tod Sloan fired the puck through a maze of bodies and past goaltender Gerry McNeil. All across Canada, old-timers prepared for more chest pains. Like all the contests in this series, Game 5 was headed to overtime.

Had these been any other NHL teams, the pressure would have been more bearable. But when Toronto and Montreal hooked up, more than hockey was on the line. Montreal, Quebec, represented French Canada, while Toronto, Ontario, was an English-speaking city. In previous centuries, wars had been fought between French and British Canadians, and in the mid-1900s a feud still existed between the two societies. In fact, throughout the 20th century, many in Quebec desired to secede from Canada; plenty of Ontarians couldn't wait to show them the door.

For Canada's French and English, hockey games were the way to vent their hostility. The Canadiens-Maple Leafs feud dated back to the inception of the NHL in 1917. Beginning in 1938, they were the only two Canadian teams left in the six-team league. Montreal and Toronto faced each other more than a dozen times a year, and each game was a war. In the 1947 Stanley Cup Finals, Toronto's Bill Ezinicki and Vic Lynn practically assaulted Montreal superstar Maurice Richard. "The Rocket" later retaliated with high sticks that bloodied their heads. Richard was suspended for one game, helping Toronto win the series.

In 1950-51, the Maple Leafs finished 41–16–13, far ahead of the 25–30–15 Canadiens. Yet the rivalry remained intense. "There were other teams we wouldn't get as up for, like the Chicago Blackhawks and the Boston Bruins," Toronto forward Harry Watson later told *Hockey Digest*. "But Richard's Canadiens—we were always ready for them."

A pair of Maple Leafs hoist Bill Barilko on their shoulders after his overtime goal—the fifth of the series—in Game 5 of the 1951 Stanley Cup Finals.

Montreal and Toronto made the 1951 championship round after winning six- and five-game semifinals series respectively. The Canadiens had defeated the first-place Detroit Red Wings thanks to heart-pounding triumphs in triple and quadruple overtime. Amazingly, coach Dick Irvin's team still had enough gas in the tank to keep up with the speedy Leafs.

Game 1 of the Finals opened at Maple Leaf Gardens, and it too went to sudden-death. But at 5:51 of the extra period, Toronto's Sid Smith beat McNeil for the victory. "It was," wrote Jim Vipond of the Toronto *Globe and Mail*, "as fast and exciting a hockey game as has been seen here this season."

In Game 2, the Canadiens turned the tables. With the score 2–2 in overtime, the fiery-eyed Richard challenged goalie Turk Broda, a 36-year-old fading legend. The Rocket bent the twine at the 2:55 mark, evening the series.

In Game 3 at the Gardens, Toronto coach Joe Primeau benched Broda in favor of the younger, spryer Al Rollins. The 24-year-old netminder allowed only one goal, to Richard, while the gentlemanly Sid Smith lit the lamp for Toronto. Through 60 minutes, the score was knotted 1–1. In OT, Rollins' young reflexes paid off, as he survived three onslaughts in the first four minutes. Finally, Toronto's Tod Sloan zipped a pass to Leafs captain Ted Kennedy, who beat McNeil at 4:47.

Never in Stanley Cup history had teams played four straight overtime games, until April 19, 1951, in Toronto. A goal by Montreal's Elmer Lach tied the game at 2–2, setting up another sudden-death. Watson,

"Bashin' Bill" Barilko earned high praise for his punishing body checks, but no one ever dreamed he'd be an offensive hero. His overtime winner was his 31st goal in the NHL—and his last.

in a *Hockey Digest* article, recalled the details: "There was a line change coming up, so I jumped on the ice because no one else was moving. [Max] Bentley gave me the puck and I put a low shot past [McNeil]."

Game 5, on Saturday night in Toronto, quickly turned ugly. Within the first minute, Captain Kennedy was carried from the ice on a stretcher. Leafs fans feared a serious back injury, but in old-time hockey fashion, "Teeder" returned to action. In the second period, Montreal's Bob Dawes crashed into the boards while trying to check Kennedy, resulting in a broken leg.

Toronto furiously assaulted the Canadiens' net all game, firing upwards of 41 shots. But McNeil played out of his mind, robbing a half-dozen "sure" goals. With Sloan's tally in the final minute, the game entered sudden-death. Fans wondered who would play the hero in this historic overtime session. Toronto boasted three future Hall of Fame forwards—Kennedy, Watson, and Bentley—as well as 30-goal scorers Sloan and Smith. The Canadiens featured seven future Hall of Famers who were eager to further their legend, including Richard, "Boom Boom" Geoffrion, and defenseman Doug Harvey.

Of all the skaters, Toronto rear guard "Bashin'

Maurice "Rocket" Richard, Montreal's goal-scoring terror, found the back of the net in overtime of Game 2 to even the series.

Bill" Barilko was more likely to prevent a goal than to score one. "[W]hen it came to body-checking and going down to block shots on his goal, Barilko had no peer during my time," Kennedy recalled on a tribute website to Barilko and the Toronto Maple Leafs. Yet in five seasons with the Leafs through 1950-51, Bashin' Bill had never netted more than seven goals in any campaign.

However, less than three minutes into OT, Barilko seized an opportunity. A Toronto shot ricocheted back toward the blue line. With McNeil sprawled on the ice, Barilko charged in and fired the puck to the upper-right corner of the net—an instant before tripping on teammate Cal Gardner's skate.

Lou Turofsky's photograph captured one of the most thrilling moments in hockey history: Barilko "flying" toward the goal, with the puck sailing above McNeil's outstretched arm and into the net. At 2:53 of overtime, Toronto won the all-overtime Stanley Cup Finals. Amid thunderous applause, Barilko raised his stick to the heavens while hoisted on two teammates' shoulders.

Tragically, Bashin' Bill would never play another NHL game. Four months later, he died in a plane crash.

Barilko disappears

Four months after scoring his Cup-clinching goal, Canada's newest hero decided to go fishing. Bill Barilko and his friend, a dentist named Henry Hudson, planned to fly a Fairchild 24 single-engine plane to a getaway at James Bay. Bill's mother told him that the trip was too dangerous, but off they went. On their return trip home, the plane vanished.

The disappearance sparked panic across Canada. Maple Leafs owner Conn Smythe helped fund a search team of 28

aircrafts, which scoured more than a million square kilometers of land and water. It was the largest air search in Canadian history, but neither the plane nor the bodies were found.

Barilko was of Russian descent, and rumors circulated that he had defected to the Soviet Union to teach hockey to young communists. Days, weeks, and months passed without a trace of evidence. As training camp began in the fall, Barilko's equipment remained in his locker room

stall, no one wanting to touch it.

Not until June 9, 1962, nearly 11 years after the disappearance, was the Fairchild 24 discovered. A hundred kilometers north of Cochrane, Ontario, bush pilot Gary Fields discovered the wrecked aircraft. "It was hard time for my mother, who was put on sedatives," said Barilko's sister, Anne. "But I told her, 'At least now we know and we can rest in peace.'"

Eerily, the Maple Leafs won the Stanley Cup in 1962 ... their first since Barilko won it for them in 1951.

THE GOAL HEARD 'ROUND THE WORLD
Canada vs. USSR, 1972 Summit Series, September 28, 1972

A nation held its collective breath on September 28, 1972, as the seconds ticked from a scoreboard clock more than 4,300 miles away. The nation was Canada. The clock was in Moscow, where a most compelling eight-game hockey series had reached its final minute deadlocked.

The Soviet Union and Canada had skated to three wins apiece and one draw. The sides were tied 5–5 in the last game as star Soviet goalie Vladislav Tretiak made a routine save on Phil Esposito's last-minute shot. Paul Henderson, who seconds earlier had crashed into the boards behind Tretiak, had returned to his skates and picked up the rebound. Most Canadians were in front of a television or radio, many having taken the day off work or school, and they would talk for years about what happened next.

The events leading to the deciding goal in the Summit Series were as dramatic as the finish itself. Many were stunned that the series even took place. Conventional wisdom held that the Soviets would never agree to play Canada's top professionals. For decades, Canadian amateurs had dominated international hockey, but by the 1960s those days were gone. The best players from the Soviet Union and other European countries had caught up to the young Canadian amateurs. Because pros were not allowed in international tournaments, it was often the Soviets' best players—technically not "pros"—against Canadian teenagers in those events. Hockey-crazed Canadians longed to see their best, the big-name stars of the National Hockey League, skate circles around these Soviets.

That such an event was arranged in 1972, largely by NHL Players' Association head Alan Eagleson, and came as terrific news across Canada. The Summit Series would consist of eight games, four in Canada, four in Moscow, before the start of the NHL season. Reporters and fans quickly predicted an eight-game

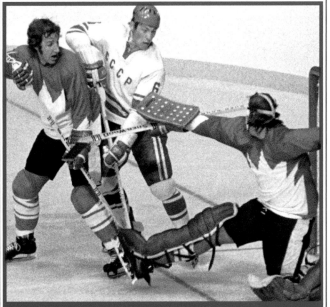

Canada defenseman Rod Seiling and goalie Ken Dryden stymie the Soviets' Valery Vasiliev. With a team loaded with NHL superstars (Dryden included) the Canadians were stunned when USSR went up 3-1-1 in the eight-game series.

sweep by the Canadians, whose roster featured not only Esposito and Henderson, but the likes of Bobby Clarke, Yvan Cournoyer, Frank Mahovlich, Ken Dryden, and Tony Esposito, to name just a few. Finding enough ice time for a collection of NHL All-Stars figured to be the biggest job for coaches Harry Sinden and John Ferguson. Winning was a given.

Bad blood developed from the start. The Soviets arrived in Montreal to find that their equipment had been seized under a Quebec court order. A young Czech immigrant had obtained a court order because the Soviet government had not paid the damages he had been awarded when a tank had run over his car in Prague. The matter was cleared up, with Eagleson supposedly writing a personal check to the man just in time to save the series. By the end of the first game, he probably wished he'd have kept the money.

The Soviets stunned Canada with their speed, their stamina, and, particularly, their crisp passing. The final score was 7–3. If Canadian fans felt let down by the outcome, they were perhaps even more disappointed with the way their heroes vented their frustration with "chippy" (a hockey term for "overaggressive") play in the third period. The final straw, for some, was the fact the Canadians headed straight for the locker room after the game while the Soviets waited on the ice for a traditional postgame handshake that never came. Recalled Dryden: "The eight-straight gang was one down now and in desperate trouble."

Among other Canadian lineup changes, Tony Esposito got the nod over Dryden in goal two nights later in Toronto. Canada bounced back with a 4–1 victory. The Soviets expressed outrage with the officiating after the game, and Team Canada agreed to scrap a planned rotation of two American crews and go with the Game 1 referees for both Games 3 and 4. The first of those games, in Winnipeg, saw the teams skate to a

4-4 tie. The final game on Canadian ice, in Vancouver, was all USSR. The 5–3 final could have been worse. Team Canada was booed off the ice by the home crowd, prompting a scolding from Phil Esposito after the game. "We cannot believe the bad press we've got, the booing we've got in our own building," he said, according to 1972summitseries.com.

Buoyed by a small group of fans that greeted them at the Toronto airport and again

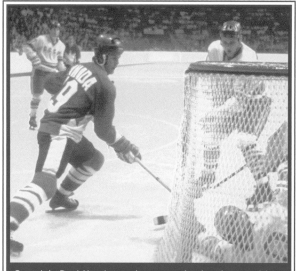

Canada's Paul Henderson became a hockey immortal in Canada when he slapped in his own rebound with 34 seconds left in Game 8 to defeat the hated Soviets 6–5.

by some 3,000 who followed them to Russia to cheer, the Canadians vowed to give everything they had to salvage the series. They built 3–0 and 4–1 leads in Game 5, only to watch the Soviets score five third-period goals on 11 shots for a 5–4 triumph. Down 3-1-1, the Canadians now had no margin for error. They won Game 6 by a 3–2 score and incensed the Soviets when Clarke took out their flashiest player with a two-handed swing of his stick to Valeri Kharlamov's ankle. Both benches emptied in the next game when Soviet captain Boris Mikhailov repeatedly kicked defenseman Gary Bergman in the shins. Order was restored and Henderson's late goal won the game for Canada. "I will never score a bigger goal than this in my life," he told himself after the game. Two nights later, he would realize that this wasn't the case.

The final game almost never happened. The night before, the Soviets decided to switch officials. The Swedish referee slated to work had come down with either the flu or food poisoning, they said, and the West German crew that had spent much of Game 6 putting Canadians in the penalty box had been called. Eagleson, with the backing of his players, said his team would rather return to Canada than play under those circumstances. After much arguing and posturing, a compromise was reached. Each side would choose one referee. The Russians kept a West German. Canada chose Czech Rudy Bata, and the puck was dropped.

Canadians remember precisely where they were when Henderson picked up that final-game rebound, had his first shot stopped by Tretiak and put home a second rebound with 34 seconds to play. Those too young to remember have surely been reminded. Many can recite Foster Hewitt's play-by-play by heart. "Here's another shot. Right in front. They score! Henderson has scored for Canada!"

Three thousand fans sang "O Canada!" in the Moscow stands after the final horn. Several Team Canada players wept on the ice. The Canada-USSR hockey rivalry would never be the same.

The rivalry skates on

The Summit Series lifted the rivalry between hockey's two most accomplished nations to a new level. Some of the most intense, talent-laden, and memorable battles in the sport's history have followed. A sampling:

1976 Canada Cup: The Soviet Union did not send its top players to the inaugural Canada Cup, but the ones who were there gave a powerhouse Canadian team a battle in the last round-robin game. Bobby Orr, playing in his first international tournament, led Canada to a 3–1 win over the Soviets en route to the final, where Darryl

Sittler scored to push Team Canada past the Czechs.

1979 Challenge Cup: Although technically not a Canada-USSR battle, the group of NHL All-Stars that took on the Soviet National Team was basically Team Canada with help from three Swedes. The opener, a 4–2 NHL win, was filled with end-to-end action. Guy Lafleur starred. The Soviets tied the series with a 5–4 victory and shocked the Madison Square Garden crowd with a 6–0 rout in the deciding game.

1981 Canada Cup: The Canadians, with a young Wayne Gretzky, handled the Soviets

7–3 in round-robin play and met them again for the final in the most anticipated Canada-USSR showdown since 1972. It was no contest. With Vladislav Tretiak stopping everything, the Soviets rolled, 8–1.

1987 Canada Cup: Many hockey fans consider this tournament's best-of-three final between the Canadians and Soviets to be the best series ever. Gretzky, Mario Lemieux, and Mark Messier were paired for Team Canada. All three games ended 6–5, the first two requiring overtime. The deciding game was tied 5-all with just over a minute to play when Gretzky dropped a perfect pass to a trailing Lemieux for the winning goal.

Edmonton Oilers teammates Mark Messier (*left*) and Wayne Gretzky helped Canada defeat the Soviets in the 1987 Canada Cup.

A CHALLENGE TO THE THRONE

Tom Watson and Jack Nicklaus, 1977 British Open

With three holes remaining in the 1977 British Open, Tom Watson and Jack Nicklaus were tied for first place, far ahead of the pack. On this sun-splashed afternoon in Turnberry, Scotland, Watson—a boyish 27-year-old—had just rolled in a 60–foot putt. The birdie elicited a roar from the gallery while sinking the spirits of his 37-year-old foe.

As they walked to the next tee, Watson said cheerfully to Nicklaus, "Isn't this what golf is supposed to be like?" "Yes," muttered Jack, and the two prepared for what the *20th Century Golf Chronicle* calls one of the greatest finishes in golf history.

Ever since defeating Arnold Palmer in the 1962 U.S. Open, Jack Nicklaus had reigned as the king of golf. From 1962 to 1977, he finished No. 1 on the money list eight times. He had won three U.S. Opens, two British Opens, four PGA Championships, and five Masters. Marveled golfing legend Gene Sarazen to *Sports Illustrated*, "I never thought anyone would ever put [Ben] Hogan in the shadows, but he did."

In 1977, however, Watson threatened to usurp Nicklaus as the world's premier golfer. Though he bore a resemblance to Huckleberry Finn, the young Missourian boasted a game that was as formidable as Jack's: long and straight drives, well-thought-out iron play, and clutch work on the greens. Watson won the '75 British Open and two early-season PGA Tour events in '77. At the '77 Masters, Nicklaus played near-perfect golf on Sunday, shooting a 66, but Watson won by a stroke. Jack's frustration carried over to Scotland that summer, where the two engaged in an epic battle.

Typically, the British Open is played in cool, damp conditions, but in '77, pleasant weather blessed the galleries and kept scores low. On Thursday and Friday, Watson and Nicklaus each carded 68–70, putting them

After matching his scores through Saturday (68-70-65), Jack Nicklaus gives Tom Watson the once-over as they tee it up on the first hole of the final round.

one shot behind Roger Maltbie. On Saturday, however, Watson and Nicklaus pulled ahead of the pack. Matching each other birdie for birdie, each shot a 65, moving three shots ahead of third-place Ben Crenshaw. Everyone sensed that Sunday's play would be a two-man grudge match for the title.

Paired together in the final round, under ideal playing conditions, Nicklaus and Watson pulled way ahead of the other competitors. On the 12th hole, Jack sank a 25-foot birdie putt to go up by two strokes. Through 14 holes, he led by one. Watson then tied the Golden Bear on the 15th with his 60-footer from off the green.

By this time, the gallery was so large and enthusiastic that it threatened to obscure the golfers' views. "It was the most electric crowd I've ever been around," Watson told the *Des Moines Register* years later.

Apparently inspired, both golfers set themselves up for birdie putts on the par-5 17th. Yet while Nicklaus two-putted from four feet for a par, Watson rolled in his putt for a birdie. With one hole remaining, the young Huck led by a single stroke.

Nicklaus needed a booming drive on the par-4 18th to have a good shot at a birdie, but he overdid it, slicing his drive into deep rough beside a stand of gorse. Watson, after drilling his tee shot right down the middle, walked over to check out his opponent's ball. "There's no question that Jack was probably the greatest player there's ever been out of the rough, but this lie was awful," Watson said. "I thought, 'If one person could do something with this thing, it's him.'"

Sure enough, Nicklaus shot the ball adroitly out of the nasty grass. It fell about 20 yards short of the putting surface, but "it rolls and rolls and rolls," Watson said. "It rolls onto the corner of the green. And I think, 'Geez, only Nicklaus.'"

Though known for blowing leads in big tournaments, Tom Watson (*pictured*) sank a two-foot putt on the final hole to defeat Jack Nicklaus by a single stroke.

Watson lofted his approach shot to within two feet of the pin. The crowd erupted; the title appeared his. As Watson and his caddie, Alfie Fyles, strode toward the green amid hearty applause, Fyles told Watson, "You've got him now, mister. You've got him now." But Watson refused to count out the master. "I said, 'Alf, he's going to make it,'" Watson said. "He gives me this look of disbelief."

To force a playoff, Nicklaus needed to hole his 40-foot-plus shot and have Watson miss his "gimme" putt. Somehow, Nicklaus properly envisioned the path of the ball on the undulating green. He then launched it on a roller coaster ride right into the hole, carding a birdie after his seemingly disastrous drive.

Watson now needed a birdie of his own to avoid a playoff. He later would admit that he was nervous as he lined up his two-foot putt. Watson had blown weekend leads in the 1974 and '75 U.S. Opens, and a last-instant twitch on this putt could have stigmatized him as golf's biggest choker. Yet, maintaining his composure, he stroked the ball smoothly into the hole.

Tom Watson blasts out of a fairway bunker in the third round. His masterful, and sometimes miraculous, iron play helped him dominate the Tour in the late 1970s.

Amid the cheers, Jack shook Watson's hand and patted his arm—the Nicklaus equivalent of a loving hug. "I gave him my best shot," Nicklaus told the press afterward. No one could deny that. In what would become known as the "Duel in the Sun," both players had demolished the British Open scoring record of 276. Watson shot 68-70-65-65—268; Nicklaus: 68-70-65-66—269. In fact, Watson also broke the major championship record of 271. Yes, conditions were ideal, but third-place finisher Hubert Green placed 11 shots back at 279.

Later that year, Watson won the Western Open. He finished first on the money list and was named the PGA Tour Player of the Year, a dual achievement that he would repeat in 1978, '79, and '80. Although Nicklaus would remain a giant in the game for years, he never again would top the money list or win Player of the Year honors.

Thus, by sinking his two-footer at Turnberry in 1977, Watson had done more than win a major tournament. He had dethroned the mighty Nicklaus and become the new king of golf.

The chip at Pebble Beach

With four straight PGA Tour Player of the Year Awards through 1980, Tom Watson reigned as the world's premier player. Or did he? As of spring 1982, Watson had never won the U.S. Open, the ultimate major that rival Jack Nicklaus had captured four times. Watson badly coveted this national championship. "Ever since I was 10 years old I had dreamed of winning the title," he said.

The 1982 U.S. Open was held at Pebble Beach, where Watson had won two Bing Crosby National Pro-Ams. Through three rounds in this event, Watson and Bill Rogers were tied for the lead, with Nicklaus three shots back. Watson played unevenly on Sunday, countering bogeys with crowd-rousing birdies—including a 40-foot downhill putt on 14. Nicklaus, whose smoking putter earned him five straight birds, finished with a 68.

On a clubhouse television, Nicklaus watched Watson tee off on the par-3 17th. At the time, Watson was tied with Nicklaus for first place, but his tee shot landed in thick fescue grass beside the green. Getting up and down for par seemed almost impos-

sible. "I thought it was over," Nicklaus said on the U.S. Senior Open website in 2002. "I thought I had won the tournament."

Bruce Edwards, Watson's caddie, told his boss to "get it close," according to pgatour.com. Watson replied, "I'm not gonna get it close; I'm gonna make it!"

Sure enough, Watson's gentle chip shot landed on the green, then curved into the hole for a birdie. Watson hoisted his club and trotted around the green in jubilation. With a birdie on 18, he beat Nicklaus by two strokes. To this day, Nicklaus calls it the toughest loss of his entire career.

"CRAZY MAN" SHOOK UP THE WORLD

Cassius Clay vs. Sonny Liston, 1964-1965

In the time that passed between the first Cassius Clay-Sonny Liston fight and the rematch, Clay changed his name to Muhammad Ali and Liston worked out to be prepared like he had for few fights in his career.

Boxing experts who saw Liston swore "The Bear" would be tough for Ali to beat the second go-around. He wouldn't underestimate Ali this time and he loathed the "Louisville Lip."

Liston had endured great embarrassment before, during, and after their first fight. Before the first bout, Clay's actions had convinced Liston that he was legitimately crazy. Fighting someone he felt was crazy unnerved even the steely-eyed Liston.

Clay had already compiled quite a resume. Growing up in Louisville, Kentucky, Clay had won 100 of 108 amateur fights, two national golden gloves championships while in high school, and a gold medal in the light-heavyweight division at the 1960 Rome Olympics—just three months after graduating from high school. The professional ranks followed, where Clay's unique style and personality drew fans like a magnet does metal. By age 22, Clay was 19-0, and had earned a title shot against Liston.

Liston had the terrifying aura of a hit man, derived from his learning how to box while serving a five-year prison sentence for robbery. Clay brought flash to the ring, but Liston brought the fundamentals of a devastating jab. His gloves housed what were alleged to be the largest fists in the history of heavyweight champions and he had a stone jaw.

Despite Clay's ring magic and charisma, most felt the champion would retain his title; the oddsmakers favored Liston 7-1. Yet Clay told anyone who cared to listen how he was going to take care of "fat bear" Liston.

When the day finally arrived for their first fight, Liston had grown weary of Clay's prefight antics.

Immediately after the opening bell, Liston stalked Clay, eagerly trying to land the blow that would end the taunts and lip service—but Liston couldn't touch him. Clay bobbed and weaved, dodging most everything Liston threw at him while stinging the champion with quick jabs that did enough damage to split one of Liston's eyebrows in the third round.

Clay was running away with the fight through three rounds, but at the end of the fourth, something got into his eyes and blurred his vision. Facing the prospect of boxing with what amounted to having a blindfold over his eyes, Clay courageously fought on—taking to heart trainer Angelo Dundee's advice to run until his eyes cleared. The fog in his eyes cleared by the middle of the fifth round and Clay once again began to stand up to Liston. The champion looked discouraged, tired, and out of shape, so it was no surprise when Liston didn't answer the bell signifying the start of the seventh round. He would say he had injured his shoulder.

Sonny Liston was so powerful that he could floor an opponent with his left jab. Yet in his first bout with Cassius Clay, Liston succumbed to a relentless barrage of punches—including this left from Clay.

When the realization hit Clay that he was the new heavyweight champion of the world, he jumped into the air and threw his arms up before proclaiming, "I shook up the world! I shook up the world!"

Liston planned to rock Clay/Ali's world in the rematch, which had been scheduled for November 16, 1964, almost a year after their first fight.

But Liston would have to wait. Ali was diagnosed with a hernia, which meant the fight would have to be delayed at least six months. In addition to fighting a battle to regain his title, Liston fought a battle few can delay and nobody can ever win: the battle against time. Liston was 33. Staying in fighting shape grew harder and harder for the former champ. The chances of maintaining his shape were remote at best.

Ali got fixed up at the hospital before getting in shape for his title defense against Liston in Lewiston,

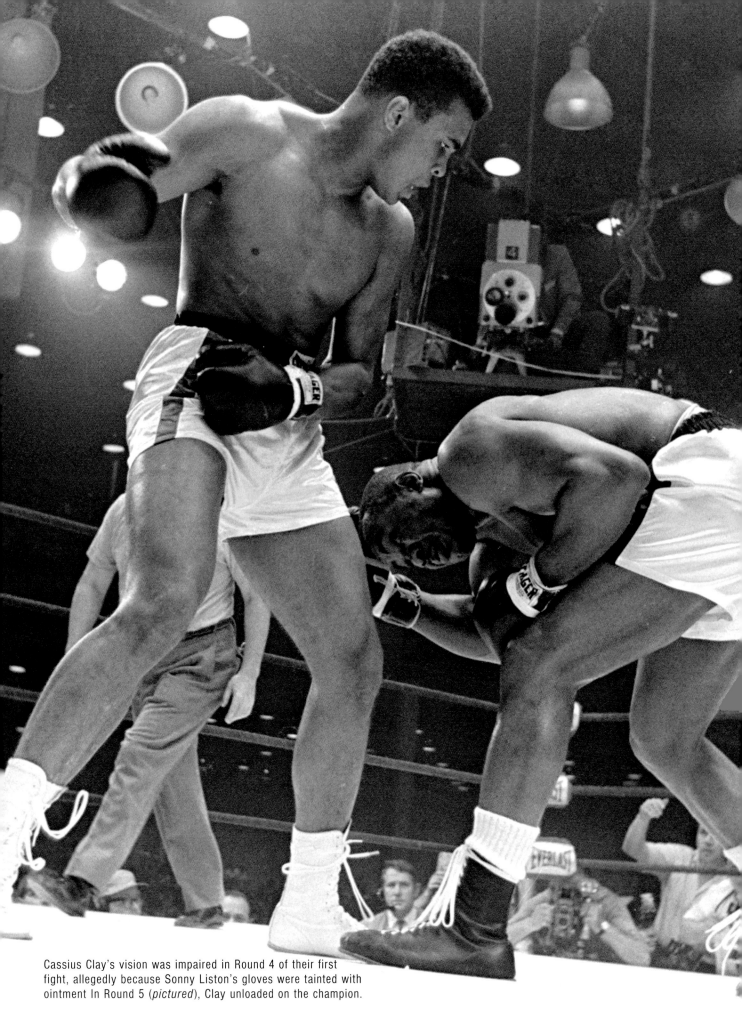

Cassius Clay's vision was impaired in Round 4 of their first fight, allegedly because Sonny Liston's gloves were tainted with ointment In Round 5 (*pictured*), Clay unloaded on the champion.

Maine. By fight time, on May 25, 1965, Ali looked refreshed, young, and vibrant—ready to once again take on the world. Liston just looked old and tired.

When the bell rang to start the fight, Ali fought the same fight he had fought in their first fight, dodging virtually any punch Liston threw while stinging Liston with quick jabs and—as it turned out—setting up a trap to spring on the former champion.

Nobody saw it coming.

Fans were still getting to their seats, the photographers around the ring were positioning themselves for the shots they would take

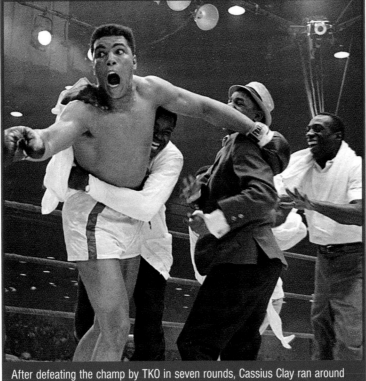

After defeating the champ by TKO in seven rounds, Cassius Clay ran around the ring screaming, "I shook up the world!" His first-round KO in 1965 would be an even bigger surprise.

in the later rounds—and suddenly, Liston was on the deck. Ali had employed an old trick of his, stinging Liston with a straight right as he backed against the ropes. When Ali bounced forward he landed a starch-filled right to Liston's jaw. Liston rolled around on the canvas while Ali looked down on him and shouted for him to get up.

Former heavyweight champion Jersey Joe Walcott

was the referee during the match. Oddly, he motioned Ali to a neutral corner so he could start the count, but Ali didn't go; Liston remained on the canvas waiting. After approximately 17 seconds passed, and no visible count by Walcott, the fight was stopped.

In later years, when Liston appeared before the California Boxing Commision to apply for a license to fight, he was asked why he didn't get up when he wasn't hurt.

"Commissioner, Muhammad Ali is a crazy man," Liston said, according to *The 12 Greatest Rounds of Boxing*. "You can't tell what a crazy man is going to do. He was standing over me, Jersey Joe couldn't control him, and if I got up, I got to put one glove on the canvas to push myself up, and as soon as my knee clears the canvas Ali is going to be beating on me. The man is crazy, and I figured I ain't getting up till someone controls him."

Thus came the ending of the Clay/Ali-Liston rivalry, a grudge match Sonny Liston could never win.

The Bear

Sonny Liston seemed destined for a sad, tragic life from the day he came into the world as the 24th in a family of 25 children. And from his early years, the man with the daunting stare was bad news.

At age 13, Liston traveled from Arkansas to St. Louis where he became involved in the trouble that defined his life. Liston committed an armed robbery

and was sentenced to a stint in a Missouri prison, where he learned to box. Once he got out of prison, Liston began his professional boxing career, stalking the heavyweight title with a seldom-seen relentlessness.

After battering his way through the heavyweight division, Liston fought Floyd Patterson for the heavyweight championship in Chicago in 1962. Liston finished off the champion in two minutes, six seconds. Patterson got a rematch with Liston in

1963, and this time Patterson managed to last a whole *four seconds* longer than in his previous fight against the imposing Liston.

Liston retired from boxing in 1969 after 17 years in the sport; he lost just four times in 54 fights.

It once was said of Liston that he died the day he was born. In truth, less than a year after retiring from boxing, Liston passed on, allegedly of a drug overdose. On his gravestone, the simple inscription reads:

"Charles 'Sonny' Liston. A man."

As they raced to the finish line of the 1976 Daytona 500, Richard Petty bumped his car (*pictured*) into David Pearson's, then slammed into the wall.

BUMPER CARS
Richard Petty vs. David Pearson, February 15, 1976

Long before NASCAR made its 200-mph charge toward the front of the pack of widely popular American sports, two drivers defined its raw and rugged existence in the 1960s and '70s. Richard Petty was "The King," a Dodge-driving North Carolina product adored by media and fans alike. David Pearson was "The Silver Fox," a Mercury-revving South Carolina boy whose fearless driving earned a loyal fan following but who preferred to avoid the camera glare when possible. Several high-profile rivalries have fueled racing's soaring popularity in the years since, from Dale Earnhardt–Rusty Wallace to Dale Jr.–Jeff Gordon. It can be argued that without Petty–Pearson (or Pearson–Petty, if you prefer), none of the others would have played out before the giant television audiences and legions of fans NASCAR now claims in all corners of the country.

"Richard Petty and David Pearson dominated our sport like nothing we have ever seen before or since," Lowe's Motor Speedway president H.A. "Humpy" Wheeler told Ryan McGee for FoxSports.com. "This was before souvenir and apparel sales had really taken off, but if you walked through the grandstands, you still saw one half wearing STP hats and the other half wearing Purolator hats. And if you dared to ask the crowd who was better, you had better have your shoulder pads on, because someone was going to start fighting."

Some racing rivals choose to do their sparring in a garage, or worse yet, through the media. Petty and Pearson saved their battles for the track, treating patrons to some of the most breathtaking finishes ever witnessed. They crossed the finish line 1–2 a remarkable 63 times between 1963 and '77, with Pearson winning 33 of those races and Petty taking 30. The most memorable of those occasions—a

David Pearson celebrates his first victory in the Daytona 500. After his crash with Richard Petty, Pearson had to restart his car before crossing the finish line.

moment still widely considered the greatest finish in Daytona 500 history and among the most talked-about ever in racing—took place on February 15, 1976.

Petty was no stranger to the checkered flag at Daytona International Speedway, having won five 500s previously. Despite his decorated career, Pearson was looking for his first victory in the Great American Race. Pearson was renowned for letting races play out in front of him before zipping to the front in the late laps, when it counted. In the 1976 Daytona 500, however, it was a virtual certainty both Pearson and Petty would run up front. A particularly hostile Speedweeks leading up to the race saw the top three qualifiers, including pole sitter A.J. Foyt, have their times disqualified for car-enhancing violations. Little-known Ramo Stott, a bean farmer from Iowa, inherited the pole position. Foyt and the other two drivers were allowed to requalify, but would be no match for Pearson and Petty.

The last 100 miles of the race saw the two front-runners swap leads (though Benny Parsons led Lap 176) and set the stage for a wild finish before a typically large crowd of 125,000. Just how wild, no one could have predicted. Petty led the field with Pearson on his bumper, literally, for the 12 laps (30 miles) leading up to the white flag, which indicates there is one lap remaining. And what a lap it was. The "slingshot pass," as it's called in racing, involves a trailing driver using the air pushed by a car in front of him to his advantage. While the lead car has to slice through the air at full throttle, the car on its bumper can use the partial vacuum created to maintain the same speed at perhaps 90 percent throttle. When Pearson pulled alongside Petty entering Turn 3 of that final lap, he used that extra 10 percent to shoot past his rival.

Had the drama ended there, the 1976 Daytona 500 would have been considered a great one. The events of the next several seconds elevated it to legendary status. After making the pass, Pearson's car drifted slightly high in Turn 3. Petty noticed the slip and shot low to retake the lead. He was half a car's length in front as they exited Turn 4 and headed toward the checkered flag. Their finish line route took a dramatic turn, though, when Petty drifted high, the right rear of his Dodge hitting the left front of Pearson's Mercury, and sending Pearson nose-first into the wall. Petty tried to right his own car but "overcorrected," in his words, and he too hit the wall a few hundred yards from Pearson. Both cars went sliding back down the track.

Petty's car settled in the infield just 20 yards from the finish line, the engine dead. Pearson fared better. Though his car was mangled, the hood folded vertically, he popped the clutch as the car came off the wall, and the engine fired. Pearson radioed to his crew chief to see if Petty had crossed the finish line. As he later recalled to Mark Aumann of Turner Sports Interactive, "When they said no, I took off."

After Richard Petty (*pictured*) collided with David Pearson, Petty's crew illegally pushed his car across the finish line behind Pearson's.

With Petty stalled in the infield grass, Pearson straightened out the Mercury and coaxed it under the checkered flag at a speed that would qualify as legal in most American school zones.

Petty's crew illegally pushed his car across the line behind the winner, then a few of its members raced to Pearson's car in order to see what happened, exchange words, or cause trouble, depending on whom you believe. Petty climbed out of his car and played peacemaker. "If you want to blame somebody, blame me," he said. Pearson had what would turn out to be his only Daytona 500 victory, fans had a finish to talk about for years to come, and stock car racing's hottest rivalry had another compelling chapter.

For all the paint they traded on tracks across the land, Petty and Pearson held a unique respect for each other that lasted long after their driving careers ended. Petty, the career NASCAR leader with 200 victories, called the 105-win Pearson his favorite competitor. "We always seemed to be near each other on the track," Petty told FoxSports.com. "We both knew that was a good thing, because if you were running with Pearson, you knew you were somewhere near the front."

Daytona's bizarre finishes

Although the slow-motion, twisted-metal finish that saw David Pearson edge Richard Petty in the 1976 Daytona 500 remains perhaps the wildest finish in the history of the Great American Race, the unusual is sometimes the norm when NASCAR's best gather near Florida's east coast.

1959: After further review
When is a winner not a winner? When Lee Petty and Johnny Beauchamp take the checkered flag, along with lapped driver Joe Weatherly, three-wide in a tight finish. Beauchamp celebrates what he thinks is a close win. But the following Wednesday, after officials look over newsreel footage, Petty is declared the victor.

1979: Too violent for TV?
The first Daytona 500 televises live ends in a fistfight. Donnie Allison and Cale Yarborough are in a last-lap duel when they bump so hard that each hits the wall. Richard Petty comes on to win his sixth 500, while back on the track apron Allison, Yarborough, and Allison's brother, Bobby, are out of their cars providing the "highlights."

1990: Blown opportunity
Dale Earnhardt had been dominant in his quest for a long-awaited 500 win. His famous black car leads for 155 laps when, about a quarter-lap from the checkered flag, he blows a rear tire after running over a piece of bell housing. Derrike Cope steals the victory, delaying Earnhardt's first 500 victory.

2002: Marlin's mayhem
As Sterling Marlin tries to catch leader Jeff Gordon on a late restart, Gordon blocks him, takes a hit, and spins out. Marlin briefly grabs the lead while a separate multicar crash takes place. Under a stoppage, Marlin gets out of his car and tries to pull away his damaged fender; this rules violation results in his move to the back and a Ward Burton win.

THE MIRACLE MILE
Roger Bannister vs. John Landy, August 7, 1954

Fifty years after becoming the second man ever to run a mile in less than four minutes, Australian John Landy discussed the magic that the phrase "four-minute mile" once conjured. For starters, Landy noted, the mile has long been the standard of distance measurement. The fact that the time top runners were chasing was an even four minutes, as opposed to 3:41.8 in the 1,500 meters, for example, made it an easy mark to remember. Additionally, Landy pointed to the symmetry of the feat. Additionally, Landy pointed to the symmetry of the feat, in an interview with *The Age*. "Four minutes, four equal laps," he said. "Every lap you had to average under 60 seconds. People could understand that."

What the world came to understand about August 7, 1954, was that a once-in-a-lifetime event was about to unfold. The Mile of the Century. The Miracle Mile. The only two milers to have beaten four minutes, a time that for many years had been deemed beyond the limits of the human body, would test their wills against each other at the Empire Games in Vancouver. The hype surrounding the race turned the Games' early competitions into a mere undercard for the main event.

Roger Bannister, a British medical student, had forever etched his name in the history books three months earlier when, at Oxford University, he became the first four-minute man. Landy, who six weeks after Bannister achieved the impossible had broken his rival's record in Turku, Finland, was eager to prove the title "best miler in the world" belonged to *him*. Their meeting at the Helsinki Olympics two years before had been a disappointment, giving their meeting in Vancouver historic significance. Asked *The New York Times* six days before the race, "What happens when a 3:59.4 miler matches strides with a 3:58 miler? It is not an academic question like the time-honored poser: What would happen if Jack Dempsey fought Joe Louis? Bannister and Landy are contemporaries, and no one will have to wait long for an answer."

The runners spoke once in the days preceding the race. Bannister had just arrived in Vancouver and had spotted Landy running sprints in the grass. The two shook hands, commented on the track surface, and discussed, of all things, the weather. That was it. Bannister made the most of his training runs west of Vancouver, away from the media frenzy. Landy's workouts drew sizable crowds, but he had holed himself in the athletes' quarters as the day of the final neared. At 3 a.m. the day before the race, however, a restless Landy left his room and was jogging barefoot in the grass, trying to clear his head, when he stepped on a broken flashbulb and cut the instep of his left foot. Initially, Landy convinced a doctor to tape the wound. He felt it was high enough on his instep that it would not affect his stride. But the morning of the race, with blood flowing from the gash, Landy returned to the doctor and had it stitched. He kept it a secret and vowed he would never use it as an excuse, a promise he forever honored.

Many hyped events, for a variety of reasons, fail to live up to their billing. The Miracle Mile was not among them. The runners' contrasting styles added to the intrigue. Bannister's late kick was unparalleled, so Landy's strategy was to break his opponent's will before that edge would become a factor. Although Landy could not match Bannister's finish, his remarkable stamina would allow him to maintain a fast pace for longer. Bannister had to stay close. Finally, the starting gun sounded. Landy shot to the lead midway through a quick first lap of 58.2 seconds, not giving a single thought to his injured foot. He hit the midway mark in 1:58.2, looking strong, with Bannister slightly more than a second behind. No one else had a chance. Landy knew that if he allowed Bannister to stay within striking range, the advantage would ultimately fall to the long-legged Brit. So the Aussie kept pushing, widening his lead to 15 yards as they rounded the first turn on lap three.

Roger Bannister demonstrates his finishing power as he passes John Landy in the "Miracle Mile." At one point in lap three, Landy had led by 15 yards.

Bannister knew it was imperative to keep Landy within reach. He subtly quickened his pace and the 15-yard gap became 12, then 10, then eight, then six. By the time they turned into the straight for the bell lap, the space between them had all but evaporated. Bannister, not wanting to make his final move too soon, settled into a comfortable pace—as comfortable as one can be after circling a track three times in slightly less than 2:59. Landy was tiring, but his resolve was as strong as ever.

Now was the time, Landy thought. If he could create enough separation before the final 200 yards, perhaps the energy Bannister spent to close the gap would take its toll on that patented kick. Landy began to pull away again as they entered the backstretch of the final lap. "Landy has got a lead of three yards," BBC Radio announcer Rex Alston shouted into his microphone. "Two hundred twenty yards to go. I don't think Bannister will be able to catch him. Landy is running beautifully."

Bannister's kick, however, did not fail him. Knowing there was no time to spare, he tapped every ounce of remaining energy. He pulled to Landy's outside shoulder as they rounded the final turn. Landy, not sensing how close his opponent was, swiveled his head briefly to the left—the inside—to look for Bannister just before entering the final straight. Landy saw no one. That's because Bannister was running by him on the right, taking advantage of Landy's quick glance. Announced Alston: "It's going to be Bannister's race!" And it was.

Bannister, later to become Dr. Bannister and, in 1975, Sir Roger Bannister, collapsed into the arms of teammates after sprinting across the finish line in 3:58.8. Landy held up for a 3:59.6. The only two men ever to have run a mile in four minutes had done it again in what was truly a Miracle Mile, and each put a congratulatory arm around the other.

3:43.13 and counting

When Roger Bannister ran the world's first sub-four-minute mile in 1954, he shattered the longest-standing record in the event. Sweden's Gunder Haegg had set the previous mark of 4 minutes, 1.4 seconds on July 17, 1945, eight years and 293 days earlier.

Bannister's record of 3:59.4 fell six weeks later to John Landy, and the mark has changed hands (and nations) frequently since. Once, in 1981, England's Steve Ovett lowered the record to 3:48.40, only to have countryman Sebastian Coe (who had held the record for just a week before Ovett broke it) shave 1.07 seconds off it to regain the mark a mere *two days* later. Two men since Haegg—American Jim Ryun and Englishman Steve Cram—held the record for about eight years each. Morocco's Hicham El Guerrouj, who lowered the mark to 3:43.13 in 1999, retired in 2006.

The following is a progression of the world record in the mile beginning with Bannister's first sub-four-minute time in the event.

May 6, 1954	Roger Bannister, Great Britain	3:59.4
June 21, 1954	John Landy, Australia	3:58.0
July 19, 1957	Derek Ibbotson, Great Britain	3:57.2
Aug. 6, 1958	Herb Elliott, Australia	3:54.5
Jan. 27, 1962	Peter Snell, New Zealand	3:54.4
Nov. 17, 1964	Snell	3:54.1
June 9, 1965	Michel Jazy, France	3:53.6
July 17, 1966	Jim Ryun, United States	3:51.3
June 23, 1967	Ryun	3:51.1
May 17, 1975	Filbert Bayi, Tanzania	3:51.0
Aug. 12, 1975	John Walker, New Zealand	3:49.4
July 17, 1979	Sebastian Coe, Great Britain	3:48.95
July 19, 1980	Steve Ovett, Great Britain	3:48.8
Aug. 19, 1981	Coe	3:48.53
Aug. 26, 1981	Ovett	3:48.40
Aug. 28, 1981	Coe	3:47.33
July 27, 1985	Steve Cram, Great Britain	3:46.32
Sept. 5, 1993	Noureddine Morceli, Algeria	3:44.39
July 7, 1999	Hicham El Guerrouj, Morocco	3:43.13

On July 7, 1999, in Rome, Morocco's Hicham El Guerrouj set the still-standing record in the mile (3:43.13). He is also the world record holder in the 1,500 meters and 2,000 meters.

Roger Bannister, the first man to break the four-minute mile, did it again in this race, hitting the wire at 3:58.8.

DOUBLE-A TRILOGY
Affirmed vs. Alydar, 1978

The two fastest 3-year-old thoroughbreds on the planet thundered for home at Belmont Park, their hooves kicking up dirt at a torrid pace as their heads bobbed inches apart. Each knew the routine well, having sprinted toward the wire in this identical situation several times in less than a year. Affirmed, the brilliant front-runner, straining to keep his rival from poking a nose in front. Alydar, the classic "closer," making his patented charge, expending every ounce of energy in an effort to overtake Affirmed. It was a quest Alydar had been unable to fulfill in the Kentucky Derby or Preakness Stakes in the previous weeks.

Belmont track announcer Chick Anderson made the call: "It's Alydar and Affirmed battling back along the inside! We'll test these two to the wire! Affirmed under a lefthand whip. Alydar on the outside driving! Affirmed and Alydar, heads apart! Affirmed's got a nose in front as they come on to the wire!"

In so many ways, these two colts side-by-side in a most memorable Triple Crown series was perfectly fitting. Both were striking chestnuts with coats of burnished copper. One hailed from Louis and Patrice Wolfson's Harbor View Farm in Ocala, Florida, and the other from Kentucky's legendary Calumet Farm, but both traced their lineage to a champion named Raise a Native. While at the Ocala farm, Raise a Native sired Exclusive Native, who in turn sired Affirmed. Before Affirmed was foaled in February 1975, the Wolfsons sold Raise a Native to Calumet Farm, where the stallion sired Alydar for owners Gene and Lucille Markey.

Affirmed and Alydar's connection grew stronger when they hit the track as 2-year-olds in 1977. Affirmed easily won in his first race at Belmont and faced a debuting Alydar in his second start three weeks later. Alydar, boxed in, finished fifth in the Youthful Stakes while Affirmed won again. Their next meeting saw

Alydar rush to a 3½-length victory in the Great American Stakes.

By the time the '78 "Run for the Roses" arrived, the two horses had all but lapped the field of top 3-year-olds. They had met three more times the previous year, with Affirmed winning by half a length in the Hopeful Stakes and a neck in the Laurel Futurity, and Alydar charging to victory by a little more than a length in the Champagne Stakes, his first race with Jorge Velasquez in the saddle. Affirmed, named the country's top 2-year-old with seven wins in nine races, had the talk of the horse racing world, 18-year-old jockey Steve Cauthen, on the reins.

Such was the backdrop to the Kentucky Derby in 1978, a year in which neither horse had been beaten. Bettors made Alydar a slight favorite, but neither horse offered much value at the window in what everyone expected to be a two-horse race. As it turned out, Alydar fell 17 lengths off the lead in the early going before mounting a furious comeback to get within 1½ of Affirmed at the wire.

Alydar's charge after early difficulties was a precursor to thrills to come. Before the Preakness Stakes two weeks later, trainer John Veitch promised that Alydar would stay much closer to the lead, and he was true to his word. Before a record crowd of more than 81,000 at Pimlico, his colt was just a head behind as the two rounded the final turn. Alydar inched up, and Affirmed fought to regain those lost inches. That exchange took place three times on the way to the wire, requiring a photo to confirm that Affirmed had, indeed, held off his rival again for a win by a neck.

Edward Bowen, in *Blood-Horse* magazine, wrote: "Affirmed's and Alydar's Preakness battle was pure art." Affirmed's winning time was 1:54.24, at the time second only to that of the great Secretariat in Preakness history. That race had the horse racing

Steve Cauthen and Affirmed defeat Jorge Velasquez and Alydar in the 1978 Preakness Stakes. Affirmed and Alydar finished 1-2, respectively, in all three Triple Crown races.

After trailing by 17 lengths in the Kentucky Derby, Alydar made a ferocious comeback to lose by just 1½ lengths.

world holding its collective breath, but the Belmont Stakes three weeks later took fans for an even more thrilling ride.

At a mile and a half, the Belmont is the most grueling test of a 3-year-old's stamina. For Alydar, it meant more stretch-run real estate to chase down a front-running champion. Only three other horses entered; it might as well have been a match race between two. Alydar caught up to Affirmed in the backstretch and the two raced as one the rest of the way, the lead never more than a nose.

Cauthen, on the inside, changed to a lefthanded whip to avoid hitting Alydar, the two were so tightly jammed. Velasquez prodded Alydar with his right. Anderson's call had Alydar taking a brief lead by a nose at the $^{3}/_{16}$ pole. Others weren't so sure the Calumet

Affirmed beats Alydar at the wire at the Belmont to win the last Triple Crown of the 20th century. Down the stretch, Alydar never trailed by more than a nose.

Cut from the same cloth

Anyone who watched Affirmed and Alydar compete could see they were neck-and-neck in talent. Fast fractions were not all they had in common.

• Native Dancer was the grandsire of Alydar and a great-grandsire of Affirmed.

• Their "A" names were an obvious similarity. Alydar, a contraction of *Aly darling*, was named for the Aga Khan, a close friend of owners Lucille and Gene Markey. Affirmed's owners, Louis and Patrice Wolfson, began their horses' names with "Aff-" in honor of the mare Affectionately, a favorite of theirs.

• Affirmed defeated Alydar seven times in their 10 meetings. Those victories were reported to be by a total of 10 lengths.

• Alydar beat Affirmed to the wire twice—by a combined 4¾ lengths—and won the 1978 Travers when front-finishing Affirmed was disqualified.

• In Affirmed's first 18 career races, the only horse to finish ahead of him was Alydar. Seattle Slew became the second horse to do so in the 1978 Marlboro Cup.

• After his debut race, Alydar put together a string of 20 consecutive trips in which he was beaten only by Affirmed and one other horse: Believe It, in the 1977 Remsen.

• Both horses were heavy favorites throughout their careers. Affirmed never went off at worse than 2.3-to-1 after his first three races. Alydar was 2.1-to-1 in his second race, then never again worse than 2-to-1 in his 26-race career.

• Affirmed was the first horse to exceed $2 million in purse winnings.

• Although the horses sired by Affirmed generally preferred turf to dirt, Alydar's offspring included Kentucky Derby winners Alysheba and Strike the Gold.

• Alydar was euthanized in 1990 after shattering his hind leg in his stall. Affirmed was put down in 2001 after battling laminitis.

colt was ever in front. This much is certain: Affirmed, as usual, refused to yield. They were even with a quarter-mile to go. And at the end of what some called the most fierce battle ever staged between two race horses, Affirmed beat Alydar to the wire by a head, becoming history's 11th Triple Crown winner and making Cauthen the youngest jockey to win the Triple Crown.

Some in sports contend that no one remembers a second-place finisher. With Affirmed and Alydar, that is clearly not the case. Rarely will a conversation arise that includes one without the other. Though Alydar did not win any of the Triple Crown races, his name is forever part of the historic achievement. He became the first horse ever to finish second in all three Triple Crown jewels.

Speculated Ed Comerford in *Newsday*: "One of these days an inventive racing secretary is going to write a race for around the world, 25,000 miles on the equator. Affirmed will win it. But Alydar will be at his throat all the way, and it will take a photo to separate them at the finish."

The two dueled again at the Travers Stakes later that year at Saratoga. With Cauthen injured, Laffit Pincay took the mount for trainer Laz Barrera and rode Affirmed to an apparent 1¾-length victory. However, Affirmed had cut off the hard-charging Alydar in the stretch, and thus was placed by stewards behind Alydar on the tote board in the final meeting of these two great rivals.

THE VALENTINE'S DAY MASSACRE
Jake La Motta vs. Sugar Ray Robinson, February 14, 1951

Jake La Motta weighed 187 pounds, just right for a light heavyweight. The problem came in the fact he was preparing for a middleweight title fight against Sugar Ray Robinson, meaning he had to drop 27 pounds in order to face his bitter rival in their sixth fight in Chicago on Valentine's Day, 1951.

Nine years earlier, La Motta had faced Robinson and easily made the weight. This time he resorted to everything one is not supposed to do in order to lose weight and retain strength. In addition to starving himself, La Motta lived in the sauna while incorporating laxatives and diuretics into his diet.

Questions surrounding La Motta's meeting his weight still were circulating the day before the fight, prior to the pair weighing in. Joe Triner, chairman of the Illinois Boxing Commission, declared that in the event La Motta did not meet weight, the bout would be forfeited to Robinson, but the fight would take place anyway.

La Motta reigned as the middleweight champion, having won the title from Marcel Cerdan in Detroit, June 16, 1949, and had successfully defended his title twice. Toughness, not style, defined La Motta. Taking two punches to land one worked just fine for La Motta, and though he had lost fights in the past, he had never been knocked out. Nobody disputed the fact La Motta could take more punishment than any fighter in any weight class and remain standing.

Robinson entered the fight as the reigning welterweight champion (147 pounds) and brought along unique, stylish boxing skills. If he won the fight he would relinquish his old title to claim his new one. Robinson had defeated La Motta four times in their

Jake La Motta couldn't match punches with the quicker Sugar Ray Robinson, who teed off on "The Bull" throughout the bout.

previous meetings, losing only a 10-round decision in 1943. In that fight, "The Bull" La Motta had connected with Robinson's solar plexus in the eighth round and landed a debilitating blow that took away Robinson's breath and left him in a survival mode for the remainder of the fight. Many believed Robinson had lived too much of the good life in advance of that fight, leaving him out of shape and unprepared for the relentless La Motta. "The Bull" could not count on such an occurrence in their sixth bout.

One thing La Motta didn't count on was Robinson's playing head games with him. At a luncheon days before their sixth meeting, Robinson asked a waiter—in front of La Motta—if he could bring him a glass of beef blood. When the waiter returned with a full glass, Robinson gulped the blood, and told La Motta the blood served him as a secret weapon that fueled his strength.

La Motta countered Robinson's eccentricity with some of his own brand of craziness by drinking a few shots of courage from a cognac bottle before the fight. He later explained in his book, *Raging Bull: My Story*, "The brandy wasn't to give me strength. It was to give me false courage. And what false courage is really is true fear. What the brandy was really doing was helping me avoid the fact that I was in absolutely no shape to go against an opponent as good as Robinson."

A crowd of 14,802 showed up at Chicago Stadium to watch the final chapter of the Robinson—La Motta saga. And Robinson answered the bell from the first round and clearly looked to be the best fighter.

Robinson's punches and combinations seemed to

Jake La Motta and Sugar Ray Robinson land simultaneous blows in the first round.
La Motta's punches lacked power due to his dramatic weight loss.

land quicker while La Motta—who looked zapped of his strength—stumbled around the ring unable to land punches, at times losing his balance while flailing awkwardly at his opponent. Robinson's precision punches continued to sting La Motta through the first seven rounds, leaving visible marks on "The Bull," who continued to charge steadfastly into Robinson.

By the end of the 10th round, La Motta had nothing left even though he trailed just six rounds to four. Robinson continued to pepper him, doing whatever he wanted to his opponent. Still, La Motta refused to go down, opting instead to keep his head down and continue to charge forward.

In the 13th round, La Motta managed to cling on to the top ring rope, which allowed Robinson to beat him silly while he offered nothing back in his defense other than taunts to the effect of Robinson's inability to put La Motta on the deck and finish the job.

La Motta's nose began to bleed and his eyes were close to being swollen shut. Still, La Motta remained on his feet. Robinson unleashed a six–punch combination that staggered La Motta—who remained standing.

Robinson had La Motta in a corner and continued the assault to La Motta's body and head that thrust him from rope to rope. The middleweight champ was getting beaten to a bloody pulp. After the barrage in the corner, Robinson looked at La Motta's corner and at referee Frank Sikora. Surprisingly, La Motta's corner wasn't throwing in the towel, nor was Sikora about to stop a championship bout of such high visibility. Finally, one last onslaught by Robinson toward the end of the 13th round prompted Sikora to raise his arms to stop the fight.

Immediately after the decision to stop the fight, La Motta's corner hustled around their fighter to assist him from the ring. La Motta refused help as he left the arena to a loud ovation saluting his courage and toughness. Afterward, La Motta talked to reporters in his dressing room. Only when he felt as though he was going to collapse did La Motta agree to let his handlers give him oxygen, which he took for 40 minutes.

The final installment of Sugar Ray Robinson–Jake La Motta came to be known as the "St. Valentine's Day Massacre." Robinson had won the world middle-weight championship, but La Motta never went down.

By the 13th round, Jake La Motta's eyes were nearly swollen shut. Referee Frank Sikora stopped the fight and announced Sugar Ray Robinson the winner by TKO.

Raging Bull, the movie

Jake La Motta's life story was depicted in the 1980 Martin Scorsese film *Raging Bull*.

Robert De Niro played La Motta and won an Oscar for his portrayal.

Recognized as the best method actor of his time, De Niro gained upwards of 50 pounds in order to play La Motta in his latter years.

The film was made in black and white and provides a less than flattering depiction of La Motta, who bullied his brother, his wife, and ring opponents in a vicious, thug–like fashion. Captured in the film is the violence of boxing. Movie goers could almost feel the blows as they landed, while they could see the visual effect in the cuts, blood, and bruises. Ultimately, the movie went to the heart of La Motta, a violent man who could not turn off the violence once he left the ring.

Though the film did not show him as a very sympathetic character, La Motta helped add to the authenticity of the movie by sparring for more than 1,000 rounds with De Niro in advance of the movie's shooting.

"I swear, without exaggeration, when I got done with him he could have fought professionally," said LaMotta in a 2005 Associated Press story printed in *The Cincinnati Post*. "That's how dedicated he was."

Britain's Sebastian Coe (254) had smashed world records in the 800 meters, 1,500 meters, and the mile, but he met his match in Steve Ovett (279), a fellow Brit, at the 1980 Olympics.

RUNNING FOR GOLD

Sebastian Coe vs. Steve Ovett, 1980 Olympics

Middle-distance running had never seen anything like it. It's a safe bet the sport might never see anything like it again. Sebastian Coe and Steve Ovett, a pair of Englishmen who had spent the years leading up to the 1980 Olympics breaking and rebreaking records from 800 to 1,600 meters, staged two of history's most memorable track battles during those Moscow Games. Ovett was the prohibitive favorite to claim the 1,500 meters, Coe the 800. And if you think for one moment these two were supportive teammates racing together under the British flag, you could not be more mistaken.

"I have never witnessed such an intense rivalry," "I have never witnessed such an intense rivalry," said 1,500-meter runner Dave Moorcroft, in an interview with Yahoo! Sport UK. According to Moorcroft, who competed in the 5,000 meters in Moscow, "We knew we were part of something special. It was something of a soap opera, two competitors from the same nation who were so different. Almost the whole Games focused around the two races." Or as American miler Steve Scott put it to *The Guardian*: "It was not the Moscow Olympics. It was the Coe-Ovett Olympics."

Born in the same country, in many ways the rivals were worlds apart. Coe was a polished Loughborough University graduate whose training regimen had been laid out and supervised by his father, Peter. He got along well with the media and his charm played well for the cameras, which endlessly documented his long, rigorous workouts and his many accomplishments. Coe had shattered the world 800 record in Oslo in 1979, beginning a six-week blitz that also saw him knock off the mile and 1,500 marks to become the first man in history to hold those three records simultaneously.

Ovett hailed from more of a working-class back-

Both Steve Ovett and Sebastian Coe surged at the end of their 800-meter race, but Ovett won in an upset to claim the gold medal.

ground. The son of a Brighton market trader, Ovett went years without speaking to the media. He once trained on the sand dunes of South Wales, far from the limelight. There was no denying his talent. Ovett excelled in distances from 400 meters to the half-marathon, and his trademark wave to the crowd as he approached the finish line was considered great showmanship by some, outright cockiness by others. He entered the Moscow Games holding the world record in the 1,500, having not lost in that event or the mile in three years.

Though their rivalry seemed to divide English fans right down the middle, it was a rare occasion when the two actually met on the track. That added to the intrigue of the 1980 Olympics, when the two greats would meet in their prime—twice—on the world's biggest sports stage. The fact that there was no American contingent, because of a boycott of the Games, hardly mattered in these two showcase events.

First up was the 800, Coe's specialty. No one in the eight-man final had ever run a time within 1.5 seconds of Coe's top clocking: 1 minute, 42.33 seconds. Some races play out entirely according to form, just as one might predict. This was not one of them. After the first of two laps, which featured contact, stumbling, and swerving from a few of the tightly-packed runners, Ovett was running in sixth place and Coe bringing up the rear.

Coe took both turns of the final lap wide and found himself "boxed in" when the time came to make a move. He watched Ovett close with a winning kick, surging past leader Nikolai Kirov of the Soviet Union. Ovett's time was 1:45.4. Coe, too, overtook Kirov, but it was not enough. He finished three meters behind Ovett. Later, on the medals stand, the two rivals answered the question on every reporter's mind when they did, indeed, shake hands.

Ovett, who had been accused by some of being too physical in gaining position during his winning 800-meter run, declined to attend the official press conference after the race. Coe showed up. One account described him as looking more like "an 8-year-old who has just been pulled out of the canal than an Olympic silver medalist." That's how he felt after falling to his chief rival in an event he had been accustomed to dominating. Coe, sitting next to his father, admitted to feeling the pressure, making tactical errors, and not responding as he should have.

Fortunately for Coe, he had a chance to redeem himself. It would, however, have to be in the event Ovett had owned on a world scale for three years. Earlier that month, Ovett had set a new world record in the mile. A writer from the *Sunday Telegraph* predicted: "No power on earth can now prevent Ovett from winning the 1,500 metres. ... That is, after all, his priority and Coe's weaker distance. Any chance of Coe beating Ovett in the 1,500 metres would have had to follow his establishing a moral ascendancy in the 800 metres, which he singularly failed to do."

Steve Ovett was supposed to be unbeatable in the 1,500 meters, but he had to settle for bronze as an ecstatic Sebastian Coe took gold and East Germany's Jürgen Straub won silver.

There would be no such failure on Coe's part the day of the second big race. He and East Germany's Jürgen Straub took the early lead and circled the track in split times. Ovett kept close to the leaders, but on the third lap Straub raised the stakes. He raced around in 54.6 seconds, taking the final-lap bell just ahead of Coe and Ovett. The blistering pace of the previous 400 meters wound up favoring Coe.

With 300 meters to go, Straub put his head down and began straining with all he had. Coe was content to stay on his shoulder until the final 200, when he started what he called a "semi-kick" and legged past the German. At the same time, unbeknownst to Coe, Ovett had begun his own assault on the leaders, but it was too late for Ovett. For the second straight time in the Coe–Ovett rivalry, the "unbeatable" runner had been defeated. Ovett settled for a bronze medal. Coe finished in 3:38.4 after the fastest final 800 meters ever in a three and a half or four-lap race. Coe covered the last two laps in 1:48.9. During his victory lap, Coe briefly put his arm around a dejected Ovett. "But," Coe would later note, "it was all reflex."

Record-setting careers

English rivals Sebastian Coe and Steve Ovett waged a few memorable battles on the track. Their duel on the world stage was every bit as noteworthy, particularly given the fact their head-to-head races were not as frequent as fans might have preferred.

Coe set his first world records in July 1979 in Oslo, Norway, smashing the 800-meter mark by more than a second in 1:42.33 and 10 days later running a record 3:49 mile. The next month, Coe's 3:32.1 in the 1,500 meters made him the first in history to carry world records in those three events at the same time.

Coe added a 1,000-meter world mark in July 1980. And in 1981, the year after his famous Moscow Olympic meetings with Ovett, he bettered his 800 mark with a time of 1:41.73, a world record that would stand for 16 years.

Though Ovett topped Coe in the Olympic 800, that race was never his specialty, nor did he ever vie for a world record at the two-lap distance. In each of his two main events, however—the mile and 1,500—Ovett broke world records set by Coe.

One year after Coe set his world mark in the mile, Ovett shaved off two-tenths of a second with a time of 3:48.8. Later that same year, he knocked Coe's name from the top of the 1,500-meter list with a run of 3:31.36, a mark he would lower to 3:30.77 in 1983.

Both runners returned to the Olympic Games in 1984 in Los Angeles. Coe's win in the 1,500 made him the first man in history with two gold medals in that event. Ovett, battling bronchitis, collapsed during that race and was taken away on a stretcher.

McENROE VS. WIMBLEDON
John McEnroe at Wimbledon, 1981

It was only the second set of his first match at Wimbledon in 1981, and already bad boy John McEnroe was ready to throttle a stuffy British official. After the volatile phenom banged his racket on his chair, umpire Edward "Ted" Jones gave him a stern warning: "You are misusing your racket, Mr. McEnroe." "Superbrat" retorted, "Man, you cannot be serious!" Two sets later, after a highly questionable call, McEnroe demanded to see the tournament referee, Fred Hoyles. "You guys are the absolute pits of the world," McEnroe exclaimed. "Do you know that?"

In the long history of tennis, no rivalry ignited more passion, anger, controversy, foul language, and press coverage than John McEnroe vs. Wimbledon—with the latter representing the All England Club, umpires and referees, the tabloid British press, and even Lady Diana. The hostilities culminated in 1981, but they had been brewing for four years.

Back in 1977, an 18-year-old McEnroe had become the youngest male ever to reach the Wimbledon semifinals. A pouty, frizzy-haired, foul-mouthed kid from Queens, New York, McEnroe acted like a tramp at a royal tea party. The Brits referred to him as "McNasty." Upon his 1979 visit to the All England Lawn Tennis and Croquet Club, he earned the nickname "Superbrat" by the tabloids. *The Sun* called him "the most vain, ill-tempered, petulant loudmouth that the game of tennis has ever known."

All true, although the British couldn't deny his phenomenal talent. "His serve is not the hardest," tennis legend Arthur Ashe said in *Oregon Insider Sports*, "but he can change speed and angle. He also has the advantage of being lefthanded, which causes his spin serves to break in the opposite direction from righthanders and confuse them."

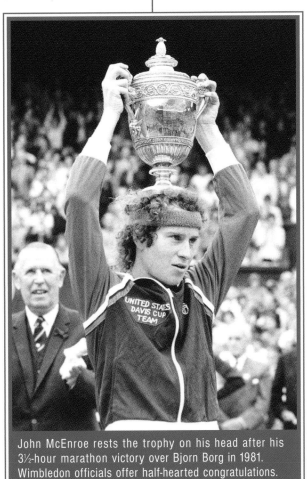

John McEnroe rests the trophy on his head after his 3½-hour marathon victory over Bjorn Borg in 1981. Wimbledon officials offer half-hearted congratulations.

McEnroe also possessed amazing footwork and hand-eye coordination, and he wowed crowds with his extraordinary shot-making. Moreover, he played with a passion that bordered on hostility—not toward his opponents but toward himself ("Play like a human being!" he'd shout after a missed shot) and the officials. Despite his outbursts, McEnroe won the U.S. Open title in 1979, his first of three straight triumphs at the American championship.

In 1980 McEnroe reached the Wimbledon Gentleman's Singles Finals for the first time. His opponent: Swedish icon Bjorn Borg. The antithesis of McEnroe, "Ice Man" never lost his cool while attracting—instead of repulsing—tennis fans. For hours in the sunshine, women swooned over Borg's perfect physique, pretty yet sometimes unshaven face, and long, golden locks.

Called "The Tennis Machine" by *Time* magazine, Borg gunned for his fifth straight Wimbledon title in 1980. The championship match between Borg and McEnroe ranks among the greatest in Wimbledon history. Borg led two sets to one, but McEnroe took the fourth set 7–6 by winning an epic tiebreaker. Saving five match points, he prevailed 18–16. Borg won the fifth set, however, 8–6—much to the delight of the tournament brass. What really burned McEnroe was that the officiating at the world's biggest tennis tournament was done by amateurs who weren't even required to have their eyesight checked until 1980. In previous years, Wimbledon officials had condemned Jimmy Connors for grunting during his play, and kicked champion Stan Smith's wife out of the tearoom because she wasn't a member, even though she was seven months pregnant. Others griped that officials gave golden boy Borg the best match times and best courts year after year. Then there was

John McEnroe drop-kicks his racquet in an early-round match against Tom Gullikson in 1981. Said Arthur Ashe, "I've never seen Wimbledon so mad, I mean burning."

the British press, who instigated an R-rated tongue-lashing from McEnroe in 1981 for hounding him with questions about his girlfriend.

In fact, tensions reached full boil during McEnroe's visit in '81. "Superbrat" called linesmen and umpires "incompetent fools" and "disgraces to mankind." In his semifinal match against Australian Rod Frawley, McEnroe spouted off 13 times. Lady Diana Spencer, the future princess, got up and left. All told during the tournament, McEnroe was slapped with $14,750 in fines. "I've never seen Wimbledon so mad," said Ashe in *Sports Illustrated*. "I mean burning."

As if the ungrateful American weren't insulting enough, the 1981 finals fell on the Fourth of July, and McEnroe strode onto the court wearing red, white, and blue. Earlier in the fortnight, McEnroe's antics had almost earned him an expulsion from the tournament, but now there was nothing Wimbledon officials could do. Only Bjorn Borg, or McEnroe's self-destruction, could prevent McEnroe from winning the ultimate prize in British tennis.

Borg, winner of 41 straight Wimbledon matches, played masterfully, but on this day his nemesis won

Bjorn Borg savors his fifth consecutive Wimbledon singles championship in 1980 after defeating John McEnroe in the "Match of the Century."

the battle of wills. After losing the first set 4–6, McEnroe took the next two sets 7–6 and 7–6, winning the tiebreakers 7–1 and 7–4.

At one crucial moment in the third set, a linesman called a McEnroe volley in but then was overruled by the umpire. All eyes turned to McEnroe. But this time, McEnroe simply bowed his head and turned away. "It's too hard to deal with other problems when you're trying to beat *him*," he explained.

With the ultimate prize in sight, McEnroe bore down and played near-perfect tennis in the fourth set. When he prevailed, winning 6–4, McEnroe praised the heavens, shook hands with Borg, and then rejoiced with his family in the visitors' box.

Normally after a player wins his or her first Wimbledon title, the All England Club immediately accords that champion honorary membership in the club. McEnroe, however, was not so honored. In turn, he skipped the traditional champions dinner that evening. Said McEnroe to ESPN: "I wanted to spend [the evening] with my family and friends and the people who had supported me, not a bunch of stiffs who are 70–80 years old, telling you that you're acting like a jerk."

At least success didn't change him.

Match of the century

Although the John McEnroe-Wimbledon feud peaked in 1981, the McEnroe-Bjorn Borg rivalry, one of the most celebrated in tennis history, had climaxed a year earlier. On July 5, 1980, at Wimbledon, the world's two top players engaged in the "Match of the Century."

Booed while entering Center Court, McEnroe was determined to win his first Wimbledon and end Borg's string of four consecutive titles. The world watched with

amazement as McEnroe, wielding a wicked lefthanded serve, cruised through the first set, winning 6–1. But the champion adjusted, relying on strong, accurate passing shots to win the next two sets, 7–5 and 6–3.

In the fourth set, Borg moved ahead 5–4 and reached two match points, only to lose them both, and the game, to his desperate opponent. The set went to 6–6, forcing a tiebreaker—or as it would come to be known, "The Tiebreaker." For 22 excruciating min-

utes, the two warriors engaged in an epic battle. Five times Borg held match point, and five times McEnroe survived. Finally, on the 34th point, McEnroe prevailed 18–16.

The fifth set was equally dramatic. Borg prevailed 8–6 for his fifth consecutive title, but he knew that McEnroe's day would finally come. After losing to McEnroe at Wimbledon and later the U.S. Open in 1981, Borg announced his retirement at age 26. McEnroe's reign as the king of tennis lasted until 1984, the year he won his third Wimbledon and fourth U.S. Open.

TONITE BOXING 15 ROUNDS
BENNY PARET ♦ EMILE GRIFFITH
NEXT SAT BOXING TIGER ♦ HANK
CIRCUS OPENS WED APRIL 4
THRU SUNDAY MAY 13 TWICE DAILY

Benny Paret's limp body was transported from the ring to the dressing room, where a Catholic priest performed last rites.

A FIGHT TO THE DEATH
Emile Griffith vs. Benny Paret, March 24, 1962

Emile Griffith and Benny Paret had fought twice before for the world welterweight title, each winning once, but their third battle took on a whole new dimension. Paret had heard that Griffith was gay, and at the prefight weigh-in for their third match-up on March 24, 1962, Paret mercilessly ridiculed his opponent.

As Griffith stood on the scale in his underwear in front of the press, Paret mocked him by gyrating his body, thrusting his pelvis, and grabbing Griffith's buttocks. "Hey, *maricón*," teased Paret, using a Spanish word that means *faggot*, "I'm going to get you *and* your husband."

As anger raged within Griffith, his trainer, Gil Clancy, stepped in. "Save it for tonight," Clancy told him. Reporters in attendance could sense Griffith's seething hostility, and they shared the same thought about that night's match-up: Lord help Benny Paret.

Before that fateful day, Griffith had enjoyed a glory-filled run in the fight business. Born in the Virgin Islands in 1938, he moved to New York City in the early 1950s, where he quickly took to boxing. Despite his 26-inch waist, Griffith boasted "shoulders that you could serve dinner for six on," wrote Bert Sugar, a Boxing Hall of Fame writer. On April Fools' Day, 1961, Griffith challenged Benny "The Kid" Paret for the world welterweight crown. Quick and powerful, Griffith handed the Cuban champ his 10th pro loss with a 13th-round knockout.

As Griffith's star soared, rumors began to circulate that he was homosexual. He had worked as a hat designer in Manhattan and had been spotted in gay clubs. At the weigh-in before their rematch on September 30, 1961, Paret mocked his opponent, uttering *"maricón"* for Griffith to hear. Paret won a split decision to take the title.

An enraged Emile Griffith pummels Benny Paret into unconsciousness in the 12th round before referee Ruby Goldstein intervenes.

A heavy underdog for their third bout in 1962, Paret decided to fluster Griffith with an even more embarrassing taunt—hence, his flamboyant act at the weigh-in. This time, however, Paret's shenanigans would come back to haunt him.

The televised Saturday night bout took place in front of 7,600 fans at New York's Madison Square Garden. Although Paret knocked down Griffith in the sixth round, the latter controlled the fight. In fact, those at ringside marveled at how much punishment Paret was absorbing. In the 12th round, however, their astonishment turned to sheer horror.

Pinning Paret in a corner, Griffith released his pent-up rage. He punished the Cuban with a powerful right uppercut to the chin ... and another ... and another. All told, Griffith unloaded at least 10 consecutive right uppercuts to the same vulnerable area, then added a brutal series of left jabs. Fans jumped to their feet, many pleading for referee Ruby Goldstein to intervene. Goldstein didn't interrupt because Paret was still standing, but the ref didn't realize that only the post was keeping him upright.

Griffith continued with a barrage of savage blows. His left and right hooks snapped Paret's head to and fro. The Kid's eyes were closed, and his hands fell to his side. Wrote *New York Times* reporter Robert L. Teague, who covered the fight, "The fact that Paret would not fall seemed to arouse the New Yorker to new heights of fury." Fans begged and screamed to stop the fight, but Goldstein didn't step in until Griffith had landed more than 20 barbaric punches. Even then, the ref had to struggle to restrain the attacker, as if prying a lion off a fresh carcass.

All eyes turned to Paret, who fell limp to the canvas. Doctors hovered over the unconscious fighter for eight minutes before transporting him on a stretcher to his dressing room. A Catholic priest performed last rites on Paret before an ambulance rushed him to the hospital. There, Dr. Lawrence Schick performed surgery to relieve pressure on his brain. Griffith, now physically and emotionally spent, was among about 15 people who gathered in the waiting room. "I'm sorry it happened," he said. "I hope everything is being done for him."

But nothing could be done. Paret lay in a coma for 10 days before dying on April 3, his wife by his side. The whole experience was sad and sickening, and it haunted those who had witnessed the sanctioned killing in person. Wrote novelist Norman Mailer, who was in attendance, "As he went down, the sound of Griffith's punches echoed in the mind like a heavy axe in the distance chopping into a wet log."

After the tragedy, outraged Americans cried for an all-out ban on boxing. Television networks refused to air any more fights, at least for a while. Moreover, New York Governor Nelson Rockefeller appointed a seven-man commission to investigate the Griffith–Paret fight as well as the sport in general.

Surprisingly, Griffith returned to the ring, fighting Ralph Dupas just four months after slaying his Cuban tormentor. In the Dupas bout, Griffith drove his challenger into a corner, but this time he backed away to let Dupas free. "After Paret," Griffith one day revealed to *Sports Illustrated*, "I never wanted to hurt a guy

Lucy Paret caresses the body of her late husband at a funeral home in the Bronx. Paret was pregnant and had a two-year-old son. She never remarried.

again. I was so scared to hit someone. I was always holding back."

Throughout his career, Griffith never admitted he was a homosexual. Any Americans who made such an admission during the 1960s risked ruining their careers. Besides, Griffith would say years later, he had been conflicted about his sexuality all his life. Griffith went on to fight for 15 years after Paret's death. He won five world titles before hanging up his gloves for good in 1977.

In 2005, while lunching with *The New York Times* columnist Bob Herbert, Griffith discussed what had driven him to such fury 43 years earlier. "I got tired of people calling me *faggot*," he said. Griffith insisted he was sorry that Paret had died, but he added, "He called me a name ... so I did what I had to do."

Moore Death

Emile Griffith's fatal blows against Benny Paret repulsed and shocked the American public. Yet Paret was hardly the first fighter to die from a beating incurred in the ring. Records are sketchy and incomplete, but large numbers of boxers have died from their beatings. One writer noted that in South Africa alone, more than 60 boxers have suffered fatal blows since 1905.

Four heavyweight champions—Bob Fitzsimmons, Jess Willard, Max Baer, and Primo Carnera—killed men with their padded fists. Yet fighters didn't have to be giant brutes to lay men to rest. On March 21, 1963, less than one year after the Paret tragedy, featherweights Davey Moore and Sugar Ramos engaged in a fatal bout.

Like the Griffith fight, this match also was televised, although it was held outdoors in Dodger Stadium. Moore reigned as the world featherweight champion, while Ramos was the undefeated No. 1 contender. Part of a "tripleheader," the bout attracted more than 26,000 fans.

In the 10th round, Ramos pleased the largely Latino crowd by knocking Moore off his feet, the back of his head banging against the bottom rope. Moore got up on the count of three, but he did not answer the bell for the 11th round.

Afterward, Moore talked in the dressing room for 40 minutes. "Sure, I want to fight him again," he said. "And I'll get the title back." After the media left, Moore dropped to the floor, unconscious. He died from brain damage four days later.

California Governor Pat Brown responded by asking the state legislature to ban the brutal sport. A year later, Bob Dylan released a song called "Who Killed Davey Moore?" The public was disgusted, but the sport continued on. In fact, Cassius Clay's TKO of Sonny Liston on February 25, 1964, ushered in a golden age of boxing.

MILITARY MIGHT
Army vs. Navy, December 2, 1950

Army vs. Navy. If there truly is a rivalry in college football where the records can be thrown out the window before the playing of the game, Army-Navy is it.

When this pair of storied military academies met in 1950 at Philadelphia's Municipal Stadium, though, the idea of a rivalry seemed like hyperbole. After all, Navy had won just two of its eight games while Army entered the game on a roll—undefeated, ranked No. 2 in the nation, and on a 28-game undefeated streak. Adding to the Navy woes was the cold, hard fact that it had not beaten its rival since 1943. But surprisingly, the Midshipmen had tied the Cadets, 21-21, in 1948.

Both teams saw red any time they played, which they had been doing since 1890, when Navy challenged West Point's Military Academy to a game of football. Army accepted the challenge even though it did not have a team.

Army put out a call to its best athletes and cobbled together a team. Despite its efforts, Navy took a 24-0 win over Army in their first-ever meeting. From there the rivalry heated up.

Shortly after the teams played in 1893, a Navy admiral and an Army general challenged each other to a duel after arguing about some aspect of the game. Grover Cleveland stepped in at this point and used his weight as President of the United States to have the game stopped. The ban lasted until 1899, when the rivalry was re-stoked with Army taking a 17-5 win.

Throughout the rivalry, both military academies have enjoyed fine football teams. During the World War II years each of the academies had an especially vibrant program. But beginning with the 1946 game, Navy had gone 7-34-3.

Nobody expected Navy to put up any kind of fight in 1950. The game appeared to be more like an Army coronation because the Cadets had a good chance to ascend to the No. 1 spot in the polls. No. 1 Oklahoma had a tester of a game in Stillwater. The Sooners had a 30-game winning streak, but the Oklahoma State Cowboys were tough at home. An upset was well within the realm of possibility. If Army did what it was expected to against its archrival, the Cadets knew they could be eating dinner ranked No. 1, well on their way to their third consecutive undefeated season—their sixth in seven seasons—and perched on the brink of a national championship.

Harry Truman and his wife, Bess, were a part of the crowd of 101,000 attending the game. The President took time to pose for pictures with team captains Tom Bakke of Navy and Dan Foldberg of Army, then sat on the Navy side because it was the home team. Truman began sitting on the home side in 1948, which seemed to improve the home team's luck.

Navy had been a big underdog in 1948, but managed a tie with Truman sitting on its side. Truman sat on the Army side the following year and Army annihilated Navy 38-0—the most lopsided score in the rivalry's history to that point. Further positive vibes for

After tying Army in 1948, this 1949 Navy team had high hopes against their rival that fall. Army responded with a 38-0 triumph—the biggest blowout in the rivalry's history.

Navy came in the form of a good-luck telegram, signed by 824 Midshipmen, that measured 813 feet and was delivered to the Navy locker room before the start of the game.

Navy won the coin toss and elected to receive. After three plays, most felt, Navy would be punting the ball, thereby triggering the start of the rout. Except that Navy came to play—at least at the start of the first quarter. The Navy offense couldn't get anything going, but its defense stopped Army's offense four times, one time after Army had advanced the ball to the Navy 9, and the game remained scoreless through the first quarter.

When would Army wake up? The inevitable had to happen sooner or later. But the clock continued to move and neither team could muster a score.

Early in the second quarter, Navy defensive back Frank Hauff recovered a fumble by Army quarterback Bob Blaik, which seemed to give the Midshipmen a much-needed boost. Quarterback Bob Zastrow led the Navy attack, marching the Midshipmen 25 yards to the Army 7 with passes to Art Sundry and Hauff. Navy then took a 7-0 lead when the junior quarterback pierced the middle of the Army defense for a seven-yard touchdown run to complete the scoring drive. Just before the half, Zastrow struck again, connecting with Jim Baldinger in the endzone. Baldinger's spectacular leaping catch, which covered 30 yards, capped the 63-yard drive that gave Navy a

During some of the worst fighting of the Korean War, and one month after an attempt on his life, President Harry Truman escaped his troubles at the 1950 Army-Navy game.

14-0 halftime lead.

Army had just one first down and three yards of total offense in the first half, which could be partially attributed to a special 6-2, 2-1 defense Navy coach Eddie Erdelatz threw at the Cadets. The unconventional alignment allowed the Navy defense to find odd angles to shoot their linebackers through Army's line. Army could not find any suitable countermeasure from its straight T formation.

Navy also employed the T formation, choosing to stray from its customary single wing, and called a selection of plays that kept the Army defense out of sync.

Army cut the lead to 14-2 in the third quarter when it collared Zastrow for a 20-yard loss in his own endzone for a safety. That set the stage for a crazed final period that saw Navy intercept three passes—giving it five for the game—and each team twice lose fumbles.

Navy began to look like a boxer dead on his feet in the final round of a prizefight, but Army couldn't land the knockout punch. The Cadets reached Navy's 21-, 15-, 6-, and 3-yard-lines during the fourth quarter and did not score. The game ended with Army trying to score from the 3 before John Gurski intercepted a Blaik pass to preserve the 14-2 victory.

Afterward, 3,700 Midshipmen dashed onto the field to celebrate what amounted to one of the biggest upsets in the history of college football.

Navy's mascot

The Navy goat has been the mascot of the Midshipmen since 1893, just three years after the first game of their rivalry with Army.

But the possibly apocryphal story of the mascot's genesis still bears telling. When the time came for the first Army-Navy contest to be played in 1890, Navy sailed up the Hudson toward West Point then marched over the plains to play the game that would begin the rivalry. En route to the contest the Navy players encountered a goat grazing in a yard. Seizing the moment, they grabbed the goat and deemed it worthy to become the team's mascot. With their new mascot on their sideline—and an experienced Navy team playing a novice Army squad—Navy and its goat got off to an auspicious beginning as Navy defeated Army 24-0. Navy's mascot had firmly entrenched itself in the fabric of the historic school.

By 1899, the Navy goat had acquired the nickname of "Billy" and Army, which did not have a mascot, found one to its liking. Army brought a mule to the game dressed in black and gold streamers. And maybe the Cadets' new mascot paid off; Army registered a 17-5 victory.

Midshipmen quarterback Bob Zastrow accounted for nearly all the points in Navy's 14-2 upset. He ran and threw for touchdowns and was sacked in his endzone for a safety.

JUST CRAZY!
North Carolina vs. Duke, February 2, 1995

When Duke's roundballers hosted North Carolina on February 2, 1995, the home team owned an 0-7 record in the Atlantic Coast Conference—and its opponent was ranked No. 2 in the nation. Yet anyone who had placed a fat wager on the visiting Tar Heels was a fool, for when these two rivals hooked up, records and rankings could be tossed onto Tobacco Road.

Duke and North Carolina, perennial basketball powerhouses located just eight miles apart, unquestionably share the greatest rivalry in all of college basketball, bigger, even, than Indiana-Purdue. "Forget the Big Ten," said Duke coach Mike Krzyewski, according to NBC Sports. "We share the same dry cleaners ... there is no other area like this. It produces things, situations, feelings that you can't talk to other people about, because they have no understanding of it."

The relationship between the state of North Carolina and college basketball is like Utah's with the Mormon faith. It's religion ... although in this case, not necessarily based on love. Recently, Will Blythe authored a book about the rivalry entitled *To Hate Like This Is to Be Happy Forever*. Summed up ESPN analyst Dick Vitale, "There is so much passion invested in these two programs, and when they meet, everyone goes bananas."

Duke ranks among the nation's most prestigious universities, yet their student fans—the famed Cameron Crazies—are notorious for their outrageous taunts and behavior. "Go to hell, Carolina," they'll chant. "Go to hell." When tongue-wagging Michael Jordan suited up for the Tar Heels in the 1980s, the Crazies mocked him by waving tongue depressors.

It's easy for fans to get psyched for Duke-UNC because their showdowns have almost always meant

Duke guard Jeff Capel sent the game into double overtime with six points in the last 10 seconds of OT—including three on a 30-foot bomb.

something, especially in the 1990s. Duke won the national title in 1991 and '92, and Carolina prevailed as NCAA champs in '93. Many of their battles have been electrifying heart-stoppers. In 1974 North Carolina beat Duke in overtime after trailing 86-78 with 17 seconds left in regulation. In the 1984 ACC Tournament, Krzyzewski led Duke to a 77-75 triumph over a Tar Heels team that boasted future NBA stars Michael Jordan, Brad Daugherty, Sam Perkins, and Kenny Smith.

This 1994-95 Tar Heels club, coached by the legendary Dean Smith, appeared destined for the Final Four. Jerry Stackhouse, hailed as the next Jordan, and Rasheed Wallace, a rim-rattling thoroughbred, highlighted a roster stacked with talent. Duke relied on big man Cherokee Parks, the savvy of coach Pete Gaudet (standing in for an ailing Coach K), and—with the game at Duke's Cameron Indoor Stadium—those zany Crazies.

At first, it looked like North Carolina was going to humiliate the Blue Devils in front of their home fans. When Stackhouse threw down a reverse dunk, then sank the free throw after drawing the foul, UNC led 26-9. But a slew of Duke three-pointers cut the 17-point lead to five by halftime. Spurred on by raucous fans, Duke roared ahead, and the Blue Devils led 70-61 with 6:18 remaining. That's when the Tar Heels staged their big run, the second of the game's trilogy of great comebacks.

Behind Stackhouse and sweet-shooting guard Donald Williams (a future Harlem Globetrotter), Carolina went on a 15-6 spurt. Dante Calabria's trey for the Tar Heels knotted the game at 76-76 just less than four minutes left. Though the Blue Devils moved ahead by three, Wallace scored twice, then nailed a free throw to put UNC up by two. After Parks hit two

UNC coach Dean Smith won an NCAA-record 879 games and appeared in 11 Final Fours. But never again in his 37 years as Tar Heels head coach did he see anything like this.

clutch free throws with 19 seconds left, the game was headed to overtime.

For the first 4:45 of the extra period, the Tar Heels dominated, taking a 95–89 lead. "I thought we just played superbly and should have won," said Coach Smith. But with just a few seconds remaining, the home team pulled a shocker. In the blink of an eye, Duke guard Jeff Capel scored on a layup and drew a foul. When he sank the free throw, the Blue Devils trailed by just three, 95–92.

The foul wasn't the only Carolina miscue in the closing seconds. The Heels' inbounds pass fell into the hands of Dutchman Serge Zwikker, who was fouled with four seconds left. At 7-foot-3, Zwikker was not exactly the man UNC wanted at the line (he had shot just 67.7 percent from the stripe in 1994-95). Zwikker needed to make just one of two free throws to secure victory, but his first shot rimmed out. With the Cameron Crazies in full voice, Zwikker uncorked another freebie that ricocheted out of the cylinder.

Hoping he could pour magic into the hole one

With less than a minute left in the second overtime, and UNC up 100–98, Jeff McInnis stole a Duke inbounds pass and converted a layup to secure the Tar Heels' victory.

more time, the Blue Devils got the ball to Capel. While on the run, he unleashed a 30-footer at the buzzer—good! The Crazies, and everyone else, went crazy. Miraculously, Capel had sent the game to a second overtime.

In this high-scoring drama, both teams struggled to put points on the board in the second OT. The score was tied at 98–98 with 56 seconds left when Donald Williams pushed UNC up by two with a 12-foot jumper. Tar Heels guard Jeff McInnis then made the play that would earn him headlines in the next day's papers. McInnis stole the Blue Devils' inbounds pass and romped to the hole for an uncontested layup. Carolina by four.

Duke's Ricky Price scored with 38 seconds remaining, but that was the last bucket of the game. After blowing two seemingly insurmountable leads, and staging their own magnificent comeback, the Tar Heels survived two overtimes in hostile territory to win 102–100. It was the highest scoring game, and the most exciting, in the history of their extraordinary rivalry. "If you don't like that," said Coach Smith, "you don't like college basketball."

Carolina classics

Though Duke has won three national championships (all since 1991), North Carolina one-upped its arch rival with a fourth NCAA crown in 2005. In head-to-head match-ups, UNC also holds the edge, 125–96. Below are some of the Tar Heels' most memorable triumphs against the school down the road:

February 9, 1957: With the score tied and just a few seconds to play, the Tar Heels' Tommy Kearns hits two free throws to secure a 75–73 win over Duke. UNC goes on to finish the season at 32-0.

January 19, 1974: The score is knotted at 71 when Duke inbounds the ball with four seconds to go. But Carolina's Bobby Jones steals the pass and converts an off-balance layup to give Carolina a 73–71 victory.

March 2, 1974: Down eight points with 17 seconds left, Carolina takes advantage of turnovers and missed free throws—and a 28-footer at the buzzer by Walter Davis—to tie Duke at 86–86. The Tar Heels then win in overtime 96–92.

February 2, 1995: Down 95–89 with just seconds left in overtime, Duke ties Carolina thanks to a three-point play and a three-pointer, both by Jeff Capel. The Tar Heels, however, prevail in double overtime, 102–100.

January 31, 1996: The Tar Heels rally from a 17-point deficit to beat Duke 73–72. Ten years later, UNC would come back from 17 down in the second half to tie their rival, but that game would eventually tip to the Blue Devils.

BASKETBRAWL
New York Knicks vs. Miami Heat, 1997-2000 NBA playoffs

Sports Illustrated called the Knicks' 1997 NBA playoff loss to Miami "the most horrifying collapse in franchise history, the instantly classic tale of how one team's infatuation with bruising, over-the-line antics ended up killing a chance to win the ultimate prize." Three years later, fans called that exhausting series something entirely different. They called it just the beginning of a long-running feud between two of the game's Eastern Conference titans.

Several classic rivalries dot NBA history. Lakers–Celtics. Bulls–Pistons. Celtics–76ers. Championships hinged on the outcomes of those meetings. The annual playoff battles, however— or were they wars?— between the Knicks and Heat began with a bruising, cheap-shot-marred melee of a seven-game 1997 series that featured as much elbow-for-elbow disdain between two opponents as any of them.

All the elements for a great rivalry were in place even before Game 1 of the '97 meeting between the Knicks and Heat. New York coach Jeff Van Gundy had been an assistant to Miami bench boss Pat Riley when Riley coached the Knicks. Both men preached physical defense as the way to win championships. Similarly, Heat center Alonzo Mourning was seen as the heir to Knicks 7-footer Patrick Ewing, having followed Ewing to Georgetown University. Both knew the value of intimidation.

So no one expected the '97 Eastern Conference semifinals to be settled on finesse. Instead, the series was decided by a Game 5 brawl that started when Heat forward P.J. Brown took exception to Knicks guard Charlie Ward's belligerent play in gaining position for rebounds. Brown flipped the smaller Ward over his head, prompting several Knicks players to race from the bench toward the shoving match, a violation of an NBA rule regarding noncombatants in a fight. Because

New York's John Wallace and Charlie Ward grapple with P.J. Brown in Game 5 of the 1997 Eastern Conference semifinals. The fight started after Brown flipped Ward over his head.

no Miami players left the bench area (largely because of to the presence of an official right in front of them), Brown was the only Heat player suspended for the incident. Meanwhile, Ward and leading scorers Ewing and Allan Houston were forced to miss Game 6 for the Knicks, while teammates Larry Johnson and John Starks were suspended for Game 7. Miami won the final three games against its suddenly shorthanded foe to overcome a 3–1 deficit and pull out the series. "It turned the whole thing around and upside down," Riley said of the incident.

It also turned two franchises against each other. The Knicks were stewing about the loss and its circumstances. Each regular-season date between the two teams was now circled on the calendar, and fate began pitting the two in playoff series every spring. New York fans needed to wait only one year for their chance at redemption, as the teams were paired in a best-of-five first-round 1998 set. The Knicks were seeded seventh, the Heat second. And once again, an altercation took center stage in the series.

This time, the two coaches did some sparring, too. Riley publicly questioned Van Gundy's self-control and coaching tactics in another physical series. Van Gundy downplayed any resentment over the comments when asked by media members, but he had to be stunned. After all, Van Gundy had given one of his daughters the middle name Riley in 1995, after his then-boss.

Soon enough, the spotlight was squarely on a fight between players. It was two big men crossing the line this time. Miami's Mourning and New York's Larry Johnson began swinging at each other in the final seconds of Game 4, and although neither landed a punch, their efforts landed each a two-game suspension. During the episode, Van Gundy had memorably raced to the scene, fallen, and grabbed hold of Mourning's leg. The Miami center dragged the Knicks coach along

Miami coach Pat Riley tries to push John Wallace out of a pile-up during their Game 5 brawl in the '97 Eastern Conference semifinals.

the hardwood trying to shake free. It made colorful footage, but the focus quickly turned to Game 5.

The Knicks had already been playing without the injured Ewing and were now especially thin up front with Johnson shelved, but it turned out the Heat were even more handicapped without Mourning. New York stormed into Miami and avenged the previous year's heartbreaking loss by a 98–81 count. If the victory came as sweet redemption for Van Gundy against Riley, he resisted the temptation to say so. His players were not so quiet. "Coach Van Gundy can downplay it and be as humble as he wants, but he took a giant step today by beating Pat Riley," Knicks forward Buck Williams said after the game.

If nothing else, their 1998 victory proved to the Knicks that, no matter their seed, setting, or expectation level, they could get the job done. They would

use the lesson well in another first-round meeting with Miami the following year. The Heat were the No. 1 seed in the 1999 playoffs. The Knicks were No. 8. Only once in NBA history had an eighth seed prevailed in that scenario, and New York would need a Game 5 win in Miami to become the second. The Heat led by one with less than a second on the clock when the Knicks' Allan Houston hit a running 14-footer to win it. New York went on to become the first No. 8 seed in history to reach the NBA Finals.

Miami was in perfect position to avenge that loss the following year, leading the Knicks 3–2 in the Eastern semifinals and up by 18 points in the second quarter of Game 6 at Madison Square Garden. But if New York felt snake-bitten by the turn of events that had decided that memorable '97 series, the Knicks stormed back, holding Miami to 25 points in the second half to win Game 6, 72–70.

For the fourth straight year, it came down to a final game in Miami. And for the third year in a row, it was the Knicks who moved on, thanks in part to a time out they were awarded with 2.1 seconds to play in Game 7, despite the contention of several Miami players that no one called it. "They had three officials in their pocket," Heat forward Jamal Mashburn said.

Van Gundy took a deep breath after the game and reflected just a bit. "It's been very, very special to be a part of this the last four years," he noted.

To the limit

The Knicks and Heat met in the playoffs for four straight seasons, with each battle going the distance.

1997 Eastern Conference semifinals
The outcome: Heat 4, Knicks 3
The story line: Miami overcomes a 3–1 deficit against undermanned New York.
The turning point: A Game 5 altercation between P.J. Brown and Charlie Ward brings several Knicks players spilling onto the court, resulting in suspensions that lead to their stunning collapse in the series.

1998 Eastern Conference first round
The outcome: Knicks 3, Heat 2

The story line: New York avenges the previous season's bitter loss against a Miami team playing without Alonzo Mourning in the deciding game.
The turning point: A Game 4 confrontation between Mourning and the Knicks' Larry Johnson earns both suspensions for a winner-take-all Game 5. That favors the Knicks, who take advantage, 98–81.

1999 Eastern Conference first round
The outcome: Knicks 3, Heat 2
The story line: New York upsets top-seeded Miami en route to becoming the first eighth-seeded team in history to reach the NBA Finals.
The turning point: The Heat are less than a

second from eliminating the Knicks, but Allan Houston's midrange jumper lifts the Knicks to a 78–77 triumph in Miami.

2000 Eastern Conference semifinals
The outcome: Knicks 4, Heat 3
The story line: After each team sweeps its first-round opponent, this series again goes the distance. This time, Patrick Ewing hits the winning shot in the Knicks' 83–82 Game 7 win.
The turning point: Even though The Heat loses the finale on its home court for the third year in a row, it is in Game 6 in New York when Miami squanders its best chance, allowing the Knicks to rally from an 18-point deficit.

Patrick Ewing roars after slamming on Miami's Keith Askins in Game 1 of the 1997 Eastern Conference semifinals.

Notre Dame captain Fred Miller poses with coach Knute Rockne before the 1928 Army game. Their win for the Gipper apparently left the Irish emotionally drained, because they were trounced the next week by Carnegie Tech.

A WIN FOR THE GIPPER

Notre Dame vs. Army, November 10, 1928

Notre Dame's George Gipp, once the most electrifying player in college football, lay in a bed at St. Joseph's Hospital in South Bend, Indiana. His coach, Knute Rockne, could see how sickly his "golden boy" had become. The Gipper looked frail and gaunt, his voice reduced to a whisper. He was dying.

Three weeks earlier, on November 20, 1920, against Northwestern, Gipp had thrown for 157 yards on six passes as the Fighting Irish fans chanted, "Gipp, Gipp, Gipp!" Days later, George began to weaken. He was tired and faint with a terrible cough. Taken to the hospital, his condition worsened. As news spread across campus, students prayed for their beloved hero. Gipp, however, knew he would never leave that hospital bed.

"Rock," he whispered to his coach, "I know I'm going to die. I'm not afraid. But someday, Rock, when things on the field are going against us, tell the boys, Rock, to go out and win just one for the Gipper."

Rockne, with tears welling, placed his hand on Gipp's brow. "Rock, one more thing, please," Gipp said. "I'd like to see a priest."

Rockne had first seen Gipp—a 21-year-old former taxi driver—in 1916. Knute was amazed by the gangly kid's 60-yard drop-kick, and Gipp soon was playing baseball and football at Notre Dame. Gipp joined the varsity football team in 1917 and became a national star a year later. He could pass, catch, kick 50-yard field goals, and elude tacklers at will. The Irish fans fell in love with him—although he remained a quiet hero. The Irish fans fell in love with him—although he remained a quiet hero. In *The Notre Dame Fighting Irish Football Team*, Rockne described Gipp as "a loner ... seemed to live for the moment."

Gipp's greatest moment would come against Army on October 30, 1920, seven years into the great Army-Notre Dame rivalry. In 1913, Army—a football power-

On his deathbed, Notre Dame legend George Gipp made one request of coach Knute Rockne: When the team was down on its imbus, he said, tell them "to win just one for the Gipper."

house—had agreed to play Notre Dame for the first time only because a date had opened up on Army's schedule. The Irish went on to stun the Cadets that year, 35–13, thanks to the forward passing of Gus Dorais to Knute Rockne. The upset made national headlines and propelled Notre Dame football to the big time. The Irish played Army five more times in the 1910s, with the Catholic school winning three of them.

In their match-up in 1920, Army resorted to dirty play against ND. This infuriated George Gipp, who became a one-man wrecking crew. He passed, ran, caught, and returned to the tune of 480 total yards. In the fourth quarter, he returned a kick 50 yards to secure a 27–17 Irish triumph.

Notre Dame fans carried Gipp off the field that day. Six weeks later, they marched with him again. Only this time, it followed a memorial service. Despite a fierce snowstorm, the Notre Dame student body escorted Gipp's casket on a solemn walk through campus.

Throughout the 1920s, the Army-Notre Dame rivalry became a "pagan autumnal rite" in New York City. In the 1924 contest, Notre Dame's "Four Horsemen" were immortalized by sportswriter Grantland Rice at the Polo Grounds as Notre Dame beat Army 13–7. The Irish won most of the teams' match-ups in the 1920s, but the Cadets forced a 0–0 tie in 1922 and enjoyed shutout victories in 1925 and 1927.

In 1928 Rockne's boys were struggling through a 4–2 season. On November 10, they faced Army, which had won six straight games and appeared unbeatable. Army halfback Christian Cagle led the charge. A three-time All-American, Cagle would grace the cover of *Time* the following fall. In this game, in front of 85,000 fans at New York's Yankee Stadium, Notre Dame and Army battled through a hard-hitting, scoreless first half. With

Army's offense surges forward during their 27–0 rout of Notre Dame in 1925. The Cadets also shut out the Irish in 1927, a year before the "Gipper" game.

his Irish decimated by injuries, Rockne feared a second-half collapse against the superior Cadets.

During halftime, Rockne cleared virtually all non-team members out of the locker room. Somber and speaking in a hushed voice, he told the story of the Gipper. He concluded: "You know, boys, just before he died, George Gipp called me over. And in phrases that were barely whispers, he said, 'Someday, Rock, when things on the field are going against us, tell the boys, Rock, to go out and win just one for the Gipper. Now, I don't know where I'll be then, Coach. But I'll know about it, and I'll be happy.'"

Coaches and players couldn't hold back their tears. Flooded with emotion, the Fighting Irish charged out of the locker room.

Army took a 6–0 lead before ND's Jack Chevigny busted in for a touchdown. "That's one for the Gipper," he proclaimed. "Let's get another." The Irish extra-point try was blocked, and the score remained

6–6 well into the fourth quarter.

Late in the game, as dusk encroached on Yankee Stadium, Notre Dame's Johnny O'Brien sat huddled under a blanket. With the Irish facing a third down on Army's 32-yard-line, Rockne ordered the 6-foot-2 pass-catcher onto the field. On the ensuing play, left half-back Butch Niemiec tossed one deep to O'Brien. The gangly receiver juggled the ball, corralled it, and dived into the endzone for the go-ahead touchdown. Rockne was so overcome that he ran to the newest Irish hero and gave him a rugged hug.

Army, though, wasn't through. Notre Dame's missed extra point kept the score at 12–6, and the Cadets drove to Notre Dame's 1-yard-line. Yet that was as far as the Irish defense would yield. Time ran out, and Notre Dame fans reveled in an extraordinary upset. The Fighting Irish had responded to Rockne's plea. They had reached deep inside themselves, and they won one for the Gipper.

Two Joe Louises

Although the Gipper game was the stuff of legend, the 1946 Army-Notre Dame match-up ranks among the most anticipated college games in history. The Fighting Irish had finished No. 1 in the country in 1943, but coach Frank Leahy and most of his best players went to fight the Axis powers in '44 and '45. Army, loaded with great athletes desiring to become officers, blew out ND those two years, 59–0 and 48–0.

At war's end, Leahy returned to South Bend, and he brought with him players from the '43 team—war veterans with college eli-

gibility remaining. Led by All-American quarterback Johnny Lujack, the Irish in 1946 crushed their first five opponents by a combined score of 177–18. On November 9 at Yankee Stadium, they would face Army, which had won 25 games in a row.

Days before the game, Irish students packed the gym for a roof-blowing pep rally. Knute Rockne's widow showed up, and the anti-Army signs were merciless: "End the meat shortage. Slaughter the Army mule." Another read, "Let's have B-L-O-O-D." Declared Army coach Earl Blaik, "This is the football epic of the century."

The "epic" resulted in a 0–0 tie. Although

the teams combined for 415 total yards, the defenses refused to break. In the second quarter, Leahy went for it on fourth-and-goal at the 3, but the Cadets held. On another play, Lujack saved a Doc Blanchard touchdown with a stunning tackle. Sportswriter Red Smith wrote that the match-up was like "two Joe Louises ... taking every punch full in the profile, and neither taking a single backward step."

Neither team was happy with the outcome, but it at least it kept their unbeaten streaks intact. Army would extend their undefeated streak to 32 games, while Notre Dame would push theirs to 39.

A THREAT TO THE DYNASTY

Boston vs. Los Angeles, 1969 NBA Finals

Only 5:45 remained in Game 7 of the 1969 NBA Finals between the Boston Celtics and Los Angeles Lakers when Wilt Chamberlain hauled in a rebound. When the Lakers center landed, he came up lame with an injured left knee. The Lakers were losing by seven points at the time, so Chamberlain tried to run it off—but with no success. Twenty-six more seconds passed before he limped to the bench.

This wasn't the way the season was supposed to end for the Lakers.

Entering 1968–69, the Celtics were coming off their 10th championship after defeating the Lakers 4–2 in the 1968 NBA Finals. To some, the Lakers were considered *the* rival of the Celtics because they had played Boston for the NBA championship five times during the 1960s, losing each series. If Celtics-Lakers was a rivalry at that point, it most definitely was a one-sided affair.

Tantamount to the Celtics' success was their unselfish team play, which

Bill Russell (*left*) and Emmette Bryant celebrate the Celtics' 11th NBA title in 13 years after defeating the Lakers in Game 7, 108–106.

started with center Bill Russell. Hoping to combat that advantage, the Lakers acquired famed center Chamberlain before the 1968-69 season. "Wilt the Stilt," combined with superstars Elgin Baylor and Jerry West, made the flashy, star-studded Lakers the antithesis of the blue-collar Celtics. Throughout the regular season, the new Lakers appeared ready to finally claim a title as they stormed to a 55-27 record.

By this time, the Celtics had grown long in the tooth, particularly Russell. He had struggled with injuries throughout the regular season, averaging just 9.9 points. John Havlicek led the Celtics' offense with 21.6 points per game. The rest of the scoring was balanced among Bailey Howell, Sam Jones, Satch Sanders, Larry Siegfried, and Don Nelson. With hardly an awe-inspiring display, the Celtics had finished the season in fourth place, nine games behind the first-place Baltimore Bullets in the Eastern Division. In the playoffs, however, the Celtics got on a roll to reach the NBA Finals.

West set the tone in the opener when he hung 53 points on the Celtics—which bested Havlicek's 39—in a 120-118 Lakers win. West continued to scorch the nets in Game 2, scoring 41 despite constant double-teams. The Lakers took a 2-0 series lead with a 118-112 win.

The series moved to the Boston Garden for the third and fourth games, and the Lakers smelled a sweep. But the Celtics took Game 3, 111-105, and Jones hit an 18-foot jumper at the end of Game 4 to give the Celtics an 89-88 win, tying the series at 2-2.

The series moved back to Los Angeles for Game 5, and the Lakers dominated to win, 117-104. But in doing so, West injured his hamstring, and the injury clearly affected him during Game 6 in Boston, where the Celtics took a 99-90 win. Still, West netted 26 points and Chamberlain scored just two. The deciding Game 7 would play out in Los Angeles.

Although the series looked up for grabs—particularly given that West's hamstring injury had worsened—it didn't stop Lakers owner Jack Kent Cooke from counting his chickens before they had hatched. On Cooke's direction, the Forum's rafters were stocked with thousands of balloons—a move that infuriated West, who had been so close so many times.

Russell arrived at the Forum wearing the black suit he always wore to Game 7s for the simple reason that he planned to bury the other team. And the Celtics began the funeral procession early.

Using the balloons in the ceiling as a motivator, the Celtics hit the floor hot, knocking down eight of their first 10 shots for a 24-12 lead. By the end of the first quarter, the Lakers had narrowed the gap to 28-25, and by halftime the Celtics led 59-56.

A critical play occurred with 3:39 left in the third quarter, when Russell took the ball inside and Chamberlain fouled him. Russell made the basket and the free throw for a 79-66 lead, and Chamberlain was saddled with five fouls.

The Celtics pushed the lead to 17 early in the final quarter before Russell and Jones were also tagged with their fifth fouls. West scored five unanswered points to cut the lead to 12. But was there enough time left for the Lakers to come back?

Jones, who had 24 points, fouled out, and the Lakers cut the lead to nine points with just over six minutes remaining. Shortly thereafter, Chamberlain hurt his knee. Lakers coach Butch van Breda Kolff sent in Mel Counts.

West continued to lead the charge. After hitting two jump shots and four free throws, he pulled the Lakers to 100–103. Counts' jumper cut the lead to one point. Meanwhile, van Breda Kolff kept Chamberlain on the bench despite his star player's expressed desire to go back in the game.

With 1:17 remaining and time running out on the shot clock, Havlicek had the ball knocked out of his hands by Keith Erickson. The ball went directly to Boston's Nelson, who launched a shot. The ball hit the rim and bounced straight up before dropping through for two points to put the Celtics up 105–102. Larry Siegfried then iced the game by sinking two free throws. When the final buzzer sounded, the Celtics had a 108–106 victory and their 11th championship.

Emmette Bryant sticks like flypaper to Jerry West. In 1969, the scoreboard-spinning West won the first NBA Finals MVP Award.

Years later, Chamberlain recalled in his book, *A View From Above:* "Russell was asked, in a postgame interview, why I wasn't put back and, infuriated, said, 'I never would have left the game with anything less than a broken back.' As if I wanted to sit down, as if I didn't want to play! I was furious. Years later Bill admitted—but not to me—that his comment was out of line. Someone asked him if he'd ever apologized to me and he said, 'No, I can't apologize. I'm not that kind of guy.'"

West finished the game with 42 points to give him a total of 556 for the playoffs—a new NBA record. Accordingly, he won the car presented by *Sport* magazine to the outstanding player of the series. West's performance and his individual award served as a microcosm for the series. In a team game like basketball, great individual accomplishments rarely conquer great team play.

Russell announced his retirement after the season, thereby ending a golden era of Celtics basketball. The team had won 11 titles in 13 seasons, six of them at the expense of the perennially frustrated L.A. Lakers.

From the Land of 10,000 Lakes to Los Angeles

The Lakers did not play in Los Angeles until the franchise moved from Minnesota for the 1960-61 season.

Led by big man George Mikan, the Minneapolis Lakers were the NBA's original dynasty. They won five titles in six seasons. The team is also remembered for several other interesting facts concerning their time in Minnesota, before they relocated to Los Angeles.

• Riding a 30-game home-winning streak at the Minneapolis Auditorium in 1950, the Lakers hosted the Fort Wayne Zollner Pistons, who decided to try stalling—a common strategy before the adopting of the shot clock—and came away with a 19-18 win.

• Beginning in 1948, West also played a series of games against the Harlem Globetrotters, who maintained they were the best team in the world. The Globetrotters won their first two contests against the Lakers, then lost six straight played over a nearly 10-year time period.

• Finally, the Lakers took part in a novel experiment in 1954, playing an official game against the Milwaukee Hawks using baskets raised to 12 feet high. At the time, college basketball was considering raising baskets to 12 feet, but following this game, most agreed that the raised basket increased the advantage for the big men.

Bill Russell attempts a hook shot over Wilt Chamberlain. "Wilt the Stilt" mustered just two points in Game 6.

'DEM BUMS' GET IT DONE
Brooklyn Dodgers vs. New York Yankees, 1955 World Series

October 1950. Bottom of the ninth, two on, score tied, last game of the season. If the Dodgers can get a run, they will force a playoff with the Phillies. Duke Snider lines a shot into center, but Richie Ashburn snags it quick and guns out Cal Abrams at home. Phillies win in 10. Dodgers go home.

October 1951. Bottom of the ninth, two on, last game of the playoffs, Dodgers up by two. Bobby Thomson homers and the Giants, not the Dodgers, go to the World Series.

To say that the Brooklyn Dodgers were the class of the National League in the late 1940s and early 1950s is a whopping understatement. They won pennants in '47, '49, '52, '53, and '55. And if not for those two plays mentioned above, they could have won the National League seven times in nine years.

But just as remarkable as their regular-season glories were their postseason ignominies. The Brooklyn boys only made it to the World Series twice in the first 40 years of the century. They lost both times. The powerful Brooklyn teams of 1947, '49, '52, and '53 kept getting knocked off in the World Series. And by the same team: the New York Yankees.

Whitey Ford spoke for the Yankees. "As a player, you couldn't help getting caught up in the rivalry. The enthusiasm was unbelievable. We especially loved it because we usually beat [them] and we got great pleasure out of kicking their ass and shutting up their fans."

Dodger fans could have been a little hopeful as Game 1 of the '55 Series started at Yankee Stadium with 18-game winner Ford starting for the Yankees and 20-5 pitcher Don Newcombe going for Brooklyn. Ford was a lefty; the Dodgers feasted on lefties. "Newk" was a money pitcher: big, strong, defiant. But on this day he gave up three home runs and six runs, and was gone before the sixth inning ended. A two-run comeback by the Dodgers in the eighth, highlighted by Jackie Robinson's steal of home, only got them to within one run. The bad blood was evident throughout. When Billy Martin tried to steal home, Roy

Jackie Robinson tries to spark the Dodgers with this successful steal of home in Game 1. The Yankees, however, won this game and the next.

Campanella whomped him with a violent tag, then said afterwards, "If it was a regular season game, I'd have punched him in the nose."

In Game 2, Dodger Billy Loes went against Tommy Byrne. Byrne's career had seemed over two years earlier. But a 20-win season in the minors in 1954 earned him a trip back to the bigs. His 16–5 record in '55 was no joke. When the dust settled, Byrne had become the first lefty all year to pitch a complete game against the powerful right-handed Dodger attack. For good measure, he knocked in the two runs that would ultimately decide the contest. The Yanks were up two games to none, and the Series was headed to Brooklyn.

Home cooking sat just fine with the Dodgers in Game 3. Twenty-three-year-old lefty Johnny Podres, who had posted a mere 9–10 record all season, baffled the big-time Yanks. Podres allowed just seven hits and three runs while his teammates brought home eight tallies, scoring in four different innings off three Yank pitchers. They continued their high-scoring ways the next game, too, as Gil Hodges belted a two-run shot, Campanella later tacked on a solo shot, and Duke Snider slammed a three-run homer. Clem Labine notched the win with 4⅓ innings of relief.

Another young pitcher stepped up for the Dodgers in Game 5. Rookie Roger Craig, who would go on to notable success as a pitching coach and manager, pitched into the seventh inning, allowing just a pair of runs while Snider was tying a record he already held with Babe Ruth and Lou Gehrig with his third and fourth homers of the Series. Brooklyn had the lead in the Series. Next stop: Yankee Stadium. And it would be the next day. The teams didn't need a "travel day" when they were playing in the same city.

Knowing that it makes sense to play a hot hand, second-year Dodger manager Walter Alston sent youngster Karl Spooner to the stadium mound. Spooner had stunned baseball by fanning 27 batters in his first two starts at the tail end of the '54 season. But

The Dodgers won Game 7 2–0 thanks to the pitching of Johnny Podres and this catch in the sixth inning by Sandy Amoros, who may not have reached it were he righthanded.

Yankees manager Casey Stengel was gunning for his sixth world title in seven years, while Brooklyn skipper Walter Alston hoped to end the Dodgers' 0-for-7 drought in World Series play.

Alston's Kiddie Korps magic didn't hold, as Spooner lasted just a third of an inning. Whitey Ford threw a second excellent game.

For Game 7, Alston selected his big winner in Game 3, Podres. Casey Stengel responded with his ace from Game 2, 35-year-old Tommy Byrne. Both pitchers were tough through the first few innings. With two out in the Yankee third, Phil Rizzuto walked, then Martin slapped a single. Stengel tried some aggressive play, having Gil McDougald bunt on a full count. The strategy looked sound, with Dodger third baseman Don Hoak playing back. But even though Hoak couldn't get to the ball, Rizzuto did. The ball and he arrived at third at the same time, and he slid into it. Out number three.

A Campanella double and Hodges single brought home Brooklyn's first run in the fourth. In the sixth, helped along by a Bill Skowron error on a bunt, Carl Furillo was walked intentionally to load the bases for Hodges, who hit a long fly to center, driving in Dodger run No. 2.

The last of that inning was the scene of one of the great plays in Series history. Alston had batted for Don Zimmer in the top of the inning, so he needed a second baseman. Alston moved left fielder Junior Gilliam to second and replaced him in left with Sandy Amoros—the lefthanded Sandy Amoros. With two Yanks on base and none out, Yogi Berra swatted a line drive down the left field line. Amoros, playing the pull-hitting Berra into left center, had a huge run to try and track it down. But his glove was on the side of the ball, so he was able to reach out and snatch it in full gallop just before it hit the fence for a game-tying double. He then wheeled and threw a strike into the infield, catch-

Years of series heartaches:

The Dodgers didn't just lose seven World Series before they won one; they usually lost them with a bizarre twist or two thrown in for good measure.

1916. The opponent: Boston Red Sox. Outcome: The Dodgers win only one of the five games, and lose Game 2 when 21-year-old Babe Ruth pitches a 14-inning, six-hit masterpiece.

1920. The opponent: Cleveland Indians. Outcome: Cleveland wins five games to two in the best-of-nine format. In Game 5, Cleveland's Elmer Smith hits the first grand slam homer in Series history, Cleveland's Jim Bagby becomes the first pitcher to homer in a Series game, and Cleveland second baseman Bill Wambsganss turns the only unassisted triple play in Series history.

1941. The opponent: New York Yankees. Outcome: Yankees, four games to one. Turning point: In the ninth inning of Game 4, Dodger catcher Mickey Owen misses a potential game-ending third strike and the Yankees rally for four runs.

1947. The opponent: New York Yankees. Outcome: Yankees four games to three. The Dodgers win Game 4 when they break up Yankees' hurler Bill Bevens' no-hitter with two out in the ninth inning. Brooklyn's Cookie Lavagetto slams a pinch double to bring home the tying and winning runs.

1949. The opponent: New York Yankees. Outcome: Yankees, four games to one. Brooklyn loses Game 1 1–0 when Don Newcombe allows a leadoff ninth-inning homer to Tommy Henrich.

1952. The opponent: New York Yankees. Outcome: Yankees, four games to three. In the seventh inning of the final game, with two outs and the Yankees up by two, Jackie Robinson lofts a popup to the right of the mound, but neither the pitcher nor the first baseman move. It takes a spectacular charge by Billy Martin to make the catch knee-high and squelch the Dodgers' hopes.

1953. The opponent: New York Yankees. Outcome: Yankees, four games to two. Yankee slugging star? None other than Billy Martin, with a .500 average and eight RBIs.

ing McDougald off first. The spectacular double play turned the tide for the Dodgers. Podres allowed a pair of hits in the eighth, but no runs, and the Yankees went up and down in order in the ninth. In their eighth try, the Brooklyn Dodgers had finally won the Series. Even better, they had done it against the Yankees. In this Series, the home team won every game. Except the last one.

RECKLESS DRIVING
Alain Prost vs. Ayrton Senna, 1988-1994

There were signs, every now and then, that Alain Prost and Ayrton Senna could coexist. When they became teammates for McLaren in 1988, the racing world braced for these master technicians and brilliant drivers to funnel their resources and leave the rest of Formula One in their fumes. After Senna won at Adelaide in 1993, he pulled Prost onto the top step of the podium with him, a gesture many took as a sign of reconciliation between the long-time rivals. When Prost arrived at the San Marino Grand Prix at Imola as a television commentator on May 1, 1994, Senna took the time to chat. And, finally, after that day's crash that took Senna's life, Prost served as a pallbearer at the funeral of the driver who had stoked his competitive fires like no one else could.

Senna's death, of course, marked the end of the greatest rivalry in Formula One history. Its beginnings were more subtle. Though they grew up half a world apart—Senna was born into a wealthy Brazilian family while Prost was the son of a kitchen furnishings manufacturer in France—their 1980s arrival at the top of their profession pitted them as adversaries. Just how deep the bad blood ran in their professional and personal relationship was something no one could have predicted. It was a passionate friction that played out on some of the grandest stages of open-wheel racing.

Prost won his first Formula One race in 1981, three years before Senna debuted on the circuit. One of Senna's greatest rookie performances in '84 saw him finish second to Prost's McLaren in the torrential rain at Monaco. Prost became the first Frenchman to win a Formula One championship in 1985, and the following year became the first back-to-back winner in a decade. Meanwhile, Senna had won six races over three years

(1985–87) with Lotus before making a decision that would propel this talented young driver to the top—while fueling the animosity between him and Prost. Senna joined McLaren in 1988; he and Prost were teammates.

As such, there was little cooperation. Each man was driven to beat the other. The team won 15 of 16 races in 1988. Senna took eight, for his first title, while Prost captured seven. At Estoril, Senna swerved in an effort to squeeze Prost into a pit wall, and the hostility between the two grew. Prost was back on top the following year, when their highest-profile confrontation took place. It was the penultimate race of the year at Suzuka on October 22, 1989. Senna knew he needed to win the last two races to beat his teammate. Prost, on the other hand, knew he would wrap up another title if neither driver was able to finish.

With less than seven laps to go, Senna shot into a sharp bend inches from Prost's rear wing, just before the pit chicane. If he assumed his teammate would give ground and allow him to complete such a move, Senna was mistaken. Prost closed the door on Senna, the two cars locking wheels and sliding right out of the race. According to Formula1.com, former F1 champ Keke Rosberg said, "You could tell Alain

A painting in São Paulo, Brazil, memorializes the late Ayrton Senna and includes his words: "Every F1 driver has a limit. Mine is a little bit higher."

had never done anything like that in his life, he did it so badly." Senna managed to rejoin the race illegally, via a run-off road, and actually crossed the finish line first, but was disqualified and had a subsequent protest thrown out. Prost had his third F1 title.

It would not be the last, however. The very next year, at the same Suzuka event, the tables turned in the Prost-Senna rivalry. Prost had left Senna and McLaren behind to join Ferrari in 1990. This time, Prost needed a win at Suzuka to retain his title hopes. He never got

Alain Prost (*pictured*) turned the tables on Ayrton Senna at Suzuka in 1989. He ran Senna off the road in order to win the Formula One championship.

sending both spinning out at high speed. Both were out of the race, and Senna was the champ. For the second straight year, a deliberate crash left the guilty party holding a somewhat tainted title. Per the Formula 1 website, Prost said, "What he did was disgusting. He is a man without value."

Those back-to-back battles were the height of the Prost-Senna rivalry, but were by no means its culmination. Ferrari struggled in 1991, and Prost failed to win a race for the first time in a decade. He took a year off, returned in '93 to capture seven races and another title for Williams–Renault, and before the '94 season had a big choice to make. With Senna also set to join Williams, Prost was faced with the prospect of the two becoming teammates for the second time. No thanks, said "The Professor." Prost decided he would rather retire.

As a broadcaster, Prost watched on the first day of May 1994 as his rival's car suddenly shot off the Imola track for no apparent reason, slamming into a concrete wall and taking the life of its driver. Prost had often accused Senna of driving as though God were his co-pilot—as if nothing could harm him, recklessness notwithstanding. According to the Formula 1 website, earlier in '94 Senna had said, "If I ever happen to have an accident that eventually costs my life, I hope it happens in one instant." Racing lost a great champion when that tragic instant arrived. "When he died," Prost told *Motor Sport* magazine, to the disbelief of some, "I felt a part of me had died also, because our careers had been so bound together."

a chance. Senna, after winning the pole, had asked that the position be moved from the traditional right side to the left. Denied, he vowed to keep Prost from grabbing the early lead. "If he gets to the first corner ahead of me," Senna was quoted as saying in *The Age*, "he'd better not turn in, because he's not going to make it." So when Prost indeed drew ahead on the left side, Senna threw his McLaren into the side of the Ferrari,

Tale of the tape

Alain Prost
Born: February 24, 1955, Saint-Chamond, France
Grand Prix Starts: 197
Grand Prix Victories: 51
Pole Positions: 33
Championships: Four
1985 (McLaren-TAG): Prost becomes the first French F1 champion in history.

Ayrton Senna
Born: March 21, 1960, São Paulo, Brazil
Died: May 1, 1994, Imola, Italy
Grand Prix Starts: 161
Grand Prix Victories: 41
Pole Positions: 65
Championships: Three

Senna finishes fourth in just his second season on the circuit.
1986 (McLaren-TAG): Prost edges Nigel Mansell by two points to become the first back-to-back champ since Jack Brabham 10 years earlier. Senna is again fourth.
1989 (McLaren-Honda): A deliberate crash

1988 (McLaren-Honda): With Senna and Prost as teammates, McLaren cruises. Senna wins eight races and his first championship. Prost wins seven for second.
1990 (McLaren-Honda): Senna exacts revenge on Prost, clinching the title

with Senna, which takes both drivers out of the penultimate race, gives Prost his third title and takes the rivalry to a new level.
1993 (Williams-Renault): Senna is second again, but this time by a wide margin as Prost comes off a one-year sabbatical to win seven races.

with an intentional wreck that sends both cars out of the race at Suzuka.
1991 (McLaren-Honda): Senna's third crown sees Prost, now driving for Ferrari, finish a distant fifth. Mansell is Senna's closest competitor, 24 points behind.

Ayrton Senna chases Alain Prost at the 1989 Japan Grand Prix at Suzuka. Prost deliberately crashed into Senna during this race as a means to secure the Formula One title.

NAMATH AGAINST THE WORLD
New York vs. Baltimore, Super Bowl III, January 12, 1969

During the buildup leading to Super Bowl III, the Jets' quarterback wasn't buying into the idea that his team would be steamrolled by the Baltimore Colts just because the Colts were from the National Football League. So the intrepid Joe Namath made the bold prediction that the Jets—18-point underdogs from the "inferior" American Football League—would defeat the Colts when the teams met on January 12, 1969, at Miami's Orange Bowl.

Namath's prediction sounded ridiculous to the old-guard NFL faction that believed the "other league" had no business being on the same field as an NFL team. To those in the AFL, as well as those who followed the AFL, Namath's words sent a liberating echo throughout the football world that the upstart league indeed was every bit as good as the NFL.

However, making predictions and backing them up were two different matters. Even some of Namath's teammates were upset with their leader for voicing his opinion. After all, the AFL was 0-2 in the first two Super Bowls and the Colts had dominated the NFL during the 1968 season.

After the Colts lost their starting quarterback, Johnny Unitas, at the start of the season because of an elbow injury, Colts head coach Don Shula inserted veteran Earl Morrall into the lineup to take his place. All Morrall did was lead the Colts to a 13-1 record after throwing for 2,909 yards and 26 touchdowns en route to winning the NFL Most Valuable Player award.

Morrall had quality targets in receivers Jimmy Orr and Willie Richardson, along with tight end John Mackey, and Tom Matte led an adequate running game. Meanwhile, the Colts' defense allowed a league-low 144 points. Leading the charge on defense were defensive tackle Bubba Smith, a giant at 6-foot-7, 295 pounds; hard-hitting linebacker Mike Curtis; and an excellent secondary led by Bobby Boyd and Rick Volk.

The Colts' only regular-season loss was a 30-20 defeat at the hands of the Cleveland Browns. The Colts exacted revenge by thrashing the Browns 34-0 in the NFL Championship Game—a game most considered to

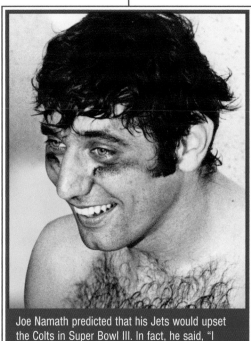

Joe Namath predicted that his Jets would upset the Colts in Super Bowl III. In fact, he said, "I guarantee it."

be more important than winning the Super Bowl.

Over in the AFL, the Jets had not been nearly as dominating as the Colts had been in the NFL. Namath threw for 3,147 yards in leading his team to an 11-3 regular-season record. But the yardage disguised several deficiencies in Namath's performance. He threw more interceptions, 17, than touchdowns, 15, and he completed only 49.2 percent of his passes. Statistics aside, Namath knew how to win and he had the players to help him do so. Don Maynard and George Sauer were excellent targets—each could make any catch and Maynard was a deep threat—while bruising running backs Matt Snell and Emerson Boozer kept defenses from thinking the Jets were a pass-only team.

The Jets' defense, with its solid line that included Gerry Philbin, Verlon Biggs, and John Elliott, led the AFL in stopping the run. And Johnny Sample led a quality Jets secondary. A 27-23 defeat of the Oakland Raiders in the AFL Championship Game earned the Jets their entry into Super Bowl III and they were immediately cast as the underdogs.

Namath's bold prediction came at the Miami Touchdown Club just three days before the game. A Colts fan had voiced his view about the whipping the Colts were going to put on the Jets. Not one to back away from a challenge, Namath guaranteed a Jets victory—a proclamation he later said would not have been made had the Colts' fan not voiced his opinion.

With 75,389 at the Orange Bowl and a national television audience watching on NBC, the Colts blew the opportunity to score first when kicker Lou Michaels missed a 27-yard field goal on the Colts' first possession. Another opportunity came the Colts' way with 20 seconds left in the first quarter, when Sauer fumbled at the Jets' 12 and the Colts recovered. But when the Colts tried to capitalize, a pass from Morrall to Tom Mitchell bounced off the tight end and into the hands of Jets cornerback Randy Beverly, who hauled in the football in the endzone for a touchback.

Taking over at their own 20, the Jets rode a combi-

Not even 6-foot-7, 295-pound Bubba Smith (No. 78) could fluster Joe Namath. Namath completed 17 of 28 passes en route to the Super Bowl MVP award.

Running back Bill Mathis (*pictured with ball*) struggled against the Colts' tough defense, but running back Matt Snell amassed 121 yards.

nation of Snell runs and Namath passes to advance to the Colts 4-yard-line. From there Snell bulled the ball into the endzone to give the Jets a 7–0 lead. The Colts' buzzard luck continued on their next possession. Morrall hit Matte with a pass that gained 30 yards and got the ball into Jets territory, where they once again stalled and Michaels missed another field goal. Namath then led his team up the field, but came up empty when kicker Jim Turner in turn missed his field goal try.

When the Colts got the football, Matte sprang loose for a 58-yard run that helped move the ball to the Jets' 16. But Sample stepped in front of a Morrall pass at the 2 to end the threat. Putting an exclamation point on the Colts' first half frustrations was Morrall's choice of receivers. He chose to throw the football to running back Jerry Hill and was intercepted while Orr stood wide open waving his arms in the endzone, which left the Jets ahead 7–0 at the half.

Turner kicked two field goals in the third quarter

to put the Jets up 13–0. After the second Turner field goal, Shula elected to change quarterbacks and inserted Unitas into the game. Unitas had pulled many miracles during his illustrious Hall of Fame career, but before he could get anything going, Turner connected on his third field goal to push the lead to 16–0.

Finally, Unitas managed to lead a touchdown drive that culminated with a one-yard run by Hill to cut the score to 16–7 Jets with 3:19 to go. The Colts then recovered an onside kick and drove to the Jets' 19 before the Colts turned the ball over on downs, ending any chance of a comeback. When the final seconds ticked off the Orange Bowl scoreboard, Namath jogged off the field holding up his finger to signify No. 1.

On the day, Namath completed 17 of 28 passes for 206 yards to earn Most Valuable Player honors. And the New York Jets had a 16–7 victory generally regarded as the biggest upset in pro football history.

Super Bowl III's MVP: Namath or Snell?

Talking smack wasn't a part of professional football back in 1969 when the Jets played the Colts in Super Bowl III. But Joe Namath backed up his big talk with a big performance. Did Namath's work on the field in Super Bowl III win him the Most Valuable Player trophy, or was his bold prediction the reason he won the award?

Before Super Bowl III Namath gave his take on the Jets, who were 18-point underdogs. Namath guaranteed a Jets win.

Establishing himself as the consummate New Yorker, Namath talked smack before Super Bowl III, then went on to back it up by completing 17 of 28 passes for 206 yards en route to leading his team to victory.

Namath, however, did not throw a single pass in the fourth quarter, relying instead on a ground game led by Matt

Snell. In addition, Namath did not throw a touchdown pass, making him the only Super Bowl MVP-winning quarterback not to have done so. Meanwhile, Snell's work was vastly undercelebrated, as he ran for a four-yard touchdown and 121 yards.

If anybody ever had a legitimate gripe about getting robbed for an award, Snell could certainly state his case after Super Bowl III.

PURE MAGIC
Larry Bird vs. Magic Johnson, 1979 NCAA Finals

One was a white player from the country who tried for a long time to avoid the media. The other was a black player from the city whose contagious smile played well for the cameras. Larry Bird grew up in French Lick, Indiana, and got so homesick in his first month at Indiana University that he decided to transfer to little-known Indiana State. Earvin Johnson earned the nickname "Magic" while dominating the Lansing, Michigan, high school ranks and made an instant impact at Michigan State, leading the school to a Big Ten title as a freshman. Though their home states border each other and their remarkable skills were obvious to anyone who watched them, it was not until their final college game that a fateful confluence united these future Hall of Famers for a game that some say forever changed the face of the NCAA Tournament.

Bird's uncanny court sense, sweet shooting stroke, and tremendous passing skills instantly elevated Indiana State. That was never more evident than during the 1978–79 season, when the Sycamores won 33 consecutive games. Even during that streak, however, few would have pegged ISU for a shot at the national championship. This was a team with a rookie coach, Bill Hodges, and a schedule that did not scream "powerhouse." The Sycamores won 18 regular-season games, 21 overall, by double-digit margins. Bird, a senior, was a one-man show at times, averaging 28-plus points per game.

Michigan State, despite returning most of the regulars from a team that fell one game short of the 1978 Final Four, did not have nearly as smooth a run in '78-79. The Spartans were 4–4 in the Big Ten at one stage, and had made a habit of losing games at the buzzer before putting it together over the second half of the season to ensure a return trip to the NCAA Tournament. Although Bird's deft touch at 6-foot-9

Larry Bird goes behind the back to set up Alex Gilbert for a shot in Indiana State's NCAA semifinal game against DePaul. The Sycamores prevailed 76–74, with Bird netting 35.

made him unique, Johnson's ability to play point guard as a 6-foot-8 sophomore truly set him apart. Magic averaged 17 points and eight-plus assists per game for a team that also featured the talents of fellow All-American Greg Kelser.

Before 1979, the NCAA Tournament was not the mass-appeal spectacle it grew to become in the 1980s and '90s. In fact, schools had never been seeded before the '79 edition, which culminated in the Final Four at Salt Lake City and included 40 teams. Indiana State was seeded No. 1 in its region. Michigan State was a No. 2 seed. Their battle for the national championship was secured when Bird led ISU to a two-point win over DePaul in one semifinal and Johnson and MSU routed Ivy League champion Pennsylvania in the other.

The title game hype surrounded the two star players. Though a rivalry between them was just beginning, already their admiration was mutual as the following quotes from Joe Gergen's *The Final Four* demonstrate. "He's so young, a sophomore, but already he plays like he's a graduate," Bird said of Johnson. Of Bird, Magic said: "I'm a fan. ... You've got to be a fan of his if you like basketball."

It was no surprise that MSU coach Jud Heathcote's game plan involved putting the clamps on Bird. Playing a match-up zone defense that called for one man to constantly shadow the National Player of the Year and at least one other to join in every time Bird had the ball, the Spartans practically dared another Sycamore to beat them. "We defensed them, and him, with an adjustment and a prayer," Heathcote said, according to *The Final Four*. "Somebody asked me if I would rather see him inside or outside. Well, I'd rather just see him on the bench."

It was not one of Bird's best games, though he did match Johnson bucket-for-bucket for a long stretch, played tough defense on Kelser, and dominated the boards. He finished with 19 points and 13 rebounds, but shot an uncharacteristic 7–of–21 from the field. By comparison, Bird had converted 16–of–19 for 35 points in the semifinal win against DePaul.

Michigan State raced to a 12-point first-half lead and maintained a 37–28 cushion at halftime. The Spartans then rattled off the first seven points of the second half to put the Sycamores in a 44–28 hole, and Johnson heated up after that. Told by Heathcote to "take over the game" in the last 10 minutes, the Magic man did just that. He hit seven of his game-high 24 points in a five-minute span, including a key slam dunk. The tournament's Most Outstanding Player's poised ball-handling under pressure kept Bird and the Sycamores at bay. The final score was 75–64.

Often, milestone moments grow to become more important with the passing of time. In this case, a long period was not required for the Bird-Magic match-up to be hailed as a significant event. Never before had the NCAA Tournament taken center stage as it did for this game. Aside from the electric atmosphere the title game generated for 15,000-plus fans at Utah's Special Events Center, it was the most

Magic Johnson flashes a winning smile after MSU's 75–64 victory over ISU. Just a year later, he would quarterback the Los Angeles Lakers to an NBA championship.

watched college basketball game in television history, and remained so more than two decades later. "College basketball will never see two big men who are better passers in the same season—maybe not even in the same decade," said Dick Enberg, who provided play-by-play for NBC Sports. "I like to think I speak for every fan when I thank them for a year of incredible 'Oh mys!'"

Of course, Bird and Johnson went on to provide basketball fans countless more jaw-dropping moments, beginning the following season when the former joined the Boston Celtics and the latter was drafted No. 1 by the Los Angeles Lakers. Bird had been selected the year before but decided to return to Indiana State for his final college season. The two went on to meet three times in the NBA Finals, captured eight NBA championships between them, and took the league to new heights through the 1980s and into the '90s. When Johnson was elected to join the previously enshrined Bird in the Basketball Hall of Fame in 2002, it was "the hick from French Lick," his long-time rival and now close friend, who served as his presenter—indeed, a fitting sharing of the stage.

Bird vs. Magic, NBA style

The NCAA showdown between Larry Bird and Magic Johnson in 1979 would not be the last time these two stars met with a championship on the line. Following is a recap of their three head-to-head NBA Finals match-ups over a four-year span in the 1980s:

1984: Celtics 4, Lakers 3
Coming off the first of his three straight MVP seasons, Bird avenges his collegiate loss to Johnson by averaging 27.4 points and 14 boards per game to add Finals MVP honors to his resume. He tallies 34 points in

Game 5, and leads Boston to a 111–102 Game 7 win with 20 points and 12 rebounds. The deciding contest draws the highest TV rating ever for an NBA game.

1985: Lakers 4, Celtics 2
Johnson's Lakers are humiliated in Game 1, dropping a 148–114 decision at the Boston Garden. Rather than hang their heads, they come out battling. Magic sets up the attack and Finals MVP Kareem Abdul-Jabbar does the bulk of the scoring over the next five games. Elbow and finger injuries limit Bird's

effectiveness during the series, hurting the Celtics.

1987: Lakers 4, Celtics 2
Johnson becomes the first three-time NBA Finals MVP in history with a terrific all-around performance. The series' most memorable moment is Magic sinking a sky hook—a la Abdul-Jabbar—with two seconds left in Game 4. "You're probably going to get beat [by the Lakers] on a sky hook," Bird said. "But you don't expect it to be from Magic."

Magic Johnson slams on Indiana State's Bob Heaton in the 1979 NCAA Championship game. Magic finished with 24 points, clinching the Final Four Most Outstanding Player award.

With victory in sight, the Wolverines celebrate on the sidelines. Though a 17-point underdog, Michigan picked off six passes en route to its 12-point victory.

KICK BUTT AND SMELL THE ROSES

Michigan vs. Ohio State, November 22, 1969

To get to Ohio State, reads the University of Michigan bumper sticker, "You Go South Until You Smell It and Then East Until You Step in It." OSU-Michigan may not be the classiest rivalry around ("Happiness is Crushed Buckeye Nuts" is another fender favorite), but it is surely the greatest. So says the United States government. In 2003, in honor of the 100th football game between the two schools, the U.S. Congress recognized Michigan-Ohio State football as the No. 1 rivalry in sports history.

Through 1951, the games usually weren't much of a contest, with the Wolverines holding a 31-12-4 edge over Ohio State. That record includes a 9-3 triumph in Columbus during the 1950 "Snow Bowl," a winter wonderland affair that featured 45 punts. That debacle inspired the Buckeyes to hire Woody Hayes as head coach. A former Lieutenant Commander in the Navy during World War II, Hayes gradually built the best program in the nation. In 1968, on its way to the national title, OSU blew out the Wolverines 50-14, prompting Michigan to hire former Ohio State assistant Bo Schembechler as head coach.

Nicknamed "General George Patton" Schembechler by Wolverines broadcaster Bob Ufer, the Michigan coach turned his first training camp into boot camp. After the worst two decades in Michigan history (just three Big Ten titles and two Rose Bowl trips from 1949 to the beginning of 1969), the new coach was determined to usurp OSU's title as conference king. To do so in 1969, however, seemed completely unrealistic.

When the Buckeyes stormed into Ann Arbor for the season finale on November 22, 1969, they were favored by 17 points over the 7-2 Wolverines. OSU had won 22 games in a row. They not only were 8-0 in 1969, but they had also averaged 46 points per game. Hayes himself would call his '69 juggernaut "probably the best team that ever played college football." Reporters joked that after they bulldozed Michigan, the Buckeyes should skip the Rose Bowl and head straight to the Super Bowl.

The media, however, underestimated the pride and

OSU coach Woody Hayes raised the Wolverines' ire in 1968 when he went for two points late in the game to give the Buckeyes an even 50 points in a blowout win.

preparedness of Schembechler's boys. As they stormed onto the field, amid the "Hail to the Victors" fight song and a record-breaking crowd of 103,588 fans, the Wolverines remembered what Hayes had done to them in the '68 game. After scoring a touchdown to go up 50-14, Hayes had tried a two-point conversion. Why? "Because they wouldn't let me go for three," he had replied. Now the Wolverines were out for blood. As Schembechler told the Ohio State newspaper, "We knew we were going to win from the very beginning."

Ohio State scored in the first quarter on a touchdown run by fullback Jim Otis. However, the way Michigan fans saw it, the Buckeyes got their just desserts when they missed the extra point. The Wolverines bounced back on their next possession with a touchdown, capped by a one-yard run by Garvie Craw. "We stuffed the ball down their throats on that drive," roared offensive lineman Dick Caldarazzo, according to *Stadium Stories: Michigan Wolverines*. When Frank Titas booted the extra point to make it 7-6, OSU trailed for the first time all season.

In the second quarter, Ohio State moved ahead 12-7 on a 22-yard pass by All-American quarterback Rex Kern. Coach Hayes again tried for two, but Kern was sacked by Mike Keller. More poetic justice, thought the Wolverines faithful. The place went nuts.

From that point on, it was all maize and blue. Said Michigan quarterback Don Moorhead, "We just went out there and punched it to them." Michigan moved ahead 14-12 after another Craw TD run. Minutes later, U of M's Barry Pierson returned a punt 60 yards to OSU's 3, setting up another touchdown: 21-12. A Tim Killian field goal made it 24-12 Michigan at halftime.

In the second half, the Michigan defense turned up the heat. The Buckeyes, who had averaged more than 500 yards per game, couldn't get out of their own territory. The Wolverines picked off six passes in the game, including three by Pierson—who also had that big punt return. "That Barry Pierson's performance was one of the greatest I've seen," Schembechler said to the *Detroit Free Press*.

No one could score in the second half. When OSU

went for it on fourth down in the fourth quarter, Michigan's Pete Newell nailed Kern for a loss. For all intents and purposes, the game was over.

Almost to a man, Wolverine players credited the victory to Schembechler, who had devised a masterful game plan. "They didn't do a thing our coach told us they wouldn't do," said Craw. "Bo's got to be coach of the year, and if they don't give him a million awards, it'll be a sin."

The game ended 24–12, in what ABC broadcaster Bill Fleming called "the upset of the century." With the Wolverines headed to the Rose Bowl, the Michigan band played "California, Here We Come." The players carried off Schembechler on their shoulders, while students tore down the goalposts. "We're going as co-champions of the Big Ten," blurted Schembechler, "and don't you forget it!"

The victory fueled the Michigan-Ohio State rivalry. Throughout the 1970s, the two powerhouses usually

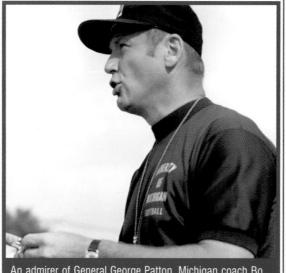
An admirer of General George Patton, Michigan coach Bo Schembechler employed whip-cracking tactics to bring the Wolverines back to national prominence.

entered their season-ending match-ups with records of 9–1 or 10–0, with the outcome of the game deciding who would go to the Rose Bowl. The rivalry reached such a high—or low—that men throughout Columbus painted M's in public urinals.

The '69 upset also marked the rebirth of a Michigan program that is the winningest in college football history. In 21 years under Schembechler, the Wolverines went 194–48–5. Fan interest swelled to unheard-of levels. From 1975 through 2005, the Wolverines attracted 193 consecutive crowds of more than 100,000. Beginning with the 1975 season, Michigan went to 31 consecutive bowl games.

Many Michigan alumni still reminisce about the Miracle of '69. "You should have seen the campus that night," recalled Bill Cusumano. "Everyone was in love with everyone else. We were fulfilled. Our time had been sanctified. We beat Ohio State!"

The Snow Bowl

On November 25, 1950, the citizens of Columbus, Ohio, awoke to their worst blizzard in 37 years. Most assumed that the Michigan-Ohio State football game scheduled for that afternoon would be canceled. That would have meant, however, that OSU would have gone to the Rose Bowl by default. Fearing the backlash from such a scenario, the Buckeyes brass decided to play the game.

The Buckeyes and Wolverines, as well the 50,000 crazies who showed up for the "Snow Bowl," ventured into a frozen hell: a temperature of 10 degrees, five inches of snow, and 30-mph winds. "My hands were numb," recalled OSU's Vic Janowicz, who would win that year's Heisman Trophy as a quarterback/kicker/punter. "I had no feeling in them and I don't know how I hung onto the ball. It was terrible. You knew what you wanted to do, but you couldn't do it."

The Buckeyes scored first when Janowicz somehow drilled a 37-yard field

goal, a play that a panel of sportswriters included among the "Greatest Feats in American Sports." Mostly, the coaches' strategy was to punt on third, second, or first down and hope the other team fumbled.

Michigan closed the gap to 3–2 on a safety, then scored a touchdown with less than a minute left in the half. On third down, Michigan's Tony Momsen blocked a

Janowicz punt in the endzone. No one scored in the second half, and the teams finished the day with a combined 45 punts. Michigan won despite no completed passes and zero first downs.

"It was a dumb football game," said Ohio State linebacker Dick Ellwood, "a really stupid football game. When you put the ball down on the field and it just blows off, that's unreal. It was a nightmare."

The Snow Bowl featured 45 punts and seemingly as many fumbles.

COLD BLOOD
Detroit vs. Colorado, 1996 to 2002

As he was moving into a new home in the Denver area after joining the Colorado Avalanche in 2001–02, NHL defenseman Todd Gill was approached by one of his new neighbors. The two exchanged handshakes, and after learning Gill was a hockey player, the neighbor asked where he played the year before. "I told him Detroit," Gill recalled, "and he told me he hated me because I played for the Red Wings."

Some rivalries bloom over time. The Boston Bruins and Montreal Canadiens, for example, grew to loathe each other over continual playoff meetings. Others are based on proximity. New York fans look for fireworks when the Rangers and Islanders square off. In the case of the Avalanche-Red Wings feud, it was one split-second hit—a single moment—on the night of May 29, 1996, that launched the most intense hockey rivalry in recent years.

Detroit's Martin Lapointe (*far left*) checks out the fight between the Red Wings' Brendan Shanahan and Colorado's Rene Corbet in Game 4 of the 1997 Western Conference finals.

It was Game 6 of the Western Conference finals at Denver's McNichols Arena. Colorado enforcer Claude Lemieux, who already had been suspended one game in the series for a sucker punch on Slava Kozlov after a Game 3 whistle, checked Kris Draper from behind, knocking him face-first into the boards. Draper underwent two and a half hours of surgery after suffering a broken nose and jaw, a concussion, and facial lacerations that required 40 stitches. He ate strained food through a straw for weeks. Colorado won, 4-1, eliminating Detroit on the way to its first Stanley Cup championship. Following the game, Red Wings coach Scotty Bowman reportedly shouted obscenities at Lemieux as the Colorado player, who was suspended for the first two Stanley Cup finals games for the cheap shot, walked to his car with his wife and child.

A rivalry was born. Over the next several years, the Red Wings and Avalanche would battle toe-to-toe in several knuckle-baring fights, some of the full-lineup variety and a couple that even had the goalies dropping their gloves. However, this cross-time zone feud was about far more than verbal and physical jabs. If these

had been two run-of-the-mill teams, their visible hatred for each other might have seemed petty, or even comical. But these were tussles with championships at stake, and the hockey that accompanied the hooliganism was among the most exciting and skilled in the NHL.

Beginning with Colorado's '96 title, the Avalanche and Red Wings won a combined five of the seven Stanley Cups through 2002. Usually, each team's path to victory traveled straight through the other. Colorado-Detroit games not only featured some of the hardest hitting in hockey, but some of the top players of the era reaching some of their greatest milestones. Red Wings star Steve Yzerman scored his 500th career goal on the Avalanche's Patrick Roy. Three years later, Roy won his 400th game against Detroit. Colorado's Ray Bourque netted his 400th career goal against the Wings, and Bowman's 200th playoff coaching win came against the Avalanche.

Still, the on-ice tension was the focus of the series. As longtime Wings analyst Mickey Redmond once noted, "With these two, we're just one high stick away from a donnybrook." With Lemieux injured when the teams met early in 1996-97, Detroit players seemed to be looking for retribution against his teammates. Aaron Ward bloodied Rene Corbet and knocked him out on one play, while Martin Lapointe sent Alexei Gusarov to the ice unconscious, gathering around him on a check that bore a resemblance to Lemieux's hit on Draper. When they finally did get a shot at Lemieux later that season, Darren McCarty made the most of it.

McCarty forever became a Detroit hero for peppering Lemieux with punches in a March 1997 game. McCarty also won that game with an overtime goal and, later that year, scored the playoff goal that gave the Red Wings their first Stanley Cup in 42 years. Which feat did Detroit fans appreciate more? "When people would come up to me," McCarty says on DetroitRedWings.com,

Detroit's Vladimir Konstantinov flips Colorado's Claude Lemieux on his head during the 1996 playoffs. Two days later, Lemieux would break Kris Draper's nose and jaw.

"they'd say, 'What you did to Lemieux, that was awesome, man; and oh, yeah, nice goal, too.'"

A mere three seconds into their first game the following season ('97-98), Lemieux and McCarty fought again, this time with Lemieux a more willing and active combatant. Roy, who had left his crease to spar with Detroit netminder Mike Vernon a year earlier, skated to center ice in a game later in that '97-98 season to call out another goaltending counterpart, Chris Osgood. This was the culmination of an incident in which all 10 skaters on the ice were engaged in a bloody slugfest in front of the benches at Detroit's Joe Louis Arena. For the record, Osgood landed nine shots before taking down Roy (who landed 11) wrestling-style, and was ejected from the game to a standing ovation.

These were the fireworks that made a seat at a Detroit-Colorado game—not that fans would spend much time *sitting* in their seats—perhaps the hottest NHL ticket. Fans knew the action would be fast, the

The Red Wings' Larry Murphy mixes it up with Avalanche superstar Peter Forsberg in Game 1 of the 1997 Western Conference Finals.

checking intense, the skill level high and the chance of a skirmish great. Lemieux left Colorado after '98-99, and fans of hockey fighting might tell you the series has not been the same since then. There was little dropoff in talent, however. After the Red Wings won consecutive Stanley Cups in '97 and '98, Colorado won its second in 2001. Not to be outdone, Detroit added another championship the following year.

"Aside from the ugliness," Avalanche center Joe Sakic told *The Sporting News*, "there has been some great hockey, great competition. If you asked any player on either team, I think you'd find out none of them wanted to miss a minute of this rivalry." And no matter the outcome, the playoff meetings between these two great adversaries (as with all Stanley Cup playoff series) always end in the same fashion: every Colorado and Detroit player lines up and sheds gloves once more for postgame handshakes. After all, it's the neighborly thing to do.

Highlights and lowlights

A breakdown of Colorado-Detroit playoff meetings:

1995-96 Western Conference finals
Colorado 4, Detroit 2
Highlight: The Avalanche win by "stealing" the first two games on the road.
Lowlight: Colorado's Claude Lemieux sets the tone when he checks Kris Draper from behind, sending the Red Wing into the boards with a concussion, broken jaw, broken nose, and facial lacerations in Game 6.
And then: Colorado beats Florida for its first Stanley Cup.

1996-97 Western Conference finals
Detroit 4, Colorado 2
Highlight: After the teams trade 6-0 routs, Detroit wraps up the series with a 3-1 home win.

Lowlight: The coaching staffs engage in a heated shouting match after a fight in which Detroit's Brendan Shanahan bloodies Rene Corbet.
And then: Detroit sweeps Philadelphia to win its first Cup in 42 years.

1998-99 Western Conference semifinals
Colorado 4, Detroit 2
Highlight: Colorado loses the first two games before winning four straight against the two-time defending champions.
Lowlight: The opener sees Detroit's McCarty draw a major boarding penalty for slamming Lemieux and Colorado's Peter Forsberg take a game misconduct for knocking Shanahan into the glass, drawing blood.
And then: Colorado loses to eventual champion Dallas in the Western Finals.

1999-2000 Western Conference semifinals
Colorado 4, Detroit 1
Highlight: Forsberg scores the winner in each of Colorado's three home wins.
Lowlight: Colorado takes seven penalties in the first period of Game 2, while the Red Wings take five.
And then: Dallas ousts Colorado in the Western Finals for the second straight year.

2001-02 Western Conference finals
Detroit 4, Colorado 3
Highlight: Three games are decided in OT in a series that is tight until the finale.
Lowlight: A great series ends with a dud, as Detroit rolls 7-0 in Game 7.
And then: The Red Wings beat Carolina in five games to win the Cup.

FIRST-CLASS ATHLETES
Rafer Johnson vs. Yang Chuan-kwang and Vassily Kuznetsov, 1960 Olympics

As a black man in a white man's world, and an American in the Soviet Union, Rafer Johnson traveled to Moscow with apprehension in 1958. Yet the decathlete displayed such scintillating talent, and exhibited such character and class, that the Russians warmly welcomed him. After his victory, his hosts bestowed him with flowers and tossed him into the air in jubilation. His No. 1 rival, Soviet Vassily Kuznetsov, kissed him on the cheek. "I'd gone over there thinking we'd be abused one way or the other," said Johnson in *Time* magazine. "But they cheered the performance, not the man or the nationality."

Johnson and Kuznetsov—and later Yang Chuan-kwang of Taiwan—battled each other as fiercely as any competitors in sports history. Yet their rivalry was not fueled by political, religious, or personal animosity. No, these were men of a higher calling. Each admired the other two, embraced his challenges, and pushed the others to extraordinary heights.

The life experiences of Johnson, Kuznetsov, and Yang—the three decathlete favorites in the 1960 Rome Olympics—could not have been more different. Kuznetsov, the "Man of Steel," grew up in the cold climate and restricted society of the Soviet Union. A science teacher, he excelled in the decathlon more on technique and regimented practice than on natural ability. The lanky and limber Yang hailed from Taiwan, an island off China's mainland. In 1958 Yang enrolled at UCLA, where he became a regular training buddy of Johnson's.

Of the trio, Johnson endured the harshest upbringing. The son of Lewis and Alma Johnson, Rafer grew up in a black ghetto in Dallas and spent time both in Oklahoma and Houston, where the family faced poverty and discrimination. In the mid-40s, Lewis, Alma, and their five kids moved to California, ending up in

the small town of Kingsburg, where Lewis worked for a railroad company. For a year the family lived in a housing unit shaped like a boxcar, They later moved to a small house, but they were threatened by Kingsburg's police chief, who seethed, "I don't want to see the sun set on any niggers in this town." The Johnsons ignored the threat, and the chief eventually left his job.

As a high school athlete, Johnson amazed onlookers with his speed and power. He averaged more than nine yards per carry in football, smashed over .400 in baseball, played basketball, and ranked among the best decathletes in the nation. In 1956 Rafer displayed the heart of a champion at the Melbourne Olympics. Despite suffering a torn stomach muscle during the long jump, Johnson won a silver medal in the decathlon. New Jersey's Milt Campbell copped the gold and Kuznetsov took the bronze.

Rafer Johnson breasts the tape to win the fourth heat of the 100-meter dash in the decathlon. Johnson won the gold by finishing only 1.2 seconds behind Yang Chuang-kwang in the 1,500 meters, the final event.

Beginning in 1958, the rivalry between Johnson and the Soviet heated up. Kuznetsov set the world record with 8,016 points, which Johnson smashed (8,302) in his visit to Moscow later that year. Also that year, Yang enrolled at UCLA. Although they could barely communicate, Rafer and Yang pushed each other on the athletic field while sharing the common bond of world-class decathletes.

In 1959, as a passenger in an auto accident, Johnson suffered a severe back injury. He was sidelined for the year, during which time Kuznetsov regained the world record with 8,357 points. Working tirelessly, Johnson returned to competition at the AAU Championships in July 1960. Stunningly, he was better than ever. After topping Kuznetsov's world record, this time with 8,683 points, Johnson dropped to his knees to pray and cry. Yang, though, still wasn't finished. With a great time in the 1,500-meter race, he could surpass Johnson's world mark. During the race, Johnson

Rafer Johnson (*center*) and Vassily Kuznetsov (*right*) had broken each other's world record in the decathlon, but Yang Chuan-kwang (*left*) proved to be Johnson's stiffest challenge in the 1960 Olympics.

actually shouted encourage-
ment to Yang: "Keep going!
Keep going!"

Yang fell short of
Johnson's record, but the
stage was set for a highly
anticipated showdown at the
Rome Olympics. It would be
all or nothing for Johnson,
who would retire after the
Games. Character-istically,
the combatants showered
one another with high
praise. "I know Kuznetsov
well enough to know three
things about him," Johnson
said in *Time*. "He's a fine
athlete. He's a gentleman.
And he's a competitor." Said
the Soviet about Johnson,
"He is a very fine, tactful
and modest young man. ... I
am sure that when we meet
again in Rome, we shall be
good friends."

Johnson, who cap-
tained the U.S. Olympic team and carried the
American flag in the opening ceremonies, was the
man to beat in Rome. However, it wasn't Kuznetsov
but Yang who emerged as Johnson's stiffest challenge.
On the first day of the two-day competition, Yang finished ahead of Johnson in four of the five events,
although Johnson led Yang by 55 points.

As if they were back at UCLA, Johnson and Yang
waged a two-man battle on the second and final day of
the decathlon. Yang moved ahead after the 110-meter

Avery Brundage, President of the International Olympic
Committee, congratulates Rafer Johnson after his triumph in the
decathlon.

hurdles, but the beefier
Johnson took the lead after
the discus throw. With a
personal-best effort in the
pole vault and a better toss
than Yang in the javelin,
Johnson maintained the
lead, but only by 67 points.

If Yang could beat
Johnson by 10 seconds in
the 1,500 meters, the final
event, he would win the
gold medal. Yang's supporters held high hopes because
he was among the best
long-distance runners
among all the competing
decathletes. But Johnson
ran the race of his life. He
crossed the finish line in
4:49.7, his fastest time ever,
to finish only 1.2 seconds
behind Yang. Johnson won
the gold medal and Yang
took the silver—the first
Olympic medal ever won by
a Taiwanese athlete.

Afterward, Johnson was physically and mentally
drained. Perhaps looking back on all the obstacles he
had overcome—and the supreme challenges from his
international rivals—Johnson was in a reflective mood.
"Tonight I'm going to shower and then just walk for
about four hours and look at the moon," he said,
according to ESPN SportsCentury. "I don't know
where—just walk, walk, walk. I've got to unwind. I'm
through, man, I'm through."

Carrying the torch

By age 25, Rafer Johnson had overcome poverty and discrimination to
become the most revered athlete in the
world. After the 1960 Games, he retired
from competition, ready to take on even
greater challenges.

Johnson was interested in pursuing a
career in international relations, potentially as
a goodwill ambassador for the U.S. State
Department. As he told *Time*, "I know that
sort of thing can do a lot to ease tensions. I

like people. I want to do all I can to help
them in whatever little way I can."

At first, Johnson found more opportuni-
ties in film and television. He appeared in
several Hollywood movies and a few TV
shows, and he later became a television
sportscaster. In 1968 he worked for
Senator Robert Kennedy's presidential
campaign, and was in the Ambassador
Hotel in Los Angeles on the night RFK was
assassinated there. Johnson helped force
the gun away from the shooter and appre-
hend him.

In the 1970s Johnson served on the
President's Commission on Olympic Sports,
and in 1984 he lit the flame at the Los
Angeles Coliseum to commence the
Summer Games. Remarkably, Johnson
raised two children who went on to
become world-class athletes—Josh in the
javelin and Jenny in beach volleyball. In
2000 Rafer attended the Sydney Games
with Jenny, who made the Olympic team.
Wrote Johnson: "Whatever I've done, this
moment being here with my daughter, this
is the greatest."

JUICED-UP RIVALS

Florida State vs. Miami, October 3, 1987

In college football, a state championship usually involves the powers of a given state vying in an annual rivalry for a year's worth of bragging rights. Normally these games take place at the end of the season, providing a crescendo to a program's accomplishments. If fortunes have not gone well, winning the rivalry game offers salvation and hope; if the season has been successful, such a win provides an exclamation point.

FSU-Miami took a different path on October 3, 1987, when they didn't wait until the end of the season to settle their business. And, the outcome of their state championship played in Tallahassee would play a large part in determining not only the bragging rights for the state of Florida, but also a college football national champion.

Where rivalries go, FSU-Miami had a past, but was just entering its heyday, given the national prominence of both schools and the growing pool of football talent in the Sunshine State. The Miami Hurricanes of coach Jimmy Johnson entered the game ranked third in the polls and were considered the most balanced college football team in the nation.

Quarterback Steve Walsh already had led the 'Canes to a 31–4 rout of Florida, relying heavily on wide receiver Michael Irvin and running back Melvin Bratton. On defense, 2–0 Miami had allowed just 429 total yards and one late touchdown by Arkansas. All-America end Daniel Stubbs led the defense that had already accrued 12 quarterback sacks. This seasoned program held the nation's longest regular-season winning streak at 23 and it held an 8–1 advantage over the Seminoles at FSU's Doak Campbell Stadium and had not lost in Tallahassee since 1979.

Bobby Bowden's 'Noles were ranked fourth in the nation and had more than a few weapons of their own. Danny McManus gave FSU experience at quarter-

back—though his tendency leaned toward streaky performances. Catching his passes were speedy receivers Herb Gainer and Ronald Lewis, while the running game fell to Dexter Carter and Sammie Smith. On defense, the 'Noles had big-play talents, none of whom could take a bigger spotlight than cornerback Deion Sanders, a fantastic athlete who had a nose for the football and a knack for providing startling results in a dramatic fashion.

In short, the contest pitted two colossal programs at the top of their games in what was billed as the biggest regular-season match-up in the history of Florida college football. A record crowd of 62,561, along with a national television audience, tuned in to see Miami take a 3–0 lead following a bizarre play by the FSU field goal team.

Even the speedy Florida State secondary couldn't keep up with Miami game-breaker Michael Irvin, who burned the Seminoles with touchdown receptions of 26 and 73 yards.

Late in the first quarter, McManus engineered a drive that led the offense into Miami territory, putting the 'Noles in position to attempt a 40-yard field goal. But center Marty Riggs made his snap prematurely sending the football sailing high over the holder's head. By the time the holder, McManus, had scrambled in a retreat down the field to recover the miscue, the 'Noles had suffered a 51-yard loss that led to a 29-yard field goal by Miami's Greg Cox.

Keeping their composure, FSU got the football back and once again drove up the field against Miami's touted defense. This time the 'Noles were rewarded with an 80-yard drive, highlighted by a 64-yard run to the Miami 17; the drive culminated with a one-yard touchdown by Dayne Williams on the first play of the second quarter.

FSU padded its lead on a 36-yard field goal by Derek Schmidt that put the 'Noles up 10–3 with 2:37 remaining in the first half. They built the lead to 19–3

Florida State won the war in the trenches, outgaining Miami 426 yards to 306, but the Hurricanes won the battle by a single point.

with 2:45 left in the third quarter, giving everyone the impression that Miami's regular-season reign would come to an end. But anyone thinking such thoughts underestimated the resolve of Walsh, the meticulous Miami quarterback.

Walsh connected with Bratton circling out of the backfield and the Miami running back beat safety Alphonso Williams in a race to the endzone for a 49-yard touchdown. A successful two-point conversion made the score 19–11.

Two minutes passed before Stubbs perfectly read a screen pass in the Seminoles' backfield. Stubbs intercepted the pass to give Miami the football at the FSU 41. Walsh once again seized the situation and hooked up with Irvin on a 26-yard touchdown before connecting with Warren Williams for their second straight two-point conversion to tie the score at 19.

FSU's offense had its chances to break the tie. First they marched up the field to put Schmidt in position to kick a 31-yard field goal with six minutes to go,

but the kick went wide. McManus blew another scoring chance when he fumbled the snap at the 'Canes' 17 with just over three minutes to go.

Walsh and Irvin once again got busy, this time on a third-and-6 from the 'Canes' 27. Walsh stepped behind center and viewed the FSU defense before changing the play. He then hit Irvin between two defenders and Irvin outraced the 'Noles defense to the endzone for a 73-yard touchdown. The extra point gave Miami a 26-19 lead.

McManus then stepped up to lead the Seminoles up the field. Early in the drive the 'Noles faced a fourth-and-8 from their own 29 and successfully negotiated a first down in advance of scoring a touchdown on the eighth play of the drive to make it 26-25 Miami.

In 1987 college football had yet to adopt overtime, which left Bowden with the weighty decision of whether to go for two points and the victory or take the tie. Settling for a tie would have put a blemish on the Seminoles' record, thereby diminishing the chances of a national championship.

Bowden first sent out Schmidt to kick the extra point. But two time outs and a world of anxiety later, the FSU offense lined up at the Miami 3 to try for the victory. Pat Carter became McManus' target despite the tight Miami coverage. McManus threw to his tight end in the right corner of the endzone anyway. Defensive back Bubba McDowell batted down the pass and Miami had a 26-25 victory.

The Hurricanes understood the magnitude of their win, celebrating the victory at midfield while holding up a sign that read "State Champions." Miami defeated Oklahoma 20–14 in the Orange Bowl at the end of the season to complete a 12–0 season and earn the right to hold up a different sign: "National Champions."

Missed kicks

Missed kicks have characterized the FSU-Miami rivalry ever since the 1987 FSU loss that saw Seminole kicker Derek Schmidt miss an extra point and two field goals. In 1991 the most famous of the misses came when Florida State's kicker Gerry Thomas stepped onto the field to try a 34-yard field goal with his team trailing 17–16 and time running out at FSU's Doak Campbell Stadium.

Talk about pressure. Everybody knew that the winner of the game would be the odds-on favorite to win the national championship.

The holder took the snap and successfully placed the football for Thomas, but his would-be game winner sailed outside the right crossbar thereby bringing to the forefront the two words that would taunt the Seminoles most: *wide right*.

Forgotten in the aftermath of Thomas' miss was the fact the goalposts had been moved in 29 inches on each side that season, reducing the kicking target by two feet. It's likely the kick would have been good a year earlier. But it wasn't to

be and Miami, as it did in 1987, went on to win a national championship.

Unbelievable as it sounds, FSU lost again against Miami the next season when FSU kicker Dan Mowrey missed a game-tying field goal from 39 yards on the final play of the game. Once again, the kick missed right and the Hurricanes won the game that would come to be known as "Wide Right II."

"Wide Right III" came in 2000 when Matt Munyon's 49-yard field goal attempt went wide right as time ran out in a 27-24 'Canes win.

Quarterback Danny McManus managed to move the ball against Miami's ferocious defense, but his attempted two-point pass late in the game was knocked down by a man named Bubba.

Sugar Ray Leonard taunts Roberto Duran during their rematch in November. Leonard humiliated Duran in Round 7 by winding up his right hand and then jabbing him with his left.

NO MÁS! NO MÁS!

Sugar Ray Leonard vs. Roberto Duran, 1980

After capturing a light welterweight gold medal at the 1976 Summer Olympics in Montreal, the talented and personable Sugar Ray Leonard turned professional. He could do no wrong and, seemingly, there were no challenges he could not meet and conquer in the ring. When his chance came to fight for the WBC welterweight title, he defeated the talented Wilfred Benitez with a knockout in the 15th round.

But Leonard's immaculate aura hit a buzz saw June 20, 1980, in Montreal, the first time he ran into Panamanian Roberto Duran, known in boxing circles for having "hands of stone" because his punches landed with such force. Although Leonard had glitz and glamour, Duran—who had held the lightweight championship for seven years, compiling a 71–1 record with 56 knockouts—had a reputation for being the rare blend of brawler and boxer, a fighter who would literally have to be knocked out before he would quit.

Duran didn't like Leonard for several reasons. First, despite Duran's extensive resume in the sweet science, he only got 20 percent of the money Leonard did for their fight. Next, Duran didn't like the glitzy world in which Leonard lived, or the hype his bouts received. During prefight press conferences Duran cursed his opponent and even included Leonard's wife in his insults. In Duran's way of thinking, getting inside of Leonard's head made the task of dethroning the champion easier.

Their fight came to be known as the "Brawl in Montreal."

Two distinctive styles were on display. Leonard danced, bobbed, and weaved against Duran, who charged in relentlessly in an attempt to turn the fight into the kind of fight he knew he could win: toe-to-toe, and inside. Duran had shown a lack of sportsmanship at the beginning of the 15th and final round by refusing

Sugar Ray Leonard lands a punch during the "Brawl in Montreal" on June 20, 1980. After Roberto Duran prevailed in a unanimous decision, fans clamored for a rematch.

to touch gloves. Duran then spent most of the round taunting Leonard. The epic battle excited fans everywhere, bringing to the ring a flavor of boxing unseen since the days of the great Muhammad Ali and Joe Frazier rivalry.

Officials scored the fight 145-144, 146-144, and 148-147. The audience approved when the ring announcer identified Duran as the winner.

Nobody disputed the decision, which had handed Leonard his first professional defeat. The only post-fight question anybody wanted answered was: When will there be a rematch?

The answer came quickly. The rematch was to take place at the Louisiana Superdome on November 25, 1980.

After the first fight, Duran had not offered any sort of consolation to the defeated Leonard and during the months that followed he talked repeatedly about his disdain for Leonard, making the prospect of the rematch even more delicious.

Duran often wrestled with his weight, so it came as no surprise that he had battled the scales before his rematch with Leonard. He had reportedly swelled to 173 pounds when he began to train for the rematch in September, and he had dropped approximately 13 pounds by the first week of November. Meanwhile, Leonard managed to keep his weight close to the 147-pound limit. Before the rematch, the former champ reported being in the best shape of his career.

On the morning of the fight, Duran was still struggling to meet the weight limit. He did that through the usual Spartan methods for cutting weight. But the last-minute work took its toll. After weighing in at 146, Duran's body was weak, prompting him to seek the necessary fuel to carry him through that night's fight. He began by consuming a large thermos of consommé with hot tea and an orange, and followed that with a

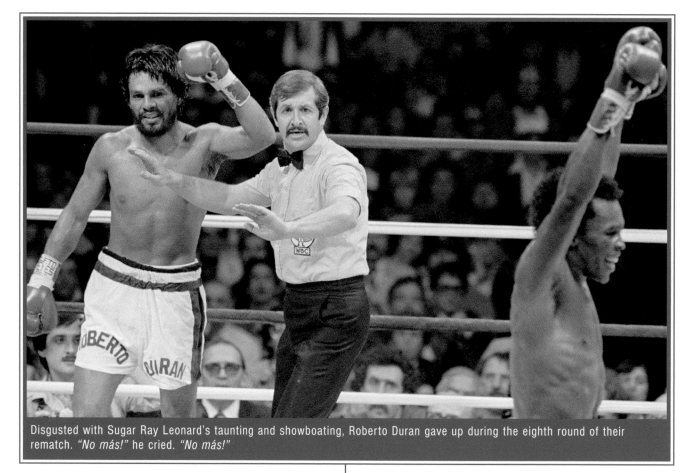
Disgusted with Sugar Ray Leonard's taunting and showboating, Roberto Duran gave up during the eighth round of their rematch. *"No más!"* he cried. *"No más!"*

lunch of two large steaks, French fries, four glasses of orange juice, water, and more tea. Duran finished his prefight dining with a half a steak and tea for dinner.

The fight began with both fighters sizing up each other before Duran coerced Leonard into the corner, much as he had done during their earlier fight. Only this time Leonard reacted differently by eluding Duran and then landing a starch-filled right. A brief exchange of punches followed before Leonard ended the round with a combination that made him appear far and away the aggressor, and the more confident of the two.

In the second round, Leonard followed with more of the same. Particularly telling was a Leonard right that snapped back Duran's head. Although Leonard seemed to have the fight in hand early, Duran had weathered many storms and knew how to handle most any situation presented him in the ring. He recovered to tag Leonard throughout the third and fifth rounds—providing hope that he might rise to take care of the challenge. Leonard never got discouraged by the rally and, unlike in their first fight, managed to dodge Duran's aggressive toe-to-toe approach, slipping his punches and keeping Duran off balance by consistently landing his hook when Duran moved inside.

Leonard knew he wanted to try to antagonize

Duran at some point during the fight and that point came in the seventh round, when Leonard began to wind up his right hand as if he were about to unleash a bolo punch. But rather than throw the bolo, Leonard delivered a jab to Duran's face. Leonard followed up the punch by taunting his opponent. He held out his chin in a showy display as if to say, "Hit me if you can." Duran couldn't and grew increasingly frustrated.

The frustration and humiliation carried over into the eighth, when Duran turned to the referee with 16 seconds remaining in the round and cried out the words that would become his legacy: "No más! No más!"

Duran had not lost a fight in eight years—not since Esteban De Jesus defeated him in a non-title bout in Madison Square Garden. Now he was quitting? Such a prospect was unfathomable, considering Duran's machismo aura. By throwing in the towel, Duran earned the notorious distinction of becoming the first fighter since Sonny Liston in his 1964 bout against Cassius Clay to give up his crown.

Leonard was once again the WBC welterweight champion. After regaining his title, Leonard reveled in his victory and noted to *Sports Illustrated*: "To make a man quit, to make a Roberto Duran quit, was better than knocking him out."

THE LITTLE HORSE THAT COULD

Seabiscuit vs. War Admiral, November 1, 1938

America had waited for the "Race of the Century" between the great War Admiral and the upstart horse with the tremendous heart, Seabiscuit. Their patience was finally rewarded with a match race between the pair on November 1, 1938, at the Pimlico Race Course in Baltimore.

The nation had worked its way through the Depression and had latched on to the underdog story of Seabiscuit, which fueled the desire for a match race between the "people's horse" and the daunting champion of thoroughbred racing, War Admiral.

War Admiral had a tremendous bloodline as the foal of famed horse Man o' War—and War Admiral's legacy began at the 1937 Kentucky Derby, when he went to the starting gate as an 8-to-5 favorite in the field of 20 horses. War Admiral wasn't challenged and took the first leg of the Triple Crown at Churchill Downs by 1½-lengths.

Pompoon played the role of War Admiral's closest adversary, finishing second at the Derby, then giving him a true run for the money the following week in the Preakness Stakes. But War Admiral managed to win by a head to take the second leg of the Triple Crown. That left just a victory in the Belmont Stakes for him to complete horse racing's grandest achievement.

On June 5, 1937, War Admiral injured his right forehoof after tripping out of the gate at the Belmont Stakes. Showing great heart, the colt quickly recovered and buried the field with a four-length victory to win the Triple Crown.

Seabiscuit's journey had a few more bumps in the road. Raised on Claiborne Farm in Paris, Kentucky, Seabiscuit had quality breeding as the foal of Hard

Tack, also a foal of Man o' War. Despite the breeding, Seabiscuit didn't have the look of a champion, from his knobby knees to his penchant for overeating and sleeping. In short, Seabiscuit had a reputation for laziness, which received fortification after he lost his first 16 races, finishing close to the rear in most.

Seabiscuit was eventually sold for $8,000 to Charles Howard, an automobile magnate in the San Francisco area. Once with Howard, who employed trainer Tom Smith and jockey Red Pollard, something clicked with the enigmatic Seabiscuit.

Seabiscuit became the leading money winner in the United States in 1937, winning 11 of the 15 races he ran, most of which were heard via the radio, seen on newsreels, and widely chronicled in newspapers. The broad exposure brought him a huge following on the West Coast. Howard felt the celebrity of his unique horse and clamored for more attention, such as what would come with a chance to beat War Admiral. A major obstacle standing in the way of such an

Trainer Tom Smith and jockey George Woolf escort Seabiscuit after his triumph over War Admiral. Most of the 40 million radio listeners reveled in the giant upset.

occasion was the less than grand standing of West Coast horses in the eyes of the more established East Coast horse racing establishment.

Such sentiments did not stop the media from calling for such a match race between the two horses, or stop the reports speculating on which horse would win and why. This dialogue began during 1937 and had reached a crescendo by 1938.

At the height of Seabiscuit's popularity, the 5-year-old had to get used to a new jockey, when a young colt threw Pollard in June of 1938. Pollard's injuries were so severe that many wondered if his career was finished. Hired to replace Pollard on

Seabiscuit's back was George Woolf, a renowned jockey and one of Pollard's good friends.

While Pollard recovered, Woolf and Seabiscuit prepared to face off with War Admiral in the "Race of the Century." Scheduled to cover 13/16 miles, the War Admiral-Seabiscuit race attracted fans from all over the country. Trains emptied in Baltimore, where the Pimlico Race Course swelled with 40,000 spectators sitting in the grandstands and standing in the infield; an estimated 40 million listened on the radio.

The race would have a walk-up start, which seemed to favor War Admiral's starting speed against Seabiscuit, who had a knack for hanging with the pack before finding some extra gear to blow past the field. Given the data, War Admiral became the clear betting favorite at 1-to-4 with most oddsmakers.

Understanding the nature of the walk-up start, Smith secretly worked with Seabiscuit to respond to the bell. Using a whip at the sound, Seabiscuit's conditioned response to the bell became akin to his stepping on hot coals. And that response carried over to the start of the race.

Johnny "Red" Pollard read poetry, boxed, and rode horses. Though partially blind, he led Seabiscuit to prominence until sidelined by a broken leg.

When the bell rang, Seabiscuit tore into the lead and continued to hold it until the backstretch, where War Admiral pulled even and eventually took the lead. Woolf did not panic; he actually had invited War Admiral to take the lead on the advice of Pollard. Pollard understood Seabiscuit's competitive nature and reasoned that once the horse saw his competition ahead of him, Woolf could squeeze more out of the horse.

Woolf went to the whip, and Seabiscuit nudged square with War Admiral as they rounded the final turn and headed down the homestretch. Both jockeys went to the whip, but War Admiral tailed off while Seabiscuit finished strong to take a four lengths victory. Seabiscuit's time of 1:56.6 broke Pompoon's track record.

A mob scene followed. Smith took the chrysanthemums awarded the winner of the race, plucked one for himself, then threw the bow into the crowd. Woolf reveled in the race's aftermath and gave all credit to Seabiscuit.

"He's the best horse in the world," Woolf told *The New York Times*. "He proved that today."

A bloodline of champions

Seabiscuit and War Admiral shared a bloodline. The great Man o' War sired War Admiral and Hard Tack, who sired Seabiscuit.

Man o' War was horse racing's first true superstar. He had the look of a champion—he stood 16.2 hands and weighed 1,125 pounds—and when he raced he had no peers.

As a 3-year-old in 1920, Man o' War won each of his 11 races, but he did not run in the Kentucky Derby, because owner Samuel Riddle didn't want such a young horse to run 1¼ miles in early May. Man o' War did race in the Preakness, taking a close win over Upset, then in the Belmont, where he won by 20 lengths.

Man o' War ran his final race at Kenilworth Park in Windsor, Ontario, against Sir Barton, who had won the Triple Crown in 1919. Man o' War won by seven lengths.

Man o' War retired to stud with 20 wins in 21 races. Of the 386 registered foals he sired, 64 were stakes winners, including Clyde Van Dusen—the 1929 Kentucky Derby winner—as well as War Admiral and Hard Tack.

Man o' War died Nov. 1, 1947 at age 30 of a heart attack.

Seabiscuit leaves the mighty War Admiral in the dust in their legendary two-horse race at Pimlico. America's favorite underdog not only won, but set the track record.

Fans at The Country Club supported their team with hoots, hollers, and American flags. But they went over the line, said the Europeans, with their heckling and spitting.

'UNITED SLOBS OF AMERICA'

Europe vs. United States, September 24-26, 1999

Following the 1999 Ryder Cup Matches, a London *Daily Mirror* headline characterized the host U.S. team as the "United Slobs of America." The tabloid continued: "Football hooligans act better than the way the Americans have treated the Ryder Cup over the last three days. Their antics whipped the crowd into uncontrollably boorish behavior. Sporting relations between the two nations have now slipped to an all-time low."

Many thought the tabloid had a legitimate gripe ... but was it sour grapes?

The event was staged at The Country Club in Brookline, Massachusetts. It attracted not just New England's upper crust but Boston's pugnacious working class, who loudly vented their hostility toward the European team. One fan yelled at Jose Maria Olazabal during his backswing. Others deliberately pointed in the wrong direction when rookie Andrew Coltart searched for his ball. Fans heckled Colin Montgomerie

Ben Crenshaw (*center*) captained the Americans to their spectacular come-from-behind victory. Young Tiger Woods (*bottom right*) was one of eight American winners on Sunday.

throughout the three-day event, so much so that Montgomerie's 70-year-old father left in disgust. On Sunday, fans were accused of vile name-calling, spitting at a player's wife, and throwing an obnoxious celebration.

On the other hand, as U.S. captain Ben Crenshaw told *Sports Illustrated*, "Ryder Cup is about partisan support. Believe me, it's no different than from when we're over there. Just ask some of the players who played at Valderrama. It's not like this has never happened before."

Clearly, this hostility is not what golf fan Samuel Ryder envisioned when he donated a gold cup for the first official Ryder event in 1927. Like the sport itself, the Ryder Cup Matches stayed more or less a gentlemanly event for decades. Americans had no complaints, as they lost to Britain in the biannual event only once from 1935 to '83. To stiffen the competition, Ireland teamed with Britain beginning in 1973. Then,

starting in 1979, the U.S. took on all of Europe. From then on, it became a biannual war.

In 1987 at Ohio's Muirfield Village, Europe defeated the U.S. 15 matches to 13, played over the course of three days. The battle at The Belfry in England in 1989 ended in a 14–14 tie.

The next three events were all decided by two points or fewer, with choke jobs deciding the finish. Germany's Bernhard Langer missed a six-foot putt at Kiawah Island in South Carolina in 1991. Italy's Costantino Rocca blew a pivotal three-footer at The Belfry in England in 1993. And Curtis Strange cost the U.S. a potential victory in 1995 at Oak Hill in New York when he failed to sink par putts on his final three holes.

Throughout, bad blood boiled between the two teams. In 1989 Paul Azinger and Seve Ballesteros accused each other of foul play—a feud that continued two years later. "I can tell you we're not trying to cheat," Azinger told Ballesteros, according to *Golf Digest*. "Oh no," the Spaniard replied sarcastically. "Breaking the rules and cheating are two different things."

In 1999, while facing the prospect of losing their third straight Ryder Cup, the U.S. team brought a war mentality to Brookline, even wearing combat-fatigue style outfits. Journalists made references to the Boston Tea Party of 1773 as well as the 1913 U.S. Open at The Country Club, when 20-year-old American amateur Francis Ouimet slayed the British giants of golf.

After Saturday's matches in '99, it appeared that the Europeans might roll to their biggest Ryder Cup victory ever, as they led 10-6. But supported by the local "hooligans," America roared back during the 12 singles matches on Sunday. In fact, they won their first seven, with Tom Lehman, Davis Love III, Phil Mickelson, Hal Sutton, David Duval, Tiger Woods, and Steve Pate thwarting their European foes.

The U.S. team, as well as their wives, caddies, and fans, poured onto the green after Justin Leonard's spectacular putt, even though his match with Jose Maria Olazabal wasn't over.

History of the Ryder Cup

Year	Site	USA	Great Britain/ Europe
2004	Oakland Hills C.C., Michigan	9½	18½
2002	The Belfry, England	12½	15½
1999	The Country Club, Massachusetts	14½	13½
1997	Valderrama G.C., Spain	13½	14½
1995	Oak Hill G.C., New York	13½	14½
1993	The Belfry, England	15	13
1991	The Ocean Course, South Carolina	14½	13½
1989	The Belfry, England	14	14
1987	Muirfield Village G.C., Ohio	13	15
1985	The Belfry, England	11½	16½
1983	PGA National G.C., Florida	14½	13½
1981	Walton Health G.C., England	18½	9½
1979	The Greenbrier, West Virginia	17	11
1977	Royal Lytham & St. Annes, England	12½	7½
1975	Laurel Valley G.C., Pennsylvania	21	11
1973	Muirfield, Scotland	19	13
1971	Old Warson C.C., Missouri	18½	13½
1969	Royal Birkdale G.C., England	16	16
1967	Champions G.C., Texas	23½	8½
1965	Royal Birkdale G.C., England	19½	12½
1963	East Lake C.C., Georgia	23	9
1961	Royal Lytham & St. Annes, England	14½	9½
1959	Eldorado C.C., California	8½	3½
1957	Lindrick G.C., England	4½	7½
1955	Thunderbird C.C., California	8	4
1953	Wentworth G.C., England	6½	5½
1951	Pinehurst C.C., North Carolina	9½	2½
1949	Ganton G.C., England	7	5
1947	Portland G.C., Oregon	11	1
1939-45	Ryder Cup canceled due to World War II		
1937	Southport & Ainsdale G.C., England	8	4
1935	Ridgewood C.C., New Jersey	9	3
1933	Southport & Ainsdale G.C., England	5½	6½
1931	Scioto C.C., Ohio	9	3
1929	Moortown G.C., England	5	7
1927	Worcester C.C., Massachusetts	9½	2½

Sunday turned into a nightmare for European captain Mark James. His strategy of playing his top players all three days, and and not using his rookies until Sunday, backfired. The stars burned out, while the youngsters—Coltart, Jean Van de Velde, and Jarmo Sandelin—struggled to navigate the course. On top of that, a young spectator spat at James' wife.

American Justin Leonard added the final insult on the 17th green of his match with Olazabal. Leonard drained a 45-foot putt to seemingly clinch victory for the U.S. You would have thought that the Red Sox had just won the World Series. U.S. players, their wives and girlfriends, caddies, and fans stormed onto the green to mob Leonard. It was a rare breach of golf decorum—especially because the competition wasn't over yet. Olazabal could have stayed alive by sinking a 20-foot putt. But after the bedlam (and perhaps because of it, European backers would say), the Spaniard missed. The United Slobs of America had won back the Cup.

"Darned if we didn't pull it off," Crenshaw said in *Sports Illustrated*.

Europeans, meanwhile, were indignant. Captain James declared that he would never again participate in the Ryder Cup on American soil. Europe vice captain Sam Torrance called the hosts' behavior "disgusting." A writer for *The Sun* of London opined, "American players and their fans belong in the gutter."

Over the following two years, Europeans contemplated the revenge they would extol on the "ugly Americans" during the final weekend of September 2001. But the event never happened; it was canceled because of the attacks on September 11. Instead, the United States and Great Britain buddied up as the closest of allies, and all the bickering at Brookline seemed, in retrospect, trivial and childish.

The Ryder Cup was postponed until September 2002 at The Belfry. The European team prevailed, and all involved were on their best behavior. As the BBC reported, Tiger Woods called it a "beautiful week," and U.S. captain Curtis Strange said, "Congratulations to everyone." Golf, once again, was a gentleman's game.

BACK FROM THE DEAD

USC vs. Notre Dame, October 15, 2005

With less than two minutes left in the game on October 15, 2005, the USC Trojans appeared doomed, their 27-game winning streak seemingly over. Trailing 31-27 at Notre Dame, with the Irish in their lucky green jerseys and the 14-story mosaic of Jesus looming in the background, Southern California faced fourth-and-9 on their own 26. Not even quarterback Matt Leinart (the 2004 Heisman winner) or tailback Reggie Bush (who would become the 2005 Heisman winner) could dig USC out of this hole. Or so it seemed.

Calling an audible, Leinart whistled one across the middle to split end Dwayne Jarrett, who had played with blurred vision throughout the fourth quarter. Nevertheless, Jarrett snatched the pass and sprinted downfield to the 40, the 30, the 20, and eventually the 13-yard-line. The Irish would need more than green jerseys to beat USC—a fact they had come to realize throughout their 80-year war.

USC–Notre Dame, one of the greatest rivalries in college football, dates back to December 4, 1926, when the Irish traveled by train all the way to Los Angeles. In front of 74,378 fans at the

Fighting Irish coach Charlie Weis ordered special green jerseys for the USC game—a move that had worked wonders for ND coach Dan Devine in 1977.

Los Angeles Memorial Coliseum, Notre Dame won a controversial game, 13-12. The next year at Chicago's Soldier Field, 120,000 fans—probably the most ever to witness an American sporting event—saw ND win another disputed nail-biter, 7-6.

Entering their 2005 grudge match, the Irish had gone 42-29-5 against USC, and many games had been epic battles. Before their 1930 game, during a practice for all the West Coast noseys to see, Notre Dame coach Knute Rockne dressed speedy back Bucky O'Connor in a teammate's jersey and reportedly told him not to run at full throttle. In the game itself, O'Connor burned past stunned USC defenders for two touchdowns. The Irish won 27-0 to clinch the national championship.

When USC ended ND's 21-game unbeaten streak in 1931, the city of Los Angeles honored the Trojans with a ticker-tape parade that drew 300,000. In 1964, USC beat the undefeated Irish 20-17 with 1:33 remaining, even though Notre Dame had dominated the game for most of the first 45 minutes.

In 1973 Notre Dame ended USC's 23-game unbeaten streak, winning 23-14, en route to its own national championship. Four years later against the Trojans, Irish coach Dan Devine outfitted his team in green jerseys for the first time in 14 years. His fired-up troops romped 49-19, kick-starting their drive to the national title. In 1986 Notre Dame won a cliffhanger, beating USC 38-37, on a John Carney field goal as time expired.

In 2005, the tables had turned. Irish fans initially dreaded the sight of USC on the Notre Dame schedule. One of the greatest juggernauts of modern times, the Trojans had won back-to-back national championships. They stormed into South Bend with a record of 5-0, a No. 1 national ranking, and averaging 51 points per game.

But this Irish team seemed poised for the challenge. Ranked ninth in the country, it was 4-1 and had upset mighty Michigan in Ann Arbor. Under new head coach Charlie Weis (who had won three Super Bowls as offensive coordinator for the New England Patriots), the Irish themselves were averaging 37 points per game.

Weis never played college football, but he graduated from Notre Dame in 1978. For a pep rally before the '05 USC game, Weis brought in two Irish players from his schoolboy days to speak: legendary quarterback Joe Montana and Daniel "Rudy" Ruettiger, Notre Dame's fabled underdog. Remembering the excitement of the green jerseys in the 1977 game, Weis unveiled them again for this game.

On a crisp, sparkling afternoon, a packed-house

Not only did Reggie Bush (the 2005 Heisman winner) run for three touchdowns in this game, but he shoved quarterback Matt Leinart across the goal line for the game-winner.

crowd of 80,795 punctuated the air with "Cheer, cheer for old Notre Dame!" Fans expected a shootout, and they got it. Midway through the first quarter, Bush romped 37 yards for a touchdown, hurdling a tackler along the way.

For the first three quarters, the teams traded touchdowns. Dramatic highlights included a 32-yard scoring pass from Notre Dame's Brady Quinn to Jeff Samardzija, a 60-yard punt return TD by ND's Tom Zbikowski, and another long run to paydirt (this one 45 yards) by Bush.

With a field goal early in the fourth quarter, Notre Dame went up 24–21. But the real drama was just beginning. Bush scored from nine yards out with 5:09 to go, making it 28–24 Trojans, before Quinn executed a gutty 87-yard drive. He capped it with his own five–yard touchdown run with 2:04 left, and he extended his arm across the goal line before hitting the ground. It was 31–28 Irish.

The game seemed hopeless for USC when it faced fourth-and-nine at its own 26. But then came Leinart's lucky strike to Jarrett. "You just have to throw it up and hope he gets it," Leinart said. His startling 61-yard pass play to the 13 put the Trojans back in business, although the Irish defense refused to break.

Two Bush rushes, of six and five yards, put the ball on the 2, but time was running out. Pulse rates quickened as the seconds diminished into single digits. Then, on what appeared to be the game's last play, Leinart ran toward the sideline before launching himself toward the endzone. The ball shot out of his hands and out of bounds, and the clocked ticked down to 0:00.

Quarterback Matt Leinart, the 2004 Heisman winner, owned one of the best arms in the nation, but this game came down to his two goal-line keepers in the final seconds.

Weis raised his hands in triumph while Irish fans stormed onto the field. But this game wasn't over! The officials huddled, put seven seconds back on the clock, and placed the ball on the 1-yard-line–claiming that Leinart had fumbled out of bounds. Down a field goal, USC coach Pete Carroll remained determined to go for the win. This time, Leinart punched it in over the middle, thanks to a push from Bush. "I used all 200 pounds of my body to push Matt in," he said.

In the realm of football, the Trojans had come back from the dead after flat-lining at 0:00. Leinart, however, was surprisingly cocky. "We just don't know how to lose," he bragged in *Newsday* afterward. Yet his words would come back to haunt him. USC lost in the national championship game when Texas's quarterback Vince Young scored on a run in the final seconds, an ironic twist that Irish fans quietly savored.

The game is on!

In 1925, the Notre Dame football team traveled to the University of Nebraska to play the Cornhuskers. It had been a long, dull train trip from South Bend, Indiana, and after the game Irish coach Knute Rockne faced a 600-mile journey home. Before leaving, however, he was approached by USC's Gwynn Wilson. Wilson, who held a position not unlike today's athletic director, had traveled all the way from Los Angeles to meet Rockne.

Wilson, on behalf of USC coach Howard Jones, invited Rockne to play the Trojans in California. Los Angeles was booming at the time, and in 1926 USC would play in the 74,000-plus-seat Los Angeles Memorial Coliseum. Coach Jones, Wilson said, would love to play a team of Notre Dame's caliber. All Rockne could think about, however, was the 2,000-mile train trip, times two. He told Wilson that the Irish were tired of long journeys and wanted to play more games close to home. So, no thanks.

But Wilson, and his wife, Marion, wouldn't take no for answer. They traveled with the Notre Dame team all the way to Chicago, and along the way Marion talked to Knute's wife, Bonnie. Like the many Los Angeles "boosters" of the period, Marion glorified L.A., adding that the hosts even "put fruit baskets in the hotel."

It all sounded glorious to Bonnie, who urged—nay, *convinced*—Knute to play USC. An elated Wilson sent a simple telegram back to USC: "The Game Is On!"

COLD WAR POWERS
United States vs. Soviet Union, 1952 Summer Olympics

On July 19, 1952, in Helsinki, Finland, a crowd of 70,000 gathered in the recently renovated Olympic Stadium for the opening ceremonies in a misty rain. The Olympic flame had just been lit to thunderous applause. There was a momentary lull in the proceedings when suddenly, a young woman dressed in long, flowing white robes leapt from her seat at one end of the stadium and began to run around the track toward the reviewing stand, where the dignitaries and officials were seated. Described as "buxom" and "titian-haired," the woman continued to run toward the podium without interference.

The audience must have assumed she was part of the ceremonies—an embodiment in white of the Olympic spirit of grace and beauty, perhaps?—and so must have the security guards and police, because no one made a move toward her. She reached the stand, bowed, and then clambered up the steps to join the astonished men sitting there. She stood at the microphone and, a little out of breath, gasped her way through something in Finnish before an official snatched her away. She smiled and waved as she was removed from the premises.

Identified later as a woman from West Germany, she caused people to wonder whether she was a communist looking to spread propaganda at the ceremony. (She wasn't.) But her act was the unofficial surprising beginning to a 15-day period during which no one had any idea what to expect.

The reason for the uncertainty was simple. This was the first Olympic Games involving athletes from the Soviet Union. Russians had last been in the Olympics when they were under Czarist rule in 1912. But these athletes weren't products of a semi-medieval state; these athletes had been conditioned and trained (and paid) as part of what Soviets liked to call "The Grand Experiment": communism. Their appearance on the world stage was clearly designed for maximum political effect. The Soviet Union had been invited to the 1948 London Games, but had sent no athletes. Instead, they had sent a reconnaissance team: dozens of scouts, coaches, and trainers, who went to school on the Olympics, taking copious notes. The following year the Communist Party "demanded" world supremacy in all sports to prove the validity of the Communist philosophy. According to *The New York Times*, the Finnish organizers said, "We're prepared for some surprises from the East. ... We don't believe the Russians would have entered the Games unless they really expected their athletes to stand up well."

Before the '52 Games, the Soviets combined boastfulness with a strange attitude of secrecy. They claimed their athletes had broken 88 track and field records in the years since London. But these were the days of the Iron Curtain. The records were set on Soviet soil, with Soviet judges and officials. No one could verify how legitimate their braggadocio was. U.S. newspapers were thick with speculation: Everyone knew the Russians had a terrific team of women in track and field events. Russians gymnasts were known for their abilities. But what about basketball? Or weightlifting? Did the Russians have distance runners or speedsters? Speculation about secret plots and Soviet trickery were everywhere. Some wondered whether the Soviets would move Communist bloc athletes around from team to team to gain strategic advantage.

When it became clear that the USSR's athletes would not stay in the Olympic village in Kapyla with athletes from capitalist countries, the columnists' hackles shot up. The collegiality of the Olympic village experience was well-known to be a symbolically significant important aspect of the Games' fellowship message. In direct contravention of all Olympic rules and ideals, the Soviets were given their own housing not far from a Soviet naval base. They were joined by other nations in the communist bloc, such as Bulgaria, Czechoslovakia, and Romania. The Soviet military provided the athletes' security.

Meanwhile, the United States team was having trouble raising enough money to pay for the trip. Newspapers ran patriotic pleas for funds. "Beat the

Americans Milton Campbell and Floyd Simmons outrun Soviet Vladimir Volkov in a hurdles event in the decathlon. Campbell took silver and Simmons won bronze in the event, while Volkov finished fourth.

In 1952, the United States could boast of having the greatest athlete in the world. Bob Mathias won his second gold medal in the decathlon after winning his first in 1948, at age 17.

Russkies" was the motivating phrase. The patent absurdity of the concept that athletic contests can determine the relative quality of two such divergent political/social/economic/moral systems seems to have occurred to no one; it was us against them. "The Cold War of Sports to Start Simmering" ran one headline as the Games began.

The intensity and unexpected nature of what was to come had its lighter moments, too. *The Washington Post* ran an article titled "Russia's Track Queen Is Big, But She's Damn Good Looking," praising the looks of the 5-foot-10, 175-pound Soviet star, especially her "poodle" haircut.

During the Games, the behavior of the Soviet team and its coaches was above reproach. Gone were the tactics of berating officials and bullying judges to get better scores that had been in evidence in other international competition involving the Soviets. Such wasn't true in the Soviet press, where the party line blasted officials daily for favoritism regarding the Americans. Its tirades were shrill and nonstop—even when the Soviet team temporarily held the overall lead in points.

All in all, 69 countries sent approximately 4,900 athletes to participate in the Helsinki Olympics. There were some amazing performances. One was from the Czech distance runner, Emil Zatopek, whose strange running motion and tortured facial expressions made

Discus flinger Nina Romaschkowa won one of 22 Soviets golds at the 1952 Summer Games. The United States won 40 gold medals.

it appear that he was suffering, when in fact he was simply outrunning everybody else. The "Czech Locomotive" took gold medals and set Olympic records in the 5,000 and 10,000 meter races, then decided fairly late in the game to run the marathon (he had never entered one before) and won that, too, also setting the Olympic record.

The star of the Soviet team was gymnast Viktor Chukarin, who took home four gold medals (pommel horse, horse vault, all-around, and team events) and two silver (rings and parallel bars.) The biggest U.S. hero was decathloner Bob Mathias, who not only repeated his victory from 1948, but did it by the largest margin ever, a world record. When the dust finally settled, the U.S. had won 40 gold medals, 19 silver, and 17 bronze. The USSR had taken 22 gold, 30 silver, and 17 bronze. Victory U.S. But wait. Instead of 10 points for first, five for second, and four for third, the Soviets suggested that first place should receive only 7 points. In fact, the 10-5-4 point system had been in effect for decades, albeit unofficially. With the new numbers in hand, the Russian press declared that they had won.

So the 1952 Olympic Games had something no Games had ever had before—a winner. It just depended on which side of the Iron Curtain you lived on as to who it was.

Final medal standings

* East Germany, West Germany, Unified Germany, Soviet Union and Russia are all considered separate nations for this comparison.

1952 Summer Olympic Games
Helsinki, Finland

Nation	Gold	Silver	Bronze
1. United States	40	19	7
2. USSR	22	30	19
3. Hungary	16	10	6
4. Sweden	12	13	10
5. Italy	8	9	4
6. Czechoslovakia	7	3	3
7. France	6	6	6
8. Finland	6	3	13
9. Australia	6	2	3
10. Norway	3	2	0

The Top 10 All-Time Olympic Medal Standings*
Winter Games

Team	Gold	Silver	Bronze	Total
1. United States	269	232	169	670
2. Great Britain	101	91	79	271
3. Sweden	80	67	76	223
4. Norway	88	76	57	221
5. USSR	87	63	67	217
6. France	63	69	56	188
7. Germany	67	67	45	179
8. Finland	52	42	40	134
9. Austria	36	38	39	113
10. East Germany	38	34	33	105

Summer Games

Team	Gold	Silver	Bronze	Total
1. United States	699	532	452	1683
2. USSR	439	356	322	1117
3. Germany	157	154	182	493
4. East Germany	153	129	127	409
5. Italy	140	116	123	379
6. China	107	85	66	258
7. Russia	86	76	82	244
8. Australia	66	70	86	222
9. France	72	56	66	194
10. West Germany	51	56	71	178

BATTLE OF THE GIANTS
Patrick Ewing vs. Ralph Sampson, December 11, 1982

There was no way to adequately prepare for a college basketball game against Ralph Sampson. How could there be? No one else was 7-foot-4 with the ability to run the floor like a guard. No one else could make scoring, rebounding, shot-blocking, and defending at dominant levels seem so effortless. And in 1982–83, no one else was on his way to a third consecutive James A. Naismith Award as college basketball's best player, a three-peat that had been accomplished only once previously, by UCLA's Bill Walton in the 1970s. Sampson, the unstoppable Virginia center, was truly head and shoulders above the competition.

If anyone *was* equipped to battle such a titan, it was Patrick Ewing. Though only a sophomore, the 7-footer had proved his mettle in his first college season when he helped Georgetown reach the national championship game. A late basket by Michael Jordan kept the Hoyas from celebrating a title, but Ewing had forcefully established himself as a rising star. The sweat that always drenched the gray T-shirt he wore under his uniform told the story of his style: physical, intense, all-out hustle, with defenders frequently absorbing an elbow or two along the way.

On the '82–83 college basketball schedule, the December 11 game at the Capital Centre in Landover, Maryland read "Virginia at Georgetown." It was billed as the "Game of the Decade." In the minds of fans everywhere, it was "Sampson vs. Ewing," and the anticipation was palpable. Not since three battles between Houston's Elvin Hayes and UCLA's Lew Alcindor in the late 1960s had a showdown of centers grabbed the spotlight like this. There were other similarities between those memorable match-ups. The second of the Hayes-Alcindor tilts, Houston's 71–69 upset of UCLA in 1968, drew more than 52,000 fans to the Astrodome and was the first nationally televised, prime-time college basketball game. The Sampson-Ewing contest was the first big

Ralph Sampson won not only the game but the statistical battle: 23 points and 16 rebounds to Patrick Ewing's 16 points and eight boards.

game for cable TV, as Ted Turner's superstation, WTBS, brought it live to fans across the country who were not among the 19,000-plus in attendance.

Virginia entered the night ranked No. 1 in the country, two places ahead of Georgetown. Predictions about the outcome varied, but most experts favored Sampson and the Cavaliers. Sampson was the more accomplished center, they argued, and his supporting cast offered more experience. The Hoyas would start two freshmen and three sophomores. At least one coach, however, predicted Ewing might just prevail if the game turned into a heavyweight bout. "If it's Marquis of Queensbury [rules]," North Carolina State coach Jim Valvano said in *Sports Illustrated,* "I like Georgetown in the fourth round. A TKO by Ewing." Sampson and Ewing tried their best to keep the focus of the game on the *teams* involved, rather than their individual match-up. It was no use, of course. The nation's eyes were on the big men when game night arrived.

Though few were aware of it until after the game, Sampson had been battling flu symptoms for days before tipoff. No one would have guessed by watching him go to work. His size, skill, and sweet-shooting teammates were too much for Ewing and the rest of the young Hoyas in the opening half. Georgetown's center got the better of his Virginia counterpart on one play a few minutes into the game. Ewing lured Sampson off his feet with a nifty pump-fake, waited for the giant to begin his descent, and made an easy underhanded shot. But it was a fleeting moment for Hoyas fans. Sampson's scoring and rebounding sparked an early Virginia surge that produced a 33–23 halftime lead that grew to 14 points, 41–27, in the early minutes of the second half.

"I thought Ralph had a really good night," Virginia head coach Terry Holland told *The New York Times.* "But as the game went on he got weaker, and by the end he had difficulty maintaining his position offen-

Ralph Sampson was used to having his way in the paint, but here the 7-4 superstar gets his layup blocked by Patrick Ewing, one of the premier college defenders in America in 1982–83.

sively or defensively. He got to the point where he was not sweating. That's bad."

While Sampson was weakening, the Hoyas were at last starting to find success with their fearsome pressure defense. They clawed their way back into the game in the second half, erasing the Virginia cushion and twice pulling even, once at 59 when David Wingate hit a 20-footer for Georgetown, and again at 61 with 3:15 to play. Had the Cavaliers not been sharp from the free-throw line, the outcome might have been different. Virginia failed to make a field goal over the final 5:50 of the night, but sank 24 of 28 shots from the charity stripe. Three close calls that went against Georgetown—a travel, a charge, and a shooting foul—in the game's last 95 seconds let Virginia ice the game on free throws.

Behind Sampson's 23 points and 16 rebounds, the Cavaliers held on for a 68–63 win. Othell Wilson added 10 points, but no other Virginia player scored in double digits. Ewing paced the Hoyas with 16 points while adding eight boards and five blocked shots

before fouling out late. Wingate, one of three Georgetown players in double figures, contributed 12 points. "Pat is an excellent player," Sampson said of Ewing in *The New York Times*. "There aren't enough words to describe the guy. He's great."

Though no championship was on the line, it was a game that merits mention among the best ever. The anticipation, the performances of its two biggest stars, and the fact it was the first cable TV event of its kind all played a part. It was also a showcase, of sorts, for the upstart Big East Conference against Virginia's more established Atlantic Coast Conference. The two leagues would battle for national supremacy often over the next two decades.

They say a picture is worth a thousand words, and the lasting image from this night shows Ewing throwing down a powerful dunk over the outstretched right arm of Sampson. In fact, it was Ewing's last basket of the game, two points that neither changed the outcome nor reflected the tone of one of the most talked-about head-to-head match-ups in the history of college basketball.

Fortunes reversed in NBA

Two years behind Ralph Sampson in college, Georgetown's Patrick Ewing had this to say about Virginia's star center before facing him for the first time in 1982. "Ralph is much more mature than I am," Ewing said in *Sports Illustrated*. "He's got more of the basics down." That changed once the two promising centers reached the NBA.

Sampson was the top pick in the 1983 NBA Draft by Houston and won the Rookie of the Year Award. The next year, Houston drafted Hakeem Olajuwon, figuring two 7-footers were better than one. However, the "Twin Towers" did not achieve the results the Rockets desired. Sampson upped his scoring average to 22-plus points in '84-85, and his tip-in at the buzzer in 1986 sent the Rockets to the NBA Finals for the second time ever. But it became clear he was uncomfortable playing forward and that Olajuwon

was the team's big man of the future. Knee injuries then took their toll, and Sampson's career spiraled. He played just 10 games for Washington in '91-92, the final season of an injury-plagued career.

While Sampson was winning NBA Rookie of the Year honors, Ewing was leading Georgetown to a 1984 national title. He, too, was a No. 1 overall pick, in '85, and won the Rookie of the Year Award with the Knicks. But Ewing's career continued to flourish. The relentless warrior was chosen for 11 NBA All-Star Games, 10 in a row, over 17 seasons and set Knicks records in virtually every significant statistical category. Ewing was honored in 1996 as one of the 50 greatest players in NBA history. He also won two Olympic gold medals, in 1984 and '92, led New York to two NBA Finals, and, in 2003, had his No. 33 retired by the Knicks at Madison Square Garden.

Ralph Sampson and Patrick Ewing continued to wage war in the NBA. Sampson was named to four All-Star Games with Houston, while Ewing became the greatest player in Knicks history.

RIVALRY INTERRUPTED
Steffi Graf vs. Monica Seles, 1995 U.S. Open Final

"Do you think you would've won if Monica were back?"

Steffi Graf became visibly tense. No matter how many times sportswriters lobbed that question at her in the winner's circle, it always gnawed at her. What should have been a moment to savor for Graf, the top-ranked tennis player on the professional women's tour, only dredged up painful memories and insecurities. It didn't seem to matter how well she had played that day, or that she had just added another Grand Slam title to her extraordinary victory tally. For the past two and a half years, sportswriters seemed perversely intent on reminding Graf that she held the No. 1 ranking partly by default, rather than on the basis of her remarkable versatility on clay and grass courts.

Truth be told, there was validity to the sportswriters' insistent questions regarding the conspicuous absence of Graf's arch rival, Monica Seles, from the tour. Seles was the only player who had ever posed a genuine threat to the tall, famously shy Manheim, Germany, native. In 1988, just six years after she had played her first professional tournament at age 13, Graf became only the third female tennis player in history to win all four Grand Slam tournaments in a calendar year. Never one to rest on her laurels—her controlling taskmaster of a father probably wouldn't have allowed it—Graf had finished her annus mirabilis with a "Golden Slam" by winning the gold medal at the 1988 Summer Olympics in Seoul.

But in 1990, a challenger to Graf emerged in the powerhouse form of teenager Monica Seles at the French Open. A year after losing to Graf in the 1989 French Open semifinal, the 16-year-old ethnic Hungarian from Serbia (then part of Yugoslavia) roared back to defeat Graf in a jaw-dropping, straight-set upset, 7–6, 6–4, to become the all-time youngest French Open champion.

Suddenly, Graf no longer appeared unbeatable.

Steffi Graf (*pictured*) rose to prominence before Monica Seles, winning not only the Grand Slam in 1988 but the gold medal in that year's Olympics.

After losing the French Open to Seles, she suffered an embarrassing defeat in the 1990 Wimbledon semifinals to American Zina Garrison. Nor did she fare much better at that year's U.S. Open, where Argentine Gabriela Sabatini bested Graf in straight sets, 6–2, 7–6. Graf's steely composure and laserlike focus on and off the court was further undermined by tabloid reports of a Playboy model's paternity suit against Graf's father.

Meanwhile, as Graf floundered, Seles soared in the rankings, proving that her French Open victory was no fluke. A giggly extrovert in interviews, Seles underwent a startling metamorphosis once she picked up a tennis racket. The teenager disappeared, replaced by a formidably aggressive competitor whose two-handed forehand and backhand shots—punctuated by loud grunts—overwhelmed her opponents. In addition to her physical strength and agility, Seles had another, arguably more important weapon in her arsenal: uncanny mental stamina. Seles appeared almost impervious to the extreme psychological and physical wear and tear of a grueling match. As Czech player Jana Novotna told *The Economist*, "Physically and mentally, it is very difficult to play her."

Novotna had fallen to Seles in the 1991 Australian Open final, the first of three Grand Slam titles Seles would claim that year as she displaced Graf from the top position in the rankings. Although shin splints had kept her from playing Wimbledon that year, Seles otherwise appeared unstoppable. She continued her dazzling winning streak by successfully defending her Australian, French, and U.S. Open titles in 1992. The French Open final pitted Seles against Graf in three exceptionally draining sets, 6–2, 3–6, 10–8. Although Graf relinquished the top spot in the rankings to Seles, she was still the far superior player on grass, as she easily proved by trouncing Seles at the 1992 Wimbledon final in two sets, 6–2, 6–1.

Monica Seles (*left*) and Steffi Graf share a laugh at the 1996 U.S. Open. Their relationship was much chillier earlier in their careers, especially after Seles was stabbed by a deranged fan of Graf.

These two rivals maintained a civil if never especially warm relationship. Gregarious and outgoing, the fashion-conscious Seles was the temperamental antithesis of Graf, an aloof, driven perfectionist who craved solitude and described her outlook as "emotionally dark." In the spring of 1993, however, their chilly relationship turned downright glacial, due to a disturbing, headline-generating incident that would haunt both women for years to come.

He was one of those paunchy, prematurely balding middle-aged men, so nondescript that you forgot him even as he stood before you. But on the night of April 30, during a changeover in Seles' quarterfinal match against Magdalena Maleeva in the Citizen Cup tournament in Hamburg, Germany, 38-year-old unemployed lathe operator Gunther Parche entered the history books. Running toward Seles as she rested, Parche thrust a nine-inch serrated boning knife into Seles' back, right below her left shoulder blade. In a lurid twist, it was soon revealed that the mentally ill Parche was an obsessive Graf fan who had only wanted to injure Seles so Graf could regain the No. 1 ranking.

No stranger to deranged fans—one had slashed his wrists before her—Graf visited Seles at Hamburg's Eppendorf University Hospital, where her injured rival was recuperating in seclusion. But as goodwill gestures go, Graf's hospital visit to her psychologically traumatized rival was a bust. In typically blunt, borderline abrasive fashion, she announced to Seles that she had to keep her visit short, because of an upcoming match. Given the bizarre circumstances surrounding Parche's attack on Seles, Graf's behavior struck many as insensitive, to say the least.

Nor would Graf make any friends in the Seles camp later, when she regained the No. 1 ranking because of a controversial, near-unanimous decision by other women players to remove Seles from the top spot during her extended convalescence. Furious about his

An affable young woman by nature, Seles turned into a ball-smashing terror on the court, punctuating her shots with loud grunts.

daughter's ouster, Karolj Seles told Matthew Cronin that Graf should instead be named "knife number one."

The Graf-Seles "Cold War" continued over the next two and a half years, as both players attempted, none too successfully, to put the attack behind them. Emotionally and psychologically traumatized, Seles withdrew from the tour. Graf soldiered on, plagued by constant insinuations that she wouldn't be numero uno if Seles were still playing. But on September 9, 1995, in the United States Tennis Association's Louis Armstrong Stadium in Flushing, New York, Graf would finally get the chance to silence her detractors: Seles was back and ready to face Graf in the 1995 U.S. Open women's final.

Neither woman was at her physical peak. Yet despite tendonitis in her left knee, Seles had wracked up 11 straight victories without losing a set since rejoining the tour just a month earlier. As for Graf, she was in chronic pain from a bone spur in her back. That ache was nothing compared to the acute humiliation of her father's latest, publicity-generating escapade. Normally a courtside fixture, Graf's father was sitting in a Manheim, Germany, jail cell, under suspicion of tax evasion.

Whatever worries both women felt seemingly evaporated, however, once the match began. A crowd of 19,883 watched the rivals battle for supremacy in a brilliant display of athleticism and resilience. Serving at speeds upwards of 100 mph, Graf countered Seles' powerful, two-handed forehand with short, backhand returns that helped Graf take the first set in a tie-breaker 7-6. The second set belonged to Seles, who blew past a suddenly rattled Graf to win it 6-0. Unfortunately for Seles, Graf shook off her nerves to take the third set—and her fourth U.S. Open title—with a score of 6-3. As she and Seles hugged and kissed each other over the net, their bitterly contested rivalry appeared forgotten—at least for the moment.

BEANBALL MEMORIES
New York Yankees vs. New York Mets, 2000 World Series

The 2000 World Series between the Yankees and the Mets was a Subway Series of a different kind. The clubs' rivalry hadn't had decades to develop. The two had met a total of just 18 times in the four years of interleague play. But make no mistake. There was a lot boiling between these two squads, and it bubbled up over just one pitch.

Actually, it was two pitches. The first was a Roger Clemens offering that Mets catcher Mike Piazza creamed into the seats for a grand slam homer in their first 2000 interleague meeting, which started off a miserable Clemens performance (5 IP, 10 H, 9R) and easy Mets win (12-2) the night of June 9. The second was another Clemens pitch to Piazza the next time they faced each other, nearly a month later. This hard one whacked Piazza in the head, leaving him dazed for several minutes. As a precaution Piazza sat out of that week's All-Star Game. He had been the leading vote-getter in the National League.

When asked about the beaning, Piazza minced no words. "It was definitely intentional." He said he had "no respect" for Clemens. When a sportswriter suggested to Piazza's teammate Todd Zeile before the Series that the three-month-old incident was already forgotten, Zeile snapped back, "Like hell it is."

For most of the season, a Yankees–Mets match-up in the Series looked unlikely. The Mets battled the Braves for the N.L. East title, but had to settle for the wild-card slot. Their division championship series featured two tight extra-inning games against Barry Bonds and the Giants. In Game 2, the Mets carried a 4-1 lead into the Giants' bottom of the ninth (sound familiar? See 1951.) A Giant hit a three-run homer this time, too, but this time it just tied the score, and the Mets took the game in the 10th. Game 3 also went extra innings, and a homer by the delightfully named Benny Agbayani ended it in the 13th. The Mets had less trouble with the Cardinals in the League Championship Series, clinching in five games.

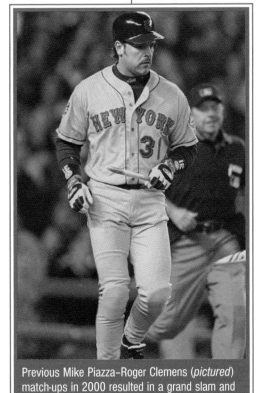

Previous Mike Piazza–Roger Clemens (*pictured*) match-ups in 2000 resulted in a grand slam and a beanball, but nothing could top their first World Series encounter.

The Yankees had been hot and cold all season, including a long losing spell in September. But taking the division series from Oakland (and winning Game 5 on the road) seemed to perk them up, and they shut out Seattle once, losing only twice in the LCS. Series commentators felt the Yankees were ready to act like Yankees again.

Game 1 in Yankee Stadium matched up lefties Al Leiter for the Mets and Andy Pettitte for the Yanks. Both men seemed at the top of their games, and through five innings neither team had scored. Oddball baserunning gaffes by Zeile in the fourth and Jay Payton in the fifth kept the Mets from moving ahead. A third one came in the top of the sixth. With two outs, Timo Perez led off first. When Zeile smacked a high fly that looked to be gone, Perez cruised. Then the ball hit the top of the padding on the wall. He tried to kick it into second gear, but it wasn't enough. Perez was easily thrown out at home.

The Yanks broke through in the bottom of the inning, on a two-run clutch double by David Justice. But the Mets came back in the top of the seventh, riding four singles and a walk to net three runs and take the lead. The Yanks manufactured a run in the bottom of the ninth off erratic Mets closer Armando Benitez to send the game into extra innings.

Loading the bases with one out in the 10th wasn't enough for the Yankees when Paul O'Neill grounded into a 4-6-3 double play. They got runners to second and third with two down in the 11th, but failed again.

In the bottom of the 12th, four hours and 51 minutes after the first pitch, surprising Yankee star Jose Vizcaino dropped a single into left, bringing home Tino Martinez. The Yankees had pocketed Game 1. It was the longest World Series game ever, and the second longest in number of innings.

Game 2 featured one of the strangest events that had or has ever happened on a baseball diamond, much less in front of millions watching. It's no surprise

The Yankees carry manager Joe Torre off the field after clinching the World Series in five games for their third straight world title.

that it involved Clemens and Piazza. Piazza was hitting against Clemens in the first inning, the first time they had faced each other since the July 8 incident. Piazza, a lifetime .583 hitter against Clemens with three homers, got around on a pitch and fouled it off, but his bat broke off near the handle. Unsure of where the ball was, he started to run to first. Clemens fielded the bat piece and fired it—toward Piazza!

The benches emptied instantly. Some Mets were livid. But wisely (or absurdly), the umpires ejected no one and things calmed down. The Yanks built up a 6–0 lead for Clemens, who allowed just two hits and no walks in eight innings. The Mets scared Yankees closer Mariano Rivera with a three-run homer in the ninth, but Rivera slammed the door shut and the Yanks took a 6–5 win. Todd Zeile was feeling snakebit. His ninth-inning loud fly to left was snatched just before it left the park, which meant he had missed two home runs in two days by a total of one foot.

The news in Game 3 was that a total of 25 strike-outs were recorded, tying a Series record. Orlando Hernandez of the Yankees had a dozen himself, but an eighth-inning double by Agbayani broke a 2–2 tie and gave the Mets a 4–2 win. But it would be their only victory in this Series.

In Game 4 Derek Jeter took center stage, hitting a leadoff homer and then a third-inning triple. The

Yanks scored one run in each of the first three innings, then handed the game to their bullpen and defense as four pitchers allowed just two Mets hits from the fifth inning on. Yanks, 3–2. *100 Years of the World Series* quotes Yank outfielder O'Neill as saying, "When you walk off the field [in this Series] you know you've been in a battle."

Game 5 was another gut-twisting affair. Leiter and Pettitte locked up again and both were marvelous. For eight-plus innings Leiter permitted just seven hits. Unfortunately for him, two were solo home runs by Bernie Williams (his first hit of the Series) and Jeter. Pettitte was even cleaner; the two runs the Mets pushed across in the second were the result of an error (his error). The game was tied till the ninth. Leiter fanned the first two Yankees, but then gave a free pass to Jorge Posada. Scott Brosius singled and so did Luis Sojo, but when Payton's throw bounced off Posada as he scored, Brosius came in to tally the insurance run.

The man who made the last out in the Mets ninth? Mike Piazza.

Crosstown series

There have been 17 World Series played between two teams from the same city. Seven were between the Yankees and Dodgers; six between the Yankees and Giants. The Yankees and Mets, the Oakland A's and San Francisco Giants, the St. Louis Browns and Cardinals, and the Chicago White Sox and Cubs have played one each.

1989. Giants/Athletics. The only notable thing about this Series is the earthquake that occurs before the third game is to start, postponing the games for 10 days.

1956. Yankees/Dodgers. The Series is tied at two games when Casey Stengel sends Don Larsen out to the mound. All he does is throw a perfect game at the befuddled Dodgers.

1936. Yankees/Giants. This Yankees club is one of the most dominant in history, and they live up to that rep in Game 2, battering five Giants pitchers for 17 hits and 18 runs, including the second grand slam in Series history, by Tony Lazzeri.

1923. Yankees/Giants. Casey Stengel is 33 years old this year, and he supplies all the fun the Giants have. His two-out ninth inning inside-the-park homer provides the winning run in Game 1, and in Game 3 his solo homer wins the game, 1–0. Those are the only two games the Giants win.

1906. Cubs/White Sox. In what is called the "David vs. Goliath Series," the already-legendary Cubs are supposed to demolish the White Sox, known as the "Hitless Wonders," who bat only .230 as a team during the season with just seven home runs. But behind spitballer Ed Walsh, the Sox prevail in six games.

Yankees catcher Jorge Posada tells Mike Piazza to back off. Piazza was furious after Roger Clemens (*right*) threw a broken bat at him in Game 2.